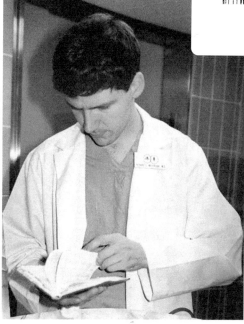

About the Author

Richard Mayerchak MD is double board certified in family medicine as well as obstetrics and gynecology. He is an Associate Clinical Professor in the Department of Obstetrics and Gynecology at the University of Minnesota where he has twice received the Leonard Lang Award as clinical faculty of the year. He is the chairman of the M Health Fairview system OB/GYN council which includes nine hospitals in Minneapolis/St. Paul. During his career he has performed thousands of surgeries and delivered thousands of babies and cared for them into adulthood. it has been a rich, rewarding, and fulfilling experience.

Rx for Success: 5 Suggestions for Surviving the Marathon Ordeal of Becoming a Medical Doctor

Richard Mayerchak MD

Rx for Success: 5 Suggestions for Surviving the Marathon Ordeal of Becoming a Medical Doctor

Olympia Publishers
London

www.olympiapublishers.com
OLYMPIA PAPERBACK EDITION

A CIP catalogue record for this title is
available from the British Library.

ISBN: 978-1-80439-634-6

This is a work of creative nonfiction. The events are portrayed to the best of the
author's memory. While all the stories in this book are true, some names and
identifying details have been changed to protect the privacy of the people
involved.

First Published in 2023

Olympia Publishers
Tallis House
2 Tallis Street
London
EC4Y 0AB

Printed in Great Britain

Dedication

Dedicated first to Carl Valentine Griesy, M.D., for years of patience, guidance, and friendship. I'm especially indebted to you for sharing your unique way of practicing the "art" of medicine that makes you humane and lovable and has earned my highest respect. You paved the way for my own foray into rural medicine.

Dedicated secondly to Gerard Thomas Parent, M.D, who inspired me to approach medicine with a disciplined mind, and to appreciate the great minds of the past, such as Osler, Cushing and Harvey, and who taught me that much can be learned through the performance of a thorough physical examination.

Dedicated also to Thomas Jeffrey Blankenship, M.D., who embraced this green, unseasoned physician early in my medical career and generously shared with me all of his practical medical knowledge and experience in managing a busy clinical practice, as well as his love of running marathons.

Finally, dedicated to Dr. Steve Hubbard, my Luther College calculus professor whose enthusiasm for teaching the beauty of mathematics inspired me greatly. He took a personal interest in making sure that I succeeded by daily opening his office for questions and taking the time to explain the difficult concepts. After all, as a pre-med I needed an A in every subject, and math was tough! He exemplifies the best of the Luther College mission to educate not only for one's career, but for succeeding in life.

Acknowledgements

I would like to thank my dear wife Mary for encouraging me to write this book and for her encouragement along every step in the process.

"The race goes not to the swift, but to those who keep on running."

–Anonymous

"Good judgment comes from experience. Experience comes from bad judgment."

–Mark Twain

"Adapt or die."

–Charles Darwin

CONTENTS

INTRODUCTION
Do you have what it takes to become a Doctor of Medicine?

The roadmap to pursuit of a medical career reveals a daunting journey. It begins early in life, because the techniques necessary to survive the immense amount of education ahead are learned as a child: the art of memorization, the ability to multi-task, the industry to buckle down and study for long hours. It boils down to the ability to delay gratification in order to achieve a goal. By the time a would-be doctor enters high school, the push is on to achieve consistently high grades. Without them, the chances of making it to college are doomed. Then, in college, the focus turns to achieving those same high grades so as to be accepted to medical school. And then residency. And so on. The bar is continually raised; the one constant through all of the journey is the need to succeed at test-taking. The exams are the great equalizer. A poor test-taker will never succeed in the quest to become a doctor.

In my estimation, the keys to surviving medical school and residency are:

1) You have to realize that it is a marathon race. Only one person wins a marathon; the rest merely survive it. Surviving the medical training marathon requires the same guts, stamina and most of all, patience. No matter how much intensity is applied to the first few miles, only those who take it one mile at a time will have something left at the end of the long journey that allows them to finish the race or the medical school/residency.

2) You have to realize that mistakes will be made. Unfortunately, sometimes the mistakes are significant and patients die or are otherwise harmed. The saying goes that, "good judgment comes from experience. Experience comes from bad judgment." No one survives medical training without making mistakes. The key is to learn from them and vow to be a better doctor from what they teach you.

3) You need to exercise regularly. It will help you maintain the stamina required for residency; more importantly, it will improve your

mental health.

4) You need to get adequate sleep. Without it, you will fail. Sleep hygiene is a critical skill that must be learned.

5) You have to adapt, or die. There will be roadblocks in every training process that takes years to complete. Those who adapt succeed, and the rest perish.

*

This is the story of my roadmap to medicine. It contains many twists and turns, and surprising obstacles along the way. During medical school I failed the practice exams for the national medical boards. Until I passed, I couldn't move on to clinical rotations, or to residency. When I got to my first residency I was fired. My medical career ended that day. My dad told me that I would either have to adapt, or I would die. I adapted. I got a second chance at residency training and I ran with it. When I finally made it out into medical practice as a family doctor, I tried a tiny town. I failed. I tried city practice. I failed at that too.

Instead of leaving medicine entirely, I adapted once again. I became a surgeon.

The following chapters chronicle my constant battle to rise to the challenge of medical training. After finishing high school, I endured a marathon of 14 more years of higher education. This included four years of college, four years of medical school, and six more years of residency. The only way to survive a marathon like this is by having guts and stamina, and patience that gets you through it one mile at a time. You adapt or you die. Along the way I discovered that good judgment doesn't come cheaply; unfortunately, I made many mistakes and sometimes patients paid the price. I learned the most from those mishaps, and they have made me a better doctor. And now, after thirty-five years of medical practice, I will share with you the secret to how I adapted and survived, so that I now embrace my job every day with joy and satisfaction, and a deep love of practicing the art of medicine.

CHAPTER 1
REALITY CHECK

I had just drifted into that wonderful fog of twilight sleep when my beeper jolted me back to reality. It was the ER again. Damn!! The ER nurse who answered my return call immediately detected the disgust in my voice.

"No time for that now", she rebuked harshly. "Get down here right away, doctor. We have a bad one..."

It still felt weird to hear someone call me "doctor". It was still my first day of internship at St Luke's Hospital In Milwaukee, technically, although I was now 21 hours into this call shift. I swung my legs over the call room bed. I was so tired that I felt sick. As if I could vomit. This pace is inhumane, I thought. Seriously? It can't be legal to work someone this hard when I am this exhausted! I noticed that I hadn't even disturbed the bedsheets – I had just plopped down on the mattress 10 minutes ago, and it remained neatly made. I eased myself off the bed slowly and ambled out the door.

At four o'clock in the morning the hospital hallways are dark. Hospitals dim the lights so that the patients can sleep. I stumbled out of the call room with my running shoes still untied, and my scrubs not quite up to my waist.

There was nobody in the hallway to see me, so it was irrelevant. Earlier in the call shift I was bounding up and down the stairwells because it was more expedient; now I gladly took the elevator so that I could wake up while I waited for it to reach the 9th floor call rooms. I took one hand and made my fingers into a comb to brush my disheveled hair, and cinched up the drawstring on my scrubs. In the elevator I stooped over to tie my shoelaces. I smelled my armpits. My sweaty body stunk from running up and down the stairs all evening. I heard the overhead speaker playing Kim Carnes' latest hit song... "she's got Bette Davis eyes..." I briefly pondered what that meant. Then the elevator door opened and I was in the ER.

At ground level where the ER was located the first thing that hit me was the bright lights. The ER never sleeps. My eyes made the painful adjustment to the intense light and I met the nurse at the control desk. See read my frown and waved it off with a disapproving nod.

"Room 3 – head laceration – bleeding quite a bit. She's a black woman age 56. Deloris Bafta. The story is that her son's best friend rang her doorbell at 3 am and she let him in. Turns out he was mad at her son and the first thing he did was hit her over the head with a tire iron. I think she has a skull fracture."

That story woke me right up again. Funny how you can be dead tired and jerked awake suddenly to fix someone's life-changing trauma. The nurse led me into room 3 and tried to introduce me to the patient Deloris. I tuned out the introduction. I was completely focused on her head wound. All I saw was that the once pristine white bedsheets on her gurney were now all red and soaked with blood. I lifted the pile of large gauze taped loosely on the center of her head. The gauzes were soaked through as well. Then I saw the enormous laceration of her scalp. It was as if someone had decided to peel off her scalp to expose the brain. The laceration extended from the back of the head, directly down the midline to her forehead. It was deep – I surmised that the skull was fractured as well.

Then I suddenly felt sick again. This time it wasn't from lack of sleep. It was the nausea of seeing gross amounts of blood on a patient writhing in pain. She was moaning and jerking. I knew I had to leave the room. This patient was depending upon my help to save her life but I knew I wouldn't be able to do it. I headed for the door of her room and told the nurse I had to leave for a moment.

I had no intention of returning. I nonchalantly strolled past the ER control desk so as to not draw attention to myself and made my way out the front entrance as if I had a purpose in mind, and then as soon as I was out of their sight I bolted down the long hallway leading away from the ER. I was queasy. I sprinted to the main hospital entrance and through the double doors to the circle driveway in front of the parking lot. There was no one outside – it was 4:15 am on a hot summer night. I sat on the curb of the driveway circle and put my head in between my knees to restore the blood flow. I was faint.

Once the blood returned to my brain, my head was flooded with thoughts. Thoughts of guilt, of panic, of self-preservation. I was done with medicine. I realized that I would not be able to take another day of this kind of stress.

My apartment was only a few blocks down the street. As I stood up from the curb and headed in that direction, I felt the immense sadness of failure. I would have to find another way to pay back med school loans, I decided, as I walked off the hospital grounds.

As I walked, I flashed back to medical school. What would Dr. Griesy think of me now?

CHAPTER 2
MEDICAL SCHOOL

The "Old Poop", the Marathon, and the Ultimate Nightmare

It was my first day of medical school at the University of Minnesota Duluth campus. Our classes were held on the south campus, the oldest of the university buildings. The brick exterior of the main med school building was partially eclipsed by a blanket of vines. The hallways had that musty smell that school hallways have when the air conditioning has been off all summer long and the air circulation is compromised.

I sat in a classroom with 47 other students who had "made the grade" and survived the awful, rigorous admissions process for medical school. There had been over 900 applications for these 48 spots. We awaited our first lecture, by Dr. T.J. Leppi, the dean of the medical school.

Dr. Leppi arrived at the stroke of 8 am and briskly strode to the front of our lecture hall. He was thin, tall, and almost bald, about 50 years old. He carried an energy about him. He wore a blue dress shirt and bright red bowtie, blue jeans, but no suitcoat. He held a pointer stick in his hand. He introduced himself, welcomed us to the school, and abruptly began our first anatomy lecture. He showed us large, oversized drawings of the anatomy of the human arm. He used his pointer stick to discuss each detail of interest. As he went through the material I realized that this was going to be the most fascinating year of my life – and possibly I would say that about each year to come. What I was learning was absolutely captivating. To see the body explained in such detail!! I sensed the inspiration and UTTER AWE that the entire classroom was feeling at that moment.

After bedazzling us for 30 minutes of rapid-fire anatomy facts, he suddenly stepped a few feet closer to the lecture seats and put down his pointer. He took a seat and addressed us very personally and from the heart: "Ladies and gents, what you are about to go through is a gauntlet, a daunting ordeal to be sure…and it will require you to apply yourselves toward your studies at a higher level than you have ever done previously. But you all know that. And you have proven that you are up to the challenge of studying long hours."

I wasn't expecting what he said next:

"Do you think you are ever going to be less busy than you are now, in the middle of medical school? You aren't. You will go on to residency, which is even more demanding of your time, and then on to medical practice which leaves you even less free time. If you don't make time now for personal development, it won't ever happen. You are kidding yourself to think you can find the time later on. So I implore you all to start running.

"Grandma's Saloon and Deli sponsored a marathon here last summer. I ran their inaugural race and it was a blast. I want to see all of you on the starting line for the second annual Grandma's marathon next June."

He continued:

"The marathon is not a race you can just enter and expect to finish. You must start running now if you want to have the stamina to make it through. You will have to make time in your busy schedules to run three to five times a week. The runs will gradually get longer. And the main benefit won't be for what it does to your bodies…"

He paused.

"It will be for what it does up here." He pointed to his head.

And so it happened that about a fourth of our medical school class took up serious training for the next marathon, which was nine months away.

And Dr. Leppi was right: it did more for keeping me sane in that first year of med school than what it did to tone my body.

I was a second-year medical student when the summer of 1978 introduced me to two things that altered my attitude toward medical school and the long road ahead of me. One was Grandma's marathon, and the other was Dr. Carl Griesy. It's wonderfully poetic that both experiences began in Two Harbors, Minnesota.

The port town of Two Harbors is primarily a tourist trap, conveniently situated north of Duluth along the expressway which continues all the way to the Canadian border. Most of the shops in Two Harbors attempt to capitalize on the rich heritage of the town's glory days when iron ore and railroads and busy shipping traffic meant plentiful jobs and a busy, growing town. In its heyday, much of the iron ore from ranges in central Minnesota was shipped to this port via a thriving railroad business. The final destination of the trains were the docks along the shore, which are still somewhat operational but on a much smaller scale than previously. In recent years, as a consequence of the railroad layoffs and dwindling industrial base, the tourist trade became a growing focus, and a large steam locomotive from the early days of logging and iron ore was planted along the shore next to the ore docks for tourists to visit. While passing through town, I visited that locomotive once, not knowing that just a hundred yards up that street was a physician's office which would someday become a second home to me, and at the other end of town was a street that would introduce me to the world of marathons.

The Marathon

In 1977, Grandma's Saloon and Deli, located next to the aerial lift bridge in the harbor of Duluth, decided to sponsor a marathon. Two Harbors was chosen for the starting point of this race because of its unique geography, situated exactly 26.2 miles north of downtown Duluth. The scenic route of old highway 61 was felt to be perfectly suited for a marathon course; undulating hills, beautiful coniferous trees, and breathtaking views of Lake Superior's rocky north shoreline might lead one to wonder if God didn't create this stretch of road with the marathon in mind. The icy cool lake breezes and occasional tailwinds have brought many runners to this section of highway to train for what is now an annual event.

The third Saturday in June 1978 rolled around, and I found myself huddled in a cluster of 680 bodies on the starting line of the marathon. None of us had the slightest notion of what the marathon gauntlet extracts from one's body during the race, or we'd have used medical school studies as an excuse to avoid the challenge.

We were packed closely together, shivering in the cool air, trying to avoid tightening up of muscles, awaiting the gun at the start of the second annual Grandma's marathon. I enjoyed the air of anticipation. Before a race runners tend to be upbeat, positive people, and it felt good to be huddled with that positive energy wave. It was very infectious – in a good way.

Not knowing what was to come, I was very relaxed and talking freely with the runners around me. I'd gone dancing with my girlfriend Toni the night before, and had slept well afterward. I hadn't worried about stressing my legs with the dancing.

My naiveté was probably quite apparent to this assemblage of mostly seasoned runners, who were sporting brightly colored outfits with matching

22

shoes and sweat suits. I wore a tattered pair of old Brooks' running shoes held together with athletic tape. An oversized shirt and boxer shorts completed my ensemble. I had no idea that my running equipment was inadequate by comparison to the serious runners. As one runner was changing his shirt, I noticed that his nipples were taped, which confused me.

A train which traveled the scenic route along Lake Superior brought tourists from Duluth to watch the start of the race at the outskirts of Two Harbors. The bushes along the side of the road were lined with men relieving their bladders, while the women and a few modest men waited in long lines to use the satellite porta-potties.

I shivered as I waited for the gun to signal the start. It was barely 50 degrees, with a moderate breeze, and I had no protective clothing to warm my muscles. I saw a runner cupping both hands around a Styrofoam cup with hot apple cider, the steam rising off the cup. The apple aroma wafted past my nose and I felt warmer for just a second. The colder I got, the more nervous I got, and my psyche began to falter. I'd been on the cross-country team in high school, and on the swimming team. I was used to races, so why the nerves? I knew it was because I had no clue whatsoever what this distance would do to me. 26.2 miles…TWENTY-SIX MILES!! I was very scared of failing. Fear always irritates my bladder. I briefly considered standing in line for the port-potty, but looked at my watch and knew that the gun would soon go off.

The gunshot rang out. The front runners broke immediately into a fast-paced pack well ahead of the rest of us, who were moving forward slowly, almost walking, trying to fight our way through the mass of bodies in front of us. The beginning is the most dangerous time of a marathon, when a runner can step on the hind leg of a runner in front of him and unintentionally cause injury. From where I started near the back of the pack, it took almost a minute just to cross the starting line. I was already a minute behind!

After several miles, the hoard of runners fanned out, and I was able to pick up my stride. I was in the middle of the pack of almost 700 runners, trying to hold pace with those around me, wondering all the while if I would be able to go the distance. The longest I had run in practice was thirteen miles. I had been informed that doing half the distance at least once was all that was necessary to finish a marathon, and that training runs that were over fifteen miles or so were actually harmful because they broke the body down. Smart runners avoided long training runs close to the race date. I was very insecure about my chances of finishing, but that was a mixed blessing. On one hand, not knowing my capacity for this type of endurance was unsettling, but on the other hand, not knowing the agony that was to come was fortuitous.

I hadn't conceived of a strategy for pacing myself because I had had no race experience. Fortunately, I began at a slow pace, eight minutes per mile, and held it for the first nine miles.

It was a beautiful day, sunny, and the temperature quickly rose to the mid 60's. I remembered Dr. Leppi's advice to drink lots of water along the way, even if I didn't feel thirsty. By the time I felt thirsty, he'd warned, it would be too late to correct it and my muscles would shut down.

Because of the gradually increasing temperature, many of the runners had taken off their shirts, which gave me the chance to observe how muscular and fit many of them seemed as they strode comfortably ahead of me. At first, I noticed only the women, slender and lithe, like gazelles effortlessly "dusting" me. Then I realized that even the well-toned men were beautiful, in the sense that they had obviously invested a lot into their bodies, as each rippling muscle and tendon attested to. And no fat! I had imagined that I was thin, but I felt obese in this crowd.

At mile nine, as I gazed out across the Lake Superior harbor, I caught my first glimpse of the aerial lift bridge next to the finish line. That psyched me up, so I picked up my pace. Before seeing that bridge, which signaled the end, my mood was negative, mostly due to fear of failure. Despite all the beauty of the Lake Superior lakeshore with its spruce trees, and the road replete with interesting curves and rolling hills, I was feeling a big need to visualize my destination, so I could imagine the task ahead. At mile 12, three miles after first seeing that bridge in the distance, now my pace was steadily increasing. I passed two of my classmates who told me later that I looked like a spring chicken zooming by them.

Then at mile 13 I saw the first real casualties. Several runners had dropped out along the way to stretch cramped up hamstrings and other sore muscles. But now I saw a guy sitting beside a tree and he looked completely exhausted – I knew he wasn't coming back to finish the race. His girlfriend had dropped out to be with him. It was my first encounter with "road kill". I worried that I was in store for that same fate down the road somewhere.

24

By mile 15, I wondered if that darned aerial lift bridge in downtown Duluth was ever going to appear any bigger in size. It HAD to get bigger, to prove to me that I was getting closer to my Duluth endpoint. My legs were still in the race, but my mind was feeling the strain, as doubt was setting in.

Then suddenly I realized that I had been drinking too much at the water stops; my bladder would not hold out until the finish line. Horrible thought! I was in a pack of runners 12–15 wide across the road. What should I do? No port-pottys around. Finally out of desperation I moved to the side of the road, a few feet from the masses whisking by me, and pulled down my shorts and peed into the grass on the side of the road, right in front of onlookers. At that point the desperation overcame any pride. It took 15 seconds that seemed like 10 minutes. I re-joined the race and left the onlookers in my rear view mirror, and my embarrassment eased.

The best training for a marathon is to never have run one before. The saying goes that ignorance is bliss. That's because the race is mostly a mental contest, a test of willpower. Anyone who finishes the race will not soon forget the pain and mental anguish, and this memory will likely affect future marathon attempts, much as when a woman finishing childbirth vows to get her husband "fixed" and avoid that misery ever again. Obviously, an aspiring marathoner must put in long, arduous months of roadwork, but the training runs tend to be shorter than a marathon, ten to fifteen miles or less, and because the endpoint of any training run is flexible, the motivation for a training run is easier.

In contrast, even the well-trained athlete must "boot up" mentally before the marathon. The temptation to quit is enormous, especially in the middle miles, from mile 13 to 20, when psychologically there's nothing imminent to focus upon. The first few miles roll along easily, because the runners themselves are talking and supporting each other. By mile five, it's easy to start looking ahead to mile ten, which is double digits. From there, mile 13 is a goal because it's halfway. That's when the trouble starts. After 13 miles you're only halfway through the race!! By that point, the banter between runners has ceased, as each one looks within to find some motivation to continue. It's a long way to mile 20, and the body is already reminding you that you've run longer than you ever have in training, and it's time to quit and take a shower.

At mile 17 I saw an ambulance attempting to plow through a row of runners on the course. Then I spied the target – another runner collapsed on the side of the road ahead of me. This one looked even worse – she was wheezing and struggling to breathe. In the miles to come I encountered more and more scenes like this one, and several more ambulances made their way along the race road.

Mile 20 or thereabouts is usually referred to as "the wall" because it's a point in the race where the body can run out of energy, muscles "freeze up", hypothermia sets in, or any number of equally humbling and disappointing variations of physiological exhaustion. I don't remember much about running the first twenty miles, except that a fat, balding man in his mid-fifties –with a potbelly – passed me at one point and I could have cried.

Having never heard of "the wall", I was blissfully thinking at mile 17 that I had conquered this run because I was averaging almost seven minutes per mile and feeling strong. I saw my dad sitting along the side of the road at 18, and he asked if I thought I would finish. I looked at him with that "Oh, Dad!" expression as if to question his lack of faith, but perhaps he had a better feel for what lay ahead than did I.

For most, the race begins all over again after mile 20. There were still 6.2 miles to go, exactly a ten kilometer race, which in and of itself had always seemed to me to be a long distance. Veteran marathoners will often describe the marathon as "a 10K race with a 20 mile starting line." It's really bittersweet to feel the rush of pride at having accomplished twenty miles only to realize in anguish that a 10K race is left to go.

"The wall" hit me at 22 miles. Psychologically I was bankrupt. Any elation I had felt earlier about running over twenty miles was long gone now. I had been running almost three hours already, and the sun had turned the morning's chill to 70 degrees, which is too warm to run comfortably for long distance.

Time seems most relative in moments of pain or stress. Each mile marker now seemed farther away than the last, and each minute of running seemed to take four or five. I had learned to use my watch to estimate when the next mile marker would come into view; those mile markers were my life now.

At 23 miles, I passed someone with a hose who sprayed me off for three seconds as I passed. That got me through another mile. Although there were only three miles to go, every step was becoming a challenge. I was now running through the section of Duluth along London Road where the larger mansions along the lake are located, but I didn't notice them. I passed "Glensheen", the mansion of the Congdon family, where Elizabeth Congdon had been murdered during the marathon week the previous year, but I didn't notice it either. I was living within myself now, trying to forget the distance and concentrating on putting one foot in front of the other. I knew that if I stopped, I wouldn't be able to start again.

I reached "Lemon Drop" hill, named for the Lemon Drop Restaurant located at the top of it. My legs felt like lead, so I walked and ran alternately, and noticed that each time I stopped to walk it was more difficult to pick up my legs into a running stride again. My body was "freezing up", so I reminded myself that I had to keep moving at all costs or hang it up altogether. At the top of the hill, I saw a large banner at the Lemon Drop Inn which read: "Rosie's Starting Point."

It caused me to laugh for five seconds. Rosie Ruiz was the woman who had come out of nowhere to win the Boston Marathon the year before, and subsequent checks of videotapes revealed that she had sneaked herself into the race somewhere after mile 20. She was disqualified, of course, and now she was a standing joke among marathoners.

Getting up Lemon Drop hill drained my legs, but from there it was a downhill coast along Duluth's downtown strip of hotels and fast-food places, and my mind began to dare to look for the finish. As I started down the hill, I saw Lake Superior and the aerial lift bridge, which had been hidden while I had been running through the last four miles of suburbia. Finally the bridge looked so big that I knew I was getting close.

Now I was in the heart of downtown, which promised that the agony would end soon. I didn't have the big picture of what a milestone this was in my life, or I would have taken in the crowd of people lining the street on both sides, and I would have smiled at them as they called out their cheers of encouragement.

Then we left the downtown area and wound through the final two miles of the race course. The cheers were gone. The road was cluttered with hundreds of smashed small paper cups from the water stop we passed through. I was now too nauseated to drink water. All the optimism and energy of the starting line was gone now, and the camaraderie I'd shared earlier with the runners beside was replaced by the silence of concentration, the determination to just get it over with. It is quite remarkable to compare the noise and excitement of the start of a marathon with the quiet and resignation that one witnesses at the finish line. At the beginning of every major war, there are those that cheer wildly with nationalist pride, fervor and enthusiasm. They cheer at parades. They charge forward. As the war draws to a close, the cheers and excitement are long gone. And so it was with this race. I was drained beyond the ability to express my pain. I knew I couldn't walk. That would be the kiss of death. If I walked, I would drop. So I jogged the slowest pace that would keep me moving forward.

Reaching mile 26 was incredibly positive for my morale. Running the next .2 miles should be a cakewalk, I thought, but that 2/10ths of a mile seemed the longest of all. At least ten runners passed me in the final stretch to the finish line chute; they grimaced with effort and moved past me but I didn't object. I didn't react at all. I no longer possessed the will to care, let alone the will to compete.

As I crossed the finish line just under 200th place, I heard the timekeeper call out "Three hours, fifteen minutes". I passed through the chute and someone handed me a shirt, and I sat down. Just then, I felt myself fainting, and I blacked out momentarily as the blood rushed from my head to my legs. One of my classmates came over to congratulate me and I tried to stand up, but discovered that I couldn't get up off my feet.

I looked down at my shirt and noticed two vertical red lines on my chest. I pulled off my shirt and discovered that my nipples looked like ground hamburger; they were bleeding, all the way from the nipple down to my navel. Three hours of my T-shirt rubbing my chest had destroyed my nipples. Immediately, I understood why that runner had taped his nipples before the race.

Within minutes, "rigor mortise" set in and I couldn't move without great effort. I felt like a nursing home patient with severe arthritis who was attempting to walk up the steps of the Statue of Liberty. I found my dad, with some difficulty, and limped to the van for the victory ride home. As I pondered this watershed moment, I re-lived the gut-wrenching struggle to hang on after mile 22, to avoid walking for fear that I might quit altogether. There was always doubt that I would finish. It intensified after mile 22 when I was the most exhausted. But I kept running, slowly moving forward.

My conclusion: there wouldn't be any more marathons in my future. Then I had an epiphany: that this marathon was never about racing other runners, it was a race within myself. It was a mental battle as much as a physical struggle. Finishing the race taught me something about perseverance in the face of fatigue: you succeed by putting one foot in front of the other. That lesson would soon help me when I reached residency training. Understand what it takes to finish a marathon and you will be well on your way to surviving your residency.

(*Editor's note*: I have since completed 25 more marathons, including six Boston marathons, New York City, Chicago, and 12 more Grandma's marathons. Years ago I promised to pay my sister Kathy $100 if I ran any more marathons. I was that convinced that I was finished with them. I now owe her a lot of cash. I will not let her read this book.)

The "Old Poop"

It was a cool morning in September of 1978, three months after the marathon, when I met Dr. Carl Valentine Griesy, a solo family practitioner in the tiny port town of Two Harbors. I was in my second year of med school in Duluth. My mind was inundated with trivia about anatomy and physiology, but I had no clue whatsoever about how it would all relate to actual medical practice. He was to be my introduction to the real world of medicine.

Driving into Two Harbors from my apartment in Duluth was like taking a trip back into time, as I passed under an abandoned railroad bridge into the heart of the downtown area where his office was located, just up the hill from where "the last of the world's largest steam locomotives" stood on display. He was renting space between the Moose Club and the Denny's, across the street from the drugstore, in short, in the heart of the downtown business district.

I arrived late, and his receptionist Louise greeted me in the waiting room. She was very cute, approximately mid-twentyish, petite, with dark curly hair, and she seemed very ebullient. My eye caught her left hand where I discovered to my dismay that she was married.

She smiled as she told me, "He's in a room with a patient, but he's expecting you. Come to the break room and wait."

To say I was excited was an understatement. I had never seen a doctor's office from an inside perspective. Every visit I had to the doctor was for something painful, like immunizations. I had never been allowed to pull back the curtain to see what real doctors are like, but this was my big opportunity. I understood that doctors are busy people and I wondered if Dr. Griesy would have any interest in spending time on me. My late arrival left me off to a bad start. As his receptionist Louise and I walked down the hall, I noticed that his office was not at all what I expected. It was small, and very homey, like someone's dorm room. There were jokes taped to the walls, and pictures of dozens of patients and other people filling all of the available spaces on doors, cabinets, windows. I noticed that some were pictures of babies that he'd delivered.

Louise led me down the hall past several small exam rooms and a tiny X-ray room and a little cul-de-sac in between them where the lab was nestled. A lady sat hunched over a microscope. She didn't bother to lookup as we passed.

"That's Rosie – she works in the lab and does our X-rays. I'd introduce you, but she's doing a white count."

The tour ended in the equally tiny break room, where a large bag of donuts was waiting on a card table which filled most of the room's available space. As I sat there waiting for him, I realized that the entire office was not much larger than an apartment, hardly the imposing structure befitting the pillar of the community that undoubtedly he was.

I was too nervous to eat a donut. Suddenly, he emerged from the examination room. He was a large man, six feet five inches or so, with a big boned 260-pound frame. I was intimidated until he smiled at me and introduced himself.

"Hello, sir, I'm Carl Griesy. I'll visit with you in a minute."

Already I felt more at ease. I followed him into the cul-de-sac which was his lab and work area, where he picked up a microphone attached to a tape recorder and began dictating notes about his last patient.

"Okay, now for Mrs. Jones. Aches, snuffy nose since Tuesday, kids have the same thing. Yellow sputum. Low-grade temp. On exam, TMs are slightly injected, clear rhinorrhea, a bit of a smoker's palate, and the throat is injected with some exudate, Strep culture taken, mild shotty anterior nodes, no posterior nodes, chest is clear and heart sounds are normal, no murmur..."

He was talking a mile a minute, with such ease that it was obvious he had done this a thousand times, if not ten thousand. I wondered how the transcriptionist could understand that rapid banter to type it into the patient's chart. I couldn't keep up with what he was saying, but I was impressed by it. As he talked, I scanned the small lab area. To the right stood a refrigerator with frozen medications, immunizations injections and culture plates on the bottom shelf, and Dairy Queen dilly bars on the top shelf. On the center shelf stood a large glass full of iced tea which he grabbed halfway through his dictation. He took a giant gulp, and placed it back in the fridge. On the outside of the fridge were Xeroxed pictures of jokes, cute sayings, and ads for drugs. Three walls of the cul-de-sac which was his laboratory area had cupboards filled to bursting with free samples of drugs. They had been given to him by the drug company salespersons who frequently visited to promote their latest medications.

I noticed also that on top of the cupboards was a stack of cartons of tootsie roll pops and little toys. Did he have that much of a sweet tooth? I wondered. Just then, he finished dictating.

I bravely offered him a compliment. "Wow, you talk fast. I couldn't keep up with you, Dr. Griesy."

He laughed. He struck me as almost jolly, but also serious, as appropriate to his trade.

"After a few hundred of those, you'll get the hang of it." He proceeded to sermonize.

"I tell all of my students the same thing: Learn medicine from me if you will, but don't imitate my style of practice. The solo practitioner is a thing of the past. The hours are long and it's a crazy lifestyle."

I later learned that Dr. Griesy was born in Belmond, Iowa in 1928. He graduated from high school at the age of 16, and attended Luther College In Iowa before enlisting in the United States Army in 1946 as a surgical technician. For much of that time he was deployed in Okinawa. After receiving a World War II Victory Medal, he was discharged in 1948. He then left the Army to attend medical school at the University of Iowa. He then moved to Rock Rapids, Iowa to begin a solo practice as a family doctor. In the early 1970s he moved his family to Two Harbors because of his love of the north shore of Lake Superior.

Dr. Griesy and I chatted a bit more and discovered that we'd both graduated from Luther College in Decorah, Iowa. He said that he'd barely made it through, but I didn't quite believe him. (I later learned that he'd scored near the top of his family practice recertification boards.) His humility was disarming, and steadily I felt more comfortable around him, as if being in the home of a longtime friend.

He took me into the next room. Without looking at the chart, he said:

"Hello Mrs. Hank, Hi Jeremy, and little Josh. Looks like you have a sick punk in here. I have a student doctor with me today – Rich Mayerchak."

I was surprised and impressed that he never once had to look at the chart to remember their names, or mine. They all seemed as at ease with him as I felt, which was easy to understand.

He proceeded to examine Josh, the little boy, who was flushed and had a fever. I noticed as he leaned over the almost three-year-old that there was a picture on the wall of a Norman Rockwell painting showing a doctor listening to the heart of a little girl's doll. It seemed to fit the scene before me.

Josh's problem was an infected left ear. I stood off to the side and watched, and to my surprise, Dr. Griesy asked me to take a look at the ear. I couldn't see in the ear very well at first. He noticed my struggle, and then he showed me how to pull the lobe of the ear to straighten out the canal to get a better look. Then I saw the bright red eardrum. My first real diagnosis! My faced beamed with excitement.

Dr. Griesy proceeded to the lab where he grabbed a bottle of Amoxicillin.

He explained. "The old man isn't working and they have more kids at home, so I'm going to help them out with this free sample, which is enough for ten days. Then I'll recheck the ear."

For me, that small act of benevolence symbolized the virtue of family practice, which is patient-oriented care enhanced by intimate knowledge of the patient's family of origin and their unique circumstances and needs.

But that wasn't all. After giving Mrs. Hank the free samples, he sat down and wrote out prescriptions for Josh and Jeremy.

"You take these to the Dairy Queen – it's pretty warm out there today."

He told me they were prescriptions for ice cream cones. He had an arrangement with the Dairy Queen up the street which allowed free ice cream cones for anyone with a handwritten Dr. Griesy prescription.

Suddenly I realized what the tootsie roll pops and toys were for. No wonder the kids felt at ease coming to see him. This guy understood people. His practice flourished because he was an astute student of human nature, able to personally relate to the human predicament.

As they left, he headed for the iced tea in the fridge and grabbed the Dictaphone and whipped off another note at blinding speed. Halfway through it, he was paged overhead for a phone call. It was the pharmacy down the street.

"Hello, sir…, oh, not too bad for an old poop… yes, give her the extend tabs, number 60, one b.i.d., non-rep… any new jokes? Okay, (chuckle), bye-bye…"

Without losing his stream of thought, he went right back to his dictation. Wow, what a memory, I thought. As he finished, he said, "…and thank you ma'am." He was courteous even to his typist.

We saw a few more patients and I asked if I could spend some time looking through all the cabinets in the lab which were crammed full of drugs. My pharmacology classes were coming alive as I saw the drugs in real life for the first time. I had learned all the generic names, but these had trade or brand names which I was unfamiliar with. For example, I had studied the generic antibiotic doxycycline, but the brand name drug he had in his cabinet was Doryx, which was the same thing. I was surprised that Dr. Griesy knew not only both sets of names, but also what most of the pills looked like, from the color, to the shape, to the markings. Where did he have room in his brain for all of that trivia?

As I buried myself in the drug cabinets, he went to the break room where Louise, the receptionist (who was also the insurance lady, billings/accounts person, and office organizer), was close to tears. He closed the door and they talked for a few minutes. When he emerged, she seemed more composed. Later in the day, I noticed him in the back room talking to Rosie, who worked in the lab. She was also close to tears, and after their conversation, seemed more in control. I didn't ask him about it, but after we finished up for the day and the staff left, he commented:

"One thing about having employees, if you spend some time with one, you have to do the same with another. They're like cats and they don't like favoritism. Louise was having some marital problems she wanted to tell me about, but that made Rosie jealous. You have to walk a tightrope around here sometimes."

So, not only did he understand the science of medicine, and the psychology of little kids, he understood the diplomacy of running a business and the daily fires that needed extinguishing.

It was already evening when I left the clinic that first day, but it had gone fast. So much to absorb! I knew I would learn a lot from Dr. Griesy if I got the chance to spend more time with him.

I drove home along the scenic route from Two Harbors to Duluth, where I had an apartment near the medical school. It was the first time I'd passed that way since the marathon in June. I was hoping that viewing the course would jar some memories that I couldn't seem to recall, maybe some faces of supporters lining the road, or one of the many sailboats and yachts anchored along the shoreline for the race, but to no avail. All I could remember was the agony of the last four to six miles. The pain was still vivid. As I arrived in Duluth, I was stupefied that I'd actually run that far, as the drive itself seemed to take forever. Dr. Leppi, our medical school dean, was now talking about the Boston marathon, and it fascinated me, but after the drive to Duluth I realized that the marathon was just too long a run for anyone with any common sense, and I would never be stupid enough to attempt it again.

When I reached my apartment, I called my girlfriend Toni. It was such a beautiful evening, that we decided to camp out at Park Point and watch the stars. One of the things I loved most about Duluth was the canopy of stars reflecting on a still Lake Superior on a windless night, best appreciated on the beach they called Park Point.

We fired up "Mighty Achilles", my dented in, beat up '68 Ford LTD that used more oil than gasoline, and headed for the shore. It was clear and crisp, and the Northern Lights – the Aurora Borealis – made a spectacular appearance as we watched in delight, quite alone in our sleeping bags on that long stretch of beach. Toni was still in college, trying to make up her mind about what to do with her life. I'd met her at church. She was intelligent, beautiful, and very high spirited. We both desired spiritual growth, and spent a lot of time on Lake Superior's shores talking about God. She added a lifesaving element of reality to what otherwise seemed for me to be a surrealistic world.

In the morning, after driving Toni to school, for some strange reason I decided to drive the marathon course again on my way up to Two Harbors. I was due to spend the day with Dr. Griesy again. Call it curiosity, or call it amnesia, but I wanted to see the marathon course. During the drive, a light bulb turned on and it dawned on me that the secret to completing the marathon was to break it into small pieces. I had succeeded by fooling myself that I was only going out for a five-mile run, and after that I had talked myself into five more miles, and so on. After seeing what lay ahead of me with almost three more years of medical school and three of

34

internship and residency, I decided to treat the education process as a marathon, and look only to the end of the year as my goal, much like looking for the next mile marker. If eventually I could make it all the way to a practice like Dr. Griesy had in the real world, I would be in heaven, and the race would be won.

An ore boat making its way into the Duluth harbor let out a booming groan to signal the aerial lift bridge of its arrival. The bridge began the slow ascent for which it was famous – the largest aerial lift bridge of its kind in the world.– After it had fully ascended, traffic on both sides came to a halt to allow passage of the 1,000-foot-long vessel. My arrival to the clinic was less heralded. Dr. Griesy was already in a room, so I visited with his lovely receptionist Louise in the front office. She was definitely in better spirits than the afternoon before, and as we talked, I noted that there was nothing pretentious or arrogant about her, which made her even more attractive.

Since I had some time to kill, she showed me how the billing and insurance forms were handled.

Stacks of horizontal files neatly alphabetized were testimony that Dr. Griesy had an enormous following in the town. I flipped through several charts to get a feel for his style of dictating. Then I came across the "G" section and discovered that he had a chart on himself! I opened it and read the first entry:

"The old poop is sick today. Non-productive cough. White count 4,000. Probably viral. Rx amantadine 100 mg b.i.d. Throat culture pending."

His routine was so consistent that he didn't even allow himself to slack off when self-medicating! He had to record it. Why so compulsive? I remembered something he had told me the day before about doing things the same way every time so I wouldn't forget something. For instance, when examining the patient, always starting with the head and working my way down so as not to forget what I'd covered.

My knowledge of his past history was sketchy, but I knew that he'd practiced in small towns in Iowa and South Dakota before migrating northward to Two Harbors, where he'd spent the last decade or so. Was his compulsive behavior a reflection of past mistakes? In his South Dakota days, had he neglected to record some important detail in someone's chart, or had he forgotten to examine someone's ears and, in the process, missed something significant? Time and again he showed me the correct way to hold an otoscope to protect myself from piercing a patient's ear. Had he done that by mistake? Although I had no evidence of mistakes or "skeletons" in his closet, I suspected that Carl Griesy was a living example of the axiom:

"Good judgement comes from experience. Experience comes from bad judgement." This was an experienced doctor who seemed to possess great judgment.

As I was finished reading his chart notes on "the Old Poop", he came out of an exam room, dressed in a suit and tie, with a red stethoscope curled twice around his neck. It detracted from a corporate image, I thought, but it seemed to describe the merger he'd made between his formal education and his informal small-town practice style.

He had a drink of iced tea and dictated, and then said hello and took me to the break room for a donut. And then we started all over again, going from room to room, listening to problems, examining, and offering solutions, usually in the form of a prescription of some kind, although I noticed that one of his most effective treatments was his ability to listen. He was never in a hurry to leave a patient room.

The patients exploited his generosity of time, but he didn't seem to mind, even though the morning spilled over into the afternoon and lunch had to be cut short. And, they didn't seem to mind my eavesdropping on their personal problems as they unloaded them on him. Dr. Griesy's gift to his patients, as to me, was his accessibility. For a man with so much education and experience to be so approachable was no small miracle in my estimation. I had never experienced that degree of comfort with any of the physicians I had seen as a youth. This inside perspective on the medical world was fascinating, and I couldn't get enough of it. It was eye-opening to say the least.

The more I watched him, the more apparent was the methodical rote by which he practiced. "Always undress the patient," he said. "You can't find out what's wrong if you don't examine the area. You can't hear the lungs through the shirt." I had been guilty of practicing my exams with people clothed, putting my stethoscope underneath the sweater, but not beneath the shirt because it took too much time or I was too embarrassed to have the patient undress. He insisted that I learn to be methodical and thorough lest I make a costly mistake by missing something.

The last patient of the day was a ten-year-old boy with a nasty cough.

Dr. Griesy sent me in to examine him first. I was all thumbs initially, trying not to let on to his mother just how green I was, although it must have been obvious. Instead of a methodical head-to-toe approach to my exam, I started by listening to his chest, since he had a cough. Then I looked in his ears, eyes, and mouth, and excused myself to discuss my findings with Dr. Griesy. I'd never had first crack at examining someone; I found it uncomfortable as well as exciting.

Dr. Griesy was waiting for me as I exited the room. "Well, what did you find?"

I was timid in my response. "His ears are clear, his lungs sound kind of raspy, especially on the right, and I think I heard rhonchi. Oh, he's been coughing for two weeks. His throat…"

Dr. Griesy cut me off.

"Wait a minute", he blurted… "Let's start over. Haven't you ever heard of the SOAP system? The S is for "subjective", the history of the problem. The O is for "objective", your exam findings. The A is for "assessment", your working diagnosis, and P is for "plan". So, tell me about his problem before you get to your exam."

Again, the point was hammered home about being methodical, approaching every patient in an organized and consistent manner. I started over:

"Okay. He's 10 years old. He's been coughing for two weeks. No sputum. No fever. I think he's had a sore throat. On exam, his head and neck were normal, but I heard raspy lung sounds bilaterally and maybe some rhonchi on the right."

"What about his heart?" he asked.

In my haste and disorganization, I had forgotten to listen to his heart. I apologized to Dr. Griesy, as the point about examining in the same order each time was more personally received. We then entered the room together.

"Hello, Mrs. Jackson. Student doctor Mayerchak tells me you have the crud, John. How long have you been coughing?"

He went over the same questions and then proceeded to a more thorough exam than I did, in half the time it took for mine. My only consolation was that he agreed with my findings in the lungs. After we discussed the antibiotic choice and follow up management, the boy and his mother got up to leave.

"John, you're in the fifth grade, right? Have you picked out a girlfriend yet? Girls are like apples, you know… if you wait too long, all that's left at the bottom of the barrel are the rotten ones…"

John turned red with mild embarrassment, but his look turned to anticipation as he saw Dr. Griesy write out an ice cream cone prescription.

As I headed home that evening, I reflected on all the wonderful new lessons I was learning from Dr. Griesy. The past two days had provided my first glimpse of the destination, private practice, much as the nine-mile mark had given me the first glimpse of the finish line in the marathon, when the aerial lift bridge, tiny and far-off, had briefly come into view. The road ahead seemed interminable, but I vowed to break it into mini goals. The first would be to get through my second year of school and pass part 1 of the

National Boards, the mother of all nightmares. I wouldn't be back to see Dr. Griesy until – or unless – I passed. And, if I didn't pass… I shuddered even to think about it.

"The Ultimate Nightmare"

Duluth. June 12, 1979. Tuesday, 8:00 a.m.

I am no stranger to difficult exams. I am the master of exams. I have aced every exam in college. I graduated from Luther College with a 4.0 GPA, top of my class. Not a single A minus. I once took a third semester calculus exam with 10 problems. It was a 24-hour take-home exam in which I spent 19 straight hours locked in a room writing 34 pages of single-spaced math equations, integrating by parts the triple integrals and solving the complicated questions. That was a piece of cake compared to what I am about to face in this test today.

On this day the test-taking whiz is scared. This has me really rattled. I'm looking around the room and surveying the crowd. It dawns on me that everybody in this room is a gunner, an accomplished exam-taker, just like me, or they wouldn't have made it into medical school. With two years of med school behind us, these minds represent the cream of the cream of test performers.

College had been intense from day one, with 180 pre-meds the first year narrowed down to twelve by the time we were seniors. In the year I matriculated at Duluth, there had been over 900 applications for just 48 positions in the freshman medical class. Even with a 4.0 grade point average and good entrance exam scores, there wasn't any guarantee that I would be accepted. But somehow, I made the cut, as did the rest of the people now gathered in this room.

Once again, a cut will be made. This two-day, 13-hour, 1,000 question examination will determine who goes on to become third year students, and who falls behind a year while nervously waiting to retake the test in twelve months. Anyone who fails on the second try is history. He or she will no longer have an option to finish medical school.

From the first day of medical school two years earlier, they've been reminding us of this test – the National Boards Part 1 – mentioning something about it almost every day in class. The exam is to cover seven subjects: biochemistry, anatomy, physiology, microbiology, pathology, pharmacology, and psychology/behavioral science. The examinee must pass all seven parts individually or retake the entire exam. After two years of horror stories about how difficult it will be, the full weight of the pressure is now felt by everyone in the room. I try to forget it for a moment.

Imagine a moment when time is slowed, so that the second hand of a clock takes an hour to move to its next second mark. That is the moment of a thought, as your life flashes before you, the speed of a synaptic transmission of ultrafast electrochemical volleys translated into images representing memories. Such a moment can contain hundreds of pictures of past experiences.

Such a moment has occurred for me presently. I'm not sure if time is indeed passing, but my mind is flooded with images of gentler times. As I scan the room in this frozen moment, my mind does an instant replay of the past two years on ultra-fast-forward.

I remember the awe I felt during my first anatomy class, taking my dad to see my cadaver, and sneaking into the anatomy lab at 3 a.m. one night to be alone with 15 cadavers as I pondered what their lives had been about – this gathering of unlikely roommates – and grasped the meaning of the Latin inscription on the wall: "vivos mortui docenti"– "the dead teach the living".

I recall how the fascination and the novelty had turned to drudgery as the classes became intense and the cycle of memorization and regurgitation went on endlessly. In two years, we'd learned every forgotten Krebs' cycle pathway, biochemical structure, formula, and theory that could possibly show up on the boards, as well as stacks of worthless drivel concerning the respective pet research project of each professor who lectured us in his or her turn. It had been a nightmarish string of cram sessions, one night for a biochem test, the next for histology, and so on, and the pressure had been far worse than any I had encountered during my pre-med days at Luther College.

So now, after two years of this intensity, one would think that we'd seen it all. No, the worst was imminently yet to come. Failing had always been a modest concern in each of our minds, but we'd all passed, so none of us had had to face it yet. To fail would be to throw away thousands of dollars we'd invested in med school, and thousands of hours of study, yet the reality was that, by Board rules, the lowest 12% would automatically fail.

Everyone would have to scramble to score better than the bottom 12% of us. That might not seem so hard to do, but as I scanned the room, I realized that everyone in here was exceptionally bright, so it seemed grossly inappropriate that someone here should not make the cut to move on.

They had given us ten days after final exams to prepare for this test. I had studied every day from 6 a.m. to midnight. Never had I studied so long or crammed so intensely. My head was exploding with facts. At one point during that ten days, I had been so wired with anxiety that I'd downed a fifth of vodka in a half gallon of orange juice in hopes of getting some sleep, and had spent the entire next day studying with my head between my knees and coping with a massive headache.

Ironically, despite majoring in biochemistry in college, it had been my weakest subject in med school – probably because I'd taken it so much for granted. Fortunately, my girlfriend Toni had just taken biochem in college and was a pro, and she'd tutored me about all the crucial enzymes and cofactors, so I thought I was ready in that area.

Now those ten days of agony were over, and the moment of truth approached. In a sense, I was glad; I couldn't handle any more cramming. Nevertheless, I was scared as hell. I'd been the only one in my class to flunk both previous practice exams, but I knew the reason was because I hadn't taken them seriously. Still, my confidence in my ability to take standardized tests was sorely lacking at this moment.

The moment of a thousand thoughts was disrupted as the proctor handed me exam booklet 951401. I was in seat 51, specifically assigned to me by someone in Kansas City so that statistical analyses could be made comparing my answers to those of my classmates to ascertain if anyone was cheating. What a waste of my $450.00 exam fee, I thought.

The proctor made one final announcement: "Good Luck!"

The famous chemist Louis Pasteur had once stated that "Luck favors those who are prepared."

I hoped that I had prepared sufficiently.

The test began. The first block of questions were of the typical "Board format" which meant they were actually four questions in one. We all hated them, but our medical school had tested us with this same format to prepare us for this moment.

The first question read as follows:

1. True statements about vitamin B12 include:
   1) It contains a cobalt atom within a corrin ring.
   2) It is a fat-soluble vitamin stored in the liver
   3) It is an essential cofactor for the conversion of homocysteine to methionine
   4) It has no relationship to folic acid in the synthesis of DNA
      a. 1, 2, and 3
      b. 1 and 3
      c. 2 and 4 all of the above, none of the above

I stared at the question for a long time. This promised to be a rough test! I was still deciding my answer when I saw the guy next to me turn to page two. That freaked me out. I knew I had only about 20 seconds per question if I hoped to get to all of them, but this was ridiculous. One of the professors had remarked that the most common answer statistically was c, so I wrote down c for every question on the first page and moved on.

I was beginning to panic when I came across an easy one: what was the pH of blood? 7.4. – for sure!! I was on the board. Then I decided to approach this like the marathon – there were more than nine hundred questions to go, and thirteen hours – no need to panic. I would break it up into small challenges, like mile markers, and hope for endurance.

The hours passed. One section led to another. Five hundred questions later, the day ended and I went directly home and immediately to bed and fell fast asleep.

The second day's events were similar. During the last hour of the exam, on question 900-something, I fell asleep for a while. It was more like a daze

I had fallen into, but when I regained alertness, I checked my watch and was horrified to learn that I'd been out for at least ten minutes. Then, as if to seal my doom, I found a mistake I'd made in recording my last 20 answers. As I frantically tried to correct the mistake, I heard the proctor call "TIME!!", and it was all over. I'd blown at least twenty questions on a stupid mistake, and I hadn't finished about ten more. One part of me felt sick to realize that I might have to do it all over again, and the other part was too tired to care.

In the parking lot, my classmates were pouring champagne, as if we'd just won the World Series. I had a glass, then beelined home to crash once more. The wait for results promised to be interminable.

At home, on my bed, I sighed. Now I could truly relax, at least until the results came. But, what if I failed? I said a prayer asking only for a passing grade – the very bottom score would be wonderful – for indeed it had been the hardest examination I'd ever sat through. It was like the marathon – long, yet requiring alertness and a concentrated effort all along the way – and similar to the marathon, once I finished, I doubted that I could ever seriously attempt it again.

A month later, the news was out. I was the last to hear anything. Several of my classmates phoned to tell me they'd passed, which left me paranoid, because I had not been notified either way. Finally, I called the dean of the med school, who told me my scores had been sent to the wrong address. Yes, of course I'd passed! In that instant it was Christmas, the Fourth of July, my birthday and every happy day I'd ever known rolled into one. I'd made the top third nationwide. Several of the class had failed, including one that really surprised me.

That night, I sat in front of a bonfire in my back yard. I dragged out all the three-ringed binders of notes that I had taken thus far as a medical student, and systematically disassembled the notebooks and burned the contents. I read aloud many of the pages such as the various amino acid structures and Krebs' cycles, and told myself to try to forget all that worthless trivia, and THREW ALL OF MY NOTES INTO THE FIRE. It was a catharsis beyond description.

There are certain moments that stick with you forever. For me, etched right alongside the moment I sat down at the finish line of Grandma's marathon is the moment the dean told me that I'd passed my boards; both were true tests of endurance, rites of passage, that, having once been

42

hurdled, could forever be laid to rest.

October 1979 The Preceptorship

As a survivor of the traumatic National Boards ordeal, I advanced to the third year of med school, which consists of a series of clinical rotations set up in hospitals in Minneapolis and St. Paul. I had a choice of where to study independently for six weeks, so I arranged a clinical rotation in Two Harbors, Minnesota to capitalize on the wisdom of the master craftsman, Dr. Griesy.

When I began medical school, my mother gave me her 1968 Ford LTD to drive. It was very generous of her to do so, because that meant she had no car to use while my dad was at work all day. Someone had hit my front right fender while it was parked, and smashed it up severely. Also the back fender was dented noticeably. I decided to call it "Mighty Achilles" and painted that name in big bold green letters on the front right side of the car panel. When I drove down the streets of Duluth, every passing car saw the large dents, and gave me wide berth. Nobody was going to mess with "Mighty Achilles".

The air was again crisp and the sky was the deep blue that comes with autumn as I guided "Mighty Achilles" lazily northward to Two Harbors. The ore boat traffic was maximal in anticipation of season's end, and the tourist traffic to see the fall colors was equally frenetic.

I drove by the med school, and smiled victoriously as I realized that I had passed the most difficult test I would ever have to take, and I would be cruising from here on in. I paused for a moment to consider those in my class who had failed the exam. They were sentenced to spend the next nine months frantically studying the same material over again in hopes of passing their second and last shot at it. Failing a second time would disqualify them from ever graduating to third year status. How light I felt to be free of that worry!

The nightmare of studying incessantly for the National Boards exam had so colored my last six months in Duluth that I had failed to notice its beauty. Lake Superior was especially blue and the breeze was appropriately triumphant as I took my victory drive through the northern edge of town.

Instead of taking the expressway to Two Harbors, congested as it was with yuppies in Jeep Cherokees and retirees in Winnebago's, I hugged the shoreline on the scenic route to again retrace the marathon, as if helplessly

43

drawn to it like a moth to fire. It seemed even longer on this ride, and the torture of the finish was painfully fresh for an event which had occurred more than a year earlier.

After spending a couple of hospital rotations in Minneapolis as a new third year medical student, I was feeling older and more medically mature. I was curious about whether Dr. Griesy would notice the change.

Consistent with previous visits, he was occupied seeing a patient when I arrived at the clinic the next morning. Louise, looking as beautiful as ever, led me to the break room where I visited briefly with the staff.

Outwardly, everything seemed the same. The office was still bustling with activity, phones ringing, pharmaceutical reps dropping in unannounced, supplies being delivered, and the donuts were still plentiful on the break room table.

I had a Long John and quietly stood outside the cul-de-sac-like lab and read the newest sign on the cupboard:

"Life is a Test.

It is only a Test.

If this were your actual life, you would have been given better instructions."

The door opened and Dr. Griesy emerged. I had forgotten how tall and imposing he appeared. His welcoming smile relaxed any apprehension I was feeling.

"Hello sir! Glad you made it okay. The 'Funny Frau' just called and wanted to know if you'd like to join us for hangie-bers tonight.

"Sure."

He led me to the X-ray room where a film was drying. In contrast to the modern processing equipment, Dr. Griesy had an older X-ray machine with a developer that required his going into a dark room to develop the films himself. An X-ray was soaking in water, the final step before he could read it.

The film was that of a man's wrist. It was still a little wet as he put it up to the reading light.

"This is Charlie Johnson's wrist – fell on the ice last winter and it's still bothering him. Can you name the bones?"

Anatomy was still fresh in my mind, thanks to the Almighty National Boards.

"There's the navicular, that's the lunate, then the..." Right then, I discovered that I'd succeeded in forgetting the trivia I'd memorized for the Boards. Dr. Griesy could see I was faltering so he piped in:

"There's a nice mnemonic for remembering this: Never Lower Tillie's Pants – Mother Might Come Home. Navicular, Lunate, Trimetrium, etc. In this case, it's the navicular we're worried about, but it looks okay."

He strode back into Mr. Johnson's room and gave him the good news, and I noticed he had a new sign embroidered on the wall:

"Too Much of a Good Thing is Wonderful."

Typical Dr. Griesy. It was these homey touches that added so much color to this man's practice. As he was dictating his note on Mr. Johnson, Louise poked her face in the lab with the collection sheets. As receptionists often do, she collected the payments from patients and helped manage the books.

"A good day today - $1,200 dollars." Dr. Griesy was obviously pleased.

"Great – now I can pay the damn feds. I'm always up to my ass in alligators and three months behind."

Since Louise had gotten his attention, I broke in: "I saw the sign in the -ray room:

Illigitimi

Non-Carborundum

"What does it mean?" He laughed.

"Illigitimi for illegitimate. Non for no. Carborundum for a grinding wheel. Translated loosely, it means 'Don't let the bastards grind you down'."

I thought of his reference to "the feds" and his constant game of "catch up" with taxes, and I thought I understood. Or, was it the "alligators", the other stressors in his life, that were grinding him down?

We went to the next room where a lady waited for a prenatal visit.

She had a glow about her that said she was happy to be pregnant. She looked a little concerned, though, when Dr. Griesy reviewed her weight gain since the last visit.

"You're going to have to cut out the cookies and cake. You're eating for two, not three – stick to the good stuff, like milk."

He seemed to have a special rapport with his OB patients. Even when he was admonishing her, I could tell that she wasn't taking it the wrong way. Because they came in monthly at first, and weekly toward the end of the pregnancy, they became very well acquainted, he explained. As she was leaving, he imparted one last piece of advice:

"And remember… if it tastes good, spit it out!"

She laughed and frowned simultaneously. Just then, the emergency room called. He looked disappointed.

"So much for an early evening… and this was supposed to be my afternoon off. It's the horse-pital. We have a patient to see."

I was glad he said "we". He was obviously including me in his day, and I felt as if I were a part of the team. We finished the clinic and drove up the road less than a mile to the small community hospital.

A nurse met us at the entrance to the emergency room.

"Hello, Dr. Griesy, it's pretty bad…"

On the table lay a man with his right thigh flayed open, right down to the bone, the result of a chain saw accident. Dr. Griesy remarked that this was a common scenario up here on these beautiful fall woodcutting days.

I glanced unobtrusively at the patient, Connie Mattson. I tried not to dwell on the injured leg because I was quite sure I would faint from seeing the blood, which was everywhere. His wound looked like a carved Thanksgiving turkey leg, the muscle and flesh hanging loosely over the bone for twelve inches across the upper leg. The blood had oozed its way peripherally from the wound to unaffected parts of the leg and onto the exam table, and some was even dripping onto the floor. It created the illusion of a wound much worse than it was. Since it was the first trauma I'd ever seen, I was shocked. I was certain that Mr. Mattson would lose his leg.

Dr. Griesy donned a surgical gown and gloves, and surprised me by insisting that I do the same. I was expecting that the time I spent with him would be as an observer, but he was serving early notice to the contrary. As he talked to Mr. Mattson, he worked quickly to stop several of the bleeding arteries that were causing most of the mess. I noticed Mr. Mattson's jeans lying on the floor. They had a cleanly cut mark diagonally across the right upper leg where the chain saw's blade had penetrated. It must have looked a lot less severe to him before the nurses took his pants off, I deduced, because the pants had likely held the skin and muscle tightly together against the bone.

As he worked, Dr. Griesy kept Mr. Mattson occupied with conversation about each other's kids and who was up to what; apparently, most of the town was acquainted with each other. I wondered if that made it more difficult for Dr. Griesy to work on him now. I surprised myself by keeping enough cool to continue watching Dr. Griesy without fainting.

Always in the past, when watching my sisters get stitches for even tiny cuts, I'd ended up leaving the room feeling queasy, or worse.

Now, gowned and gloved like a real surgeon, I found my eyes glued to his hands, watching the way they smoothly tied knots and pulled tissues together. How could he tell what tissues he was sewing? I couldn't distinguish muscle from fascia or from fat in that bloodied mess that was once a leg.

Then, abruptly, he turned to me and handed me the needle holder with needle in place.

"Scw."

He didn't say it loudly; apparently he didn't want Mr. Mattson to notice that a novice was taking over. Or, should I say, neophyte? I'd never even sewn a stitch. I didn't know the first thing about it.

As I accepted the needle holder, my hand was shaking visibly. Dr. Griesy placed his hand over mine, and guided me through the first stitch. The needle went through the skin and out again – what a novel experience!

– and then he tied the stitch. He motioned quietly for me to try one on my own, but I fumbled with the needle holder and dropped the needle in the wound, and I was sure that the nurse and the whole world was aware of my incompetence. I retrieved the needle and secured it in the holder and awkwardly managed a stitch.

After years of practicing medicine and teaching students of my own, I would come to appreciate how difficult it must have been for Dr. Griesy to let me sew that first stitch into his patient. It would have been much easier – and definitely more expedient – for Dr. Griesy to sew him up and simply let me observe. Dr. Griesy's demeanor was remarkably calm as he watched me struggle to place each suture, and tie it with the instrument. It must have required extraordinary patience. Humphrey Bogart was once asked if he enjoyed working with Audrey Hepburn on the movie "Sabrina". His reply had been.

"She's Ok if you don't mind shooting 30 takes" – obviously annoyed at her lack of preparation before each scene. Dr. Griesy would have said the same about my shaky surgical start if he had been forced to answer honestly.

47

After a few shaky sutures placed by me, he took over again and I sighed in relief. This hands-on learning was thrilling, but as glad as I was to be involved, I was scared of the enormous responsibility and potential for error. Finally, after six years of regurgitating meaningless trivia in college and med school, I was learning something useful. Why couldn't I have skipped the first six years and started straight with this?

When the job was finished, Mr. Mattson looked down at his patched-up leg. More than 25 stitches held the flesh in place, and even more secured the inside layers. His face showed how amazed he was with Dr. Griesy's repair. I felt a real sense of accomplishment, even though I'd been an innocent bystander who'd contributed nothing more than to keep from fainting into the wound. Nevertheless, Dr. Griesy made it seem like a team effort that we could both be proud of.

"You're gonna have to stay off the leg for a few weeks, Connie. The stitches underneath the skin will dissolve, but the outside ones should come out in ten days – see me in the office next week to check the wound."

On our way home, we stopped to make a house call. Einar Nelson was in his 70s and lived alone on the outskirts of town, just a hundred yards up from the starting line for Grandma's marathon. The mile lines were clearly marked on the road year-round so that runners indigenous to the area had a clear idea of the mile markers and could train on the course.

"Einar's had some PND (paroxysmal nocturnal dyspnea) and orthopnea, and his legs are swelling. What does that tell you?", inquired my mentor.

"That he has CHF (congestive heart failure)?" I asked.

"Right. And he lives alone – hard for him to get in to see me."

Einar met us at the door, and as anticipated, his breathing was labored, his legs were swollen, and he had evidence of fluid in his lungs from his failing heart. Dr. Griesy opened a large black suitcase-like bag with lots of separate compartments inside. They stored many different drugs and needles and other emergency supplies for house calls. He drew up some morphine in a needle and injected Mr. Nelson, and gave him a lasix pill to swallow.

After ten minutes or so, the old man began to breathe easier. They visited about Two Harbors town gossip for a while.

I felt particularly proud to be with Dr. Griesy at that moment. I had grown up in a suburb of Minneapolis, where house calls were non-existent.

48

I knew how rare it was to witness a genuine house call, and I had witnessed first-hand a precious act of kindness.

Dr. Griesy dropped me at the house where I was boarding so I could unpack. Having accomplished that in minutes, I headed downtown and bought a turkey leg at the grocery store so I could begin practicing my suturing technique. Within the hour, he was back to pick me up for hamburgers at his home.

The Griesy house was large, but very "homey" and "lived in" inside, consistent with the way his office was appointed, and typical for a family of eight. As the oldest of thirteen children, I immediately felt right at home.

His wife was quiet, so we stuck to casual conversation over supper, which was interrupted several times by patient phone calls. After supper, we watched a few minutes of "Barney Miller", his favorite show, and then he took me home and headed for the office to tan his psoriatic legs with the ultraviolet lamp he kept down in the office basement. Ultraviolet light is one of the most effective treatments for psoriasis. The time he spent soaking his leg under his UV light , he said, was the only real time he had to himself. I wondered if at some point in my future I would end up escaping from all the stresses in my life by retreating into my office late at night.

After sewing some more on my turkey leg, I plopped on my bed and drifted off to sleep. The chilly Lake Superior breeze made for excellent sleeping weather. As I faded, I was reminded of another chilly autumn night not too many years ago, described in Gordon Lightfoot's haunting ballad of the wreck of the Edmund Fitzgerald:

"Superior, it is said never gives up her dead when the gales of November come early."

I awoke with a start. It was Dr. Griesy on the phone. The clock radio said 9:45 p.m.

"I'm on my way to pick you up – Mrs. Eim's in labor."

On the ride to the hospital, he reiterated the already familiar spiel.

"Don't practice like I do. It's a way of the past. Takes too much time. I'm a poor role model. Most of the students I take on end up doing family practice, but I hope they don't try to go it alone as I do."

We arrived at the hospital and donned scrub clothes. Mrs. Eim was in early labor. Dr. Griesy estimated that she wouldn't deliver for at least two hours. He introduced me to her, and instructed me to do hourly vaginal checks to chart her labor course, and to let him know when there were significant changes. He left to find a room in which to nap.

It was then that I realized that Dr. Griesy didn't need to be here for any of this; he was doing it for my benefit. He wanted me to learn the entire labor process, to sit with the patient and experience the agony, instead of merely arriving in time to do the delivery after all the significant sweating was over.

I sat with Mrs. Eim, a mother of three. Her labors had been fairly normal in the past, so she was pretty relaxed about it. When the contractions came, though, I could read the intensity of pain from her facial contortions.

I didn't envy her.

Her husband sat in the couch in the corner of the room. He explained that their kids were with a friend waiting for the arrival of their new brother or sister. Monday night football was playing on a small TV set located at ceiling height, so the father and I occupied ourselves watching the game, and simultaneously I kept one eye on the monitor which showed the fetal heart tracing. Once an hour I checked her cervix for dilatation. Her husband was noticeably uncomfortable while I checked her, and I surmised it was because of my age. I was grateful that the OB nurse didn't trust my vaginal/cervical checks, and did her own at the same time to back me up.

At 1 a.m., she let out a large cry, which startled me. A nurse ran in, checked her, and looked my way.

"Time to wake Dr. Griesy."

I felt a lump in my throat. Would he make me get involved again? I was still much more comfortable with the idea of watching from the sidelines. As I woke him, I was reminded of the story of Jesus sleeping calmly on the boat during the storm, and his disciples waking him and experiencing his calming influence. After he awoke, he sauntered nonchalantly into the labor room and checked her.

"Take her to the delivery room, please." He was obviously calm. As we scrubbed, he asked me about the labor.

"Did you learn anything?"

"Yeah – remind me not to have a baby! Actually, I'm getting a little better at the vag checks, thanks to the nurses."

"Well, you'll get lots of practice. But stay with the patients. That's the best way to really learn OB. There's a lot more to it than just helping the baby come out – especially now with fetal monitoring."

Mrs. Eim was lying on the table in the delivery room as we walked in after our scrub. We draped her bottom and Dr. Griesy anesthetized her skin so that he could cut an episiotomy if needed, to allow a larger opening through which to deliver the baby if necessary.

"Check the position and presentation," he said.

I answered. "Vertex, and I think it's LOT (left occiput transverse)."

"No, check again. You're almost right. It's ROT."

I reinserted my fingers to feel the lines on the fetal head which allowed the examiner to tell which position it was in. I realized that he was right.

There were many noises filling the delivery room. The fetal monitor let out a distinctive beep with each heartbeat, and the infant warmer had a noisy heat fan blowing as it warmed up. Mrs. Eim was now wearing an oxygen mask to facilitate her pushing, and it too was making noises.

Various nurses and aides scurried about the room bringing in supplies and communicating with Dr. Griesy via nods and nonverbal signals so as to not concern the patient or her husband. For instance, one of the nurses raised a pair of forceps as if to ask him, "should I lay these out?" and I saw him wave her off.

The fetal heartbeats slowed, which was manifest as a subtle change in the tempo of the beeps, a barely recognizable difference amid all the other noises in the room, but Dr. Griesy noted the change. Although this was a somewhat potentially worrisome occurrence, he maintained a sense of calm much as he had with Mr. Mattson, engaging in conversation and making little jokes. He sensed that Mr. Eim was getting nervous, so he gave him something to do. He asked the nurse to give the father a wash cloth so that he could wipe his wife's forehead as her brow dripped with sweat from the effort of pushing.

As much as he seemed in control, like the captain of a great ship, he later told me that it was those moments just before delivery that scared him to death, knowing all the things that can go wrong and being stuck out in the country without immediate help for OB emergencies. He told me of the nights when a shoulder had gotten stuck or there'd been an unexpected breech, and the panic he'd endured. When it went wrong in OB, he said, it really went wrong – and fast.

I again thought of the Edmund Fitzgerald, and the "captain well-seasoned". Things can go wrong in the best of hands, I realized. But, he never let his patients know that he had the least bit of doubt in the outcome.

Mrs. Eim suddenly let out a loud groan, and the head began to "crown".

Dr. Griesy placed a sterile towel in my hand and traded places with me so that I was right next to the crowning head. My heart stopped. I knew then that he intended for me to do the delivery. I'd never done one before, although I'd watched a few, and had practiced the technique. My knees were shaking.

As the head presented, he guided my hands onto it to restrain the head from shooting out too abruptly, and together we eased it out gently. Then he showed me how to free the anterior shoulder, then the posterior shoulder, and demonstrated how to trace my hand down the baby's wet back until I found the buttocks and legs, which I grabbed between my fingers to secure a grip on the baby.

Then it was out – a boy – and Dr. Griesy clamped and cut the cord while I nervously held onto the baby for dear life. It would take years before I could appreciate how much patience it takes for an experienced physician to trust such a delicate and litigious moment to a rookie such as I was.

Finally, he took the baby boy from my arms, placed him momentarily on Mrs. Eim's lap, and from there removed him to the warmth of an incubator at the edge of the room.

My face was as radiant as the baby's warmer. He allowed me to do several stitches of the episiotomy repair, and I found that my turkey leg practice had helped. Also, having done the delivery, I identified with this patient and felt more relaxed about working on her.

After we finished, Dr. Griesy took out his Polaroid camera and snapped a picture for me to remember my first delivery by. I knew I would never forget his name: Chad Michael Eim.

As we retreated to the doctor's lounge, I felt unusually cocky, as if I had done all the work myself. Dr. Griesy handed me the telephone.

"Dictate the report so we can get out of here."

My ego plummeted to earth and dug a deep crater. What did I know about dictating? Apparently Dr. Griesy was not aware of just how green I truly was.

I had never dictated anything, let alone an operative report, so I fumbled, jumping from finish to start to somewhere in the middle. Dr. Griesy looked at me quizzically. Finally, he took the phone, erased my report, and demonstrated an appropriate approach, based on the SOAP system which was familiar to me from my earlier visits to his office.

His dictations defined the scientist and the clinician in him: always methodical, taking the thrill of the moment and breaking it into concise, descriptive language that excluded any hint of personal involvement. But, to describe his abilities as a physician in such limited terms betrayed his depth. I saw beyond those narrow qualities a humble, sincere, empathetic human being who admitted vulnerability, and who demonstrated that the science of medicine was practiced best by someone who understood the art of medicine.

After he dropped me off that night, I called my parents to tell them that I'd delivered my first baby. It was one of the milestones in my life. Then I called my former girlfriend Toni, who was finishing her last year of college in Minneapolis. She was now a senior in college and expecting to hear any day about medical school. My relationship with Toni was one of the unfortunate casualties of this intense medical training. We broke up when the demands of med school overloaded me. But I just had to share this moment with her. I woke her up, but I could tell that she shared my excitement. This Two Harbors rotation was living up to my expectations. I knew that what I learned up here would surpass the best experiences of all my other hospital rotations.

Now I felt a definite direction to point my studies toward. When I'd run the marathon, I'd had trouble convincing myself that the endpoint was worth achieving. The time I spent with Dr. Griesy convinced me beyond any doubt that family medicine was my calling. In my estimation, he had become the ultimate role model for a family physician.

The road ahead for my medical career loomed long, and I was sure that there were unforeseen obstacles around the curves. Now that aerial lift bridge in downtown Duluth which signified the end of the race was finally in sight. I was learning how to reach for the finish line, one mile at a time.

Foreword to Chapter 3

Residency training is always evolving. In the early years of the twentieth century, it was possible to enroll in a one-year hospital-based internship before entering a private practice. A doctor recently related a story to me regarding his wife's grandfather, one of the founding physicians of North Memorial Hospital, which is one of our most prominent Minneapolis hospitals. This physician is now 97 years old. He was trained in that era of a one-year internship, and yet he performed a variety of surgeries, including appendectomies, Cesarean sections, etc. This physician tells a story that on one occasion early in his career, when he was completing a Cesarean section, after he had removed the baby, the placenta was stuck, and couldn't be removed. His patient was bleeding critically, and to save her life he needed to perform a hysterectomy. However, she had lost so much blood that she required a blood transfusion. He had the nurse remove several units of his own blood to give immediately to his patient, and then he continued to operate. He then fainted while operating, because he had donated blood, and after the nurses revived him, he got up and finished the surgery. It sounds too far-fetched to be valid, but to this day he insists that it is a true story.

While the veracity of this tale cannot be verified, it underscores the fact that the training in those earlier days was so much more of a hands-on approach. Those early interns were managing patients and performing procedures that interns and residents today are never allowed to see or do until they are actually out in a real practice. It was the era of, "see one, do one, teach one."

The most significant change in residency training occurred about ten years ago, early in the 21st century. The nature of the change was a mandate from the official organization which accredits residency training. It announced a strict policy that interns and residents could not be required to work after they had spent a night on call. They must then be allowed at least 4–8 hours off to rest. The change was dramatic and life-altering. It meant that no longer would residents be required to work for 36–48 hours straight, without a break, as was often the case in both of my residency training programs.

For a person in residency training today, it may be difficult to appreciate the severity of the conditions that residents in that former era endured, as attested to in the following chapters. It seems almost inhumane to consider the environment in which I was required to train. From my first night on call as an intern, I was handed the reins and asked to perform medical procedures that the most senior resident would probably not be allowed to perform now. There were no staff physicians in the hospital at night. The most senior physician was a senior resident, and they often delegated duties to the interns without any further supervision. Many mistakes made by residents were made simply a case of lack of sleep. I know that I made many mental errors due to sleep deprivation. But the training also hardened me in a way that is not possible in the present-day training of residents. I am able to endure countless hours in the OR even after working a 24-hour overnight shift, because it is still second nature to me. I am still able to focus when my brain has had no sleep. I have been trained to fall back on my experience when I am stressed beyond belief, thanks in large part to the countless sleepless nights I endured in six years of residency when I had to perform despite my exhaustion. As you read the following pages, keep in mind that this type of hands-on residency training no longer exists, and that is in large part a good thing, for the added safety of patients, but it is also a trade-off, because the experience I gained with all of the hands-on work is what gave me the confidence and competence that I possess today. As the saying goes,

"Good judgment comes from experience, and experience comes from bad judgment."

CHAPTER 3
RESIDENCY TRAINING

<u>Day 1 Summer 1981 St. Luke's Hospital Milwaukee, Wisconsin</u>

I yawned. It was still dark outside, but my day was in full swing already. The other three interns – Doug Landers, Josie Ramirez, and Konrad Krawczyk – and I were sitting at the table on 6JK (the sixth floor, JK wing) in the conference room, waiting for Jill Harman, our senior resident. The air was tense with apprehension as Jill sauntered in. I was scared out of my wits. They say that life begins at the edge of your comfort zone. I was well beyond that edge, believe me.

My senior resident wasted no time. "Hi – I'm Jill – listen you guys, there's a lot of work to do, so let's divvy these patients and get to it. We're probably gonna get bombed with admissions this month, so get rid of these guys as fast as you can – half of these guys should've been gone already.

Rich, since you're on call tonight, you get the lightest load."

I sized up Jill in a non-threatening way. She was blonde, mid-height and slender. Her glasses made her look smart but by the way she was talking, I already had no doubt of that. Earlies thirties, I guessed. And VERY sure of herself. Jill handed me eight index cards. On each card was the name of a patient, his/her diagnoses, current medications, and results of tests completed so far. Doug got 13 cards and the other two interns 12 each – all of them flashed me a quick look of jealous disapproval.

I took it in stride; I was glad to have five patients less than Doug – heck, I was on call tonight! My yawn earlier had reminded me that I hardly slept at all last night, worrying about how bad tonight might be. The little sleep I did get was plagued with the sort of bad dreams I used to have before organic chemistry finals or national boards – like showing up for rounds without any clothes on, or two hours late.

Medicine wards – what a lousy way to start internship! And, why did I have to have the first call night? After making patient assignments, Jill got up to leave. I likened her to a flight squadron commander during a briefing:

56

"Any other questions? My pager number is 9846. Call me at the clinic if you need me. You guys had better get busy – you should see everyone before our rounds with Dr. Parent at two o'clock. We'll meet in here again. Chow, folks!"

Just as she left the room, John Holtan popped in. John had been my roommate at Luther College for two years, and he had been the one who suggested that I interview for this residency in family medicine here in Milwaukee. John had just finished the internship here, and was now a second-year resident. I could see that he was much more relaxed now that the toughest year of his life was over. It was encouraging for me to know someone who had made it through. Then again, John had always had a knack for ignoring pressure. I was still jealous of him for that.

"Richie! Ready for breakfast?"

"I don't have time, Johnnie – I'm on tonight."

"Lighten up, guy – it's too early to wake up your players anyway – besides, we'll just get something quick; I'm on my way to the clinic." We took the elevators down to the basement and over to the cafeteria. St. Luke's was a huge hospital, growing faster than a cancer, spreading out in every direction. There was obviously much financial success to the hospital, which the nurses nicknamed St. Lucrative's. Sections of the hospital were constantly being renovated and equipped with the latest technologic equipment, according to John.

My former college roomie John Holtan was very bright. He grew up on a large dairy farm in western Iowa, and made it through college in only three years – he was not only smart but also a talented musician- –and he never seemed to worry about any of the stress in front of him. I envied his sense of calm as he navigated his medical training.

It took us twelve minutes to get down to the caf. While we ate, John pointed out various people to me.

"See those two? They were caught 'in the act'."

"Yeah, right." I laughed it off.

"No, really… those two there-one night they were fooling around in the nursing offices on fourth floor and a janitor caught them.

"him?"

"You've gotta be kidding – her? She's a fox! He'd old and fat – why"

"Got me. Some people have all the luck. They're both married to other people, but they've been an item here for almost a year now. Lucky she's a nursing supervisor, or they'd both have been canned."

I was staring at John, a little skeptical. Was it all gossip? In all fairness to him, in our eight years of close friendship, he'd never told me a story without having his facts straight.

"Look over there." He was at it again, pointing to the table behind us. "See those two? That's 'Hot Rod'– Rodney Jones. The nurses call him 'Rod the Bod', he's a third-year X-rays resident, and the girl next to him is a tech. They were caught in the X-ray room during a slow afternoon last year. He's made the rounds, boy. Every year when the new ultrasound students move into the hospital apartments, he's over there helpin' 'em move in and puttin' the moves on. What kills me is, he's married to a fantastic-looking law student. He's either 4+ horny, or stupid. She's bound to find out sooner or later – he's so obvious about it."

He went on to tell about another couple that was caught, warned, and caught again, and fired on the spot. I couldn't quite absorb it – or believe it – right away, but events that occurred over the next few months convinced me that his stories were valid. St. Luke's, with its 700 beds and over a thousand employees, was a mini Peyton Place, and I had just joined the cast.

As we were walking out of the caf, John could tell that I was incredulous about what he'd told me.

"It happens, Rich. A year ago, we had a surgical intern here – her name was Julie Sargent. You can ask Dave Farrell – the surgical chief resident – if you don't believe me. This Julie was smart, and dynamite looking, but she was never around for surgery when the cases started.

Afterwards, she'd come to Dave with excuses, like her beeper wasn't working, or she didn't know they had a case to do.

One day, Dave decided to find out where she was, after she didn't show to scrub with him. He snuck upstairs to the call rooms on 9th floor and asked the operator to page her. Her beeper went off in one of the rooms, so he charged in to chew her out and found her in bed with Dr. Johnson, the cardiologist. She was fired that morning, but nothing was ever said to Dr. Johnson. He got away with it. Johnson's fiancé recently died in a plane crash – that's why he has those scars on his face – he was the only survivor now he's on the prowl a lot – always seems to have young female medical students with him."

John Holtan parted for the clinic, leaving me conspicuously on my own to tackle work rounds. My eight patients were scattered over four separate floors on six different wards. I took the 'vator to 6JK and decided to work my way down from there. That way, I could take the stairs and save valuable time not waiting for the 'vators. Time was of the essence, and I learned that the best way to save time was to learn where every stairwell was located so I could dash up and down the stairs efficiently. It was a matter of survival. The stairwells were musty and warm. Apparently they lacked air conditioning vents. After each climb up a few floors, I was sweating through my clothes.

When I got to the nursing station, a woman approached me and read my name tag.

"Hi, Dr. Mayerchak. I'm Laurie – Mr. Olson's nurse."

Doctor Mayerchak – wow, did that sound weird. My first day being called that!! That alone was a big adjustment for me. I noticed that she was cute – tall, with pretty brown eyes – but I was much too anxious to even consider my usual lustful thoughts.

"They tell me you're picking him up for this month. I need an insulin order by 6:15 every morning. He's two hours late – can you give me one now?"

My God! I felt sick, but I couldn't show it. I had never ordered insulin. I had never even had a diabetic patient. There weren't any other interns around to coach me, but the nursing station was buzzing with staff docs and nurses gliding as smoothly through their duties as ants passing mindlessly on a crowded hill. In my panic, I was afraid to let on that I was so ignorant, as if they couldn't sense it by the awkward uncertainty of my movements. I reeked of green, but pride prevented me from asking any one of them a simple question about diabetic care, which would have nipped the present problem neatly.

"Give me a minute, Laurie, and I'll take care of it." I said in my best stage voice. It was time to shrink away to a back room somewhere and find a medicine text, but I got beeped in mid-retreat.

"Doctor Mayerchak, this is X-ray. Do you want Mr. Ryan's barium enema with air contrast or without?"

Who the heck was Mr. Ryan? I paged through my cards and realized that he was one of my "players". I hadn't gotten to see him yet. I surmised that his previous intern had ordered the barium enema, but I sure didn't know what the difference in the two types were, so I punted.

"Without, please."

The "please" threw them – they weren't used to a doctor talking politely to a mere tech. I was disturbed to see this attitude developing in me. I was ignorant, but was afraid to let on to anybody how little I knew. I assumed I was supposed to know these things already. Acting like I knew what to do seemed more important than doing the right thing. Where was my senior resident when I needed her most? I was getting my feet wet the hard way. I hoped my ignorance wouldn't end up hurting somebody.

Before I could tackle Mr. Olson's insulin order, I got two more pages from nurses wanting order changes, and I started to sweat. Where should I start? How should I organize priorities? I felt like a rookie secretary answering seven office phones at once. The questions were coming in waves, and I hadn't even seen the people I was supposed to be managing.

I regained my composure and told the nurses that I would answer their questions as soon as I could. I sat down at one of the nursing desks and took a brief survey of the room. All of these nursing floors were laid out similarly – multiple wings, spacious hallways, brightly lit, and it seemed that all of the nurses were young and cute. I envied them because they seemed sure of what they were doing. I was NOT. As I compared this hospital floor to many of the hospitals I had trained at in medical school, it was clearly several standard deviations above the run-down wards I had been accustomed to working in. I grabbed a bunch of blank index cards to scribble notes to myself. My first card read:

Air contrast Barium Enema? Insulin Rx?

<u>Read up on DIABETES.</u>

Then I proceeded to read each of my patients' charts, introduce myself to them, and examine them briefly. Overshadowing every move was the dread that I wouldn't finish seeing everybody before two o'clock rounds with Dr. Parent.

(One thing to remember about 1981 is that there was no internet, no smart phones to google information about medications and treatments for diseases.

We didn't even possess cellphones. We felt we were state-of-the art because our pagers actually spoke to us instead of merely flashing a phone number.)

Mr. John Olson was first. He's a 67-year-old with diabetes just recently diagnosed after he had a foot infection that wasn't healing. Even though I walked in and introduced myself, his face and all the other fine details about his care were a blur to me – they seemed irrelevant. All I cared about at that moment was finishing a note on him so I could say I had done it – AND taking care of the insulin order the nurse was asking for. I thumbed through his order sheets for the previous three days and ordered the same amount of insulin as he'd been getting before – luckily the doses hadn't fluctuated.

The rest of the "players" fared similarly. I put everybody on hold and decided not to rock the boat by writing any new orders until I knew which end was up. I assumed that they would all coast on auto pilot until 2 p.m. rounds with Dr. Parent.

I was wrong. Before I finished orders on John Olson, 3EF (third floor, E and F wings) called. Viola Anderson, a 72-year-old stroke rehab patient, was having bouts of ventricular tachycardia – a heart rhythm irregularity that can be fatal. I hadn't seen her yet, but her nurse needed stat orders to stop this ominous heart rhythm. She suggested lidocaine. It sounded good to me – I remembered seeing it used somewhere as a student, but I couldn't remember any of the details. Where was that blasted senior resident when I needed her most? Why couldn't I be eased slowly into this stressful decision making? Nurses got a three-month orientation here – we were doing the job cold from day 1. They shadowed a seasoned nurse during that entire orientation. We interns were thrust immediately into the deep end of the pool. My feet were getting wet so fast that I thought I would drown.

Just then, I spied my fellow intern Konrad Krawczyk heading toward me.

He was hard to miss, because he was moderately overweight, to put it politely. His white lab coat hugged his waist so tightly that he looked uncomfortable. He had a calm about him and seemed to be more at home here on the first day than I was.

"Hey, Con Man!" I'd dubbed him that at rounds this morning.

"What do you want, Caddychak?" Krawczyk and I had an immediate affinity for each other. We were both of Czechoslovakian origin, which fit right in with this South Milwaukee Polish town. A number of the docs had Polish names also – Wengelewski, Owsiak… we hoped our Polish names would earn us a modicum of credibility, neophytes that we were.

"Do you know how to use lidocaine for V-tach?" I asked.

Konrad didn't hesitate.

"Sure. Bolus the patient with one milligram per kilogram IV and then start a two to four milligram drip – most people use two, I think."

I acted as if I knew that already. "Oh yeah, that's right. Now I remember." What a lifesaver he was – I relayed the order to the nurse on 3EF, told her I'd be right down, and finished with Mr. Olson.

Viola Anderson, the lady in the stroke rehab wing, was in normal sinus rhythm by the time I got down to 3EF. I walked into her room and got my first look at her. She was thin, elderly, and looked frail. There was no one in the room with her. Poor thing, I thought – a widow all alone in later life. I realized that all of these cards I had in my white coat with patient names on them were just that- names – I had no faces to put to them. And yet here I was ordering tests and medications on them without having even the slightest clue who they were. Hopefully the next few hours and days would change that. I introduced myself to her, but she stared blankly back at me; it was obvious that hers had been a major stroke. Nevertheless I gave her the benefit of the doubt and talked to her as if she could understand me; just in case she really could. Her stroke had occurred suddenly during a bridge game two weeks ago, and her entire right side was paralyzed. That meant that the damage involved the left side of her brain, the half that also controls language function.

During med school, I'd learned that the left side of the brain controlled language function, but the right half controlled motivation; since Viola still had her right side intact, her motivation to recover would be optimal, in contrast to people who suffered strokes on the right side, that preserved their abilities to speak, but often they had no desire to rehabilitate themselves.

Viola couldn't get her thoughts across to me or anyone else, so we weren't sure of whether she understood us or not, but it was obvious that she had thoughts, and was very frustrated with her condition. I spent fifteen minutes going over her chart, and then hurried on to meet the other patients. It was already 10:15 a.m.

Jack Larson was a haggard-looking 49-going-on-80-year-old with pancreatitis resulting from years of alcoholism. He'd been in the hospital for three days now, and my main concern was to keep him from going into DTs-delirium tremens- now that he was without his daily fifth of scotch.

When an alcoholic dries out, the DTs can cause seizures which can be fatal.

Agnes Jones was 38, rather rotund, and almost ready for discharge after gallbladder surgery eight days ago. The rule of thumb med students learn for diagnosing gallbladder disease is the four Fs: female, fat, fertile, and forty. The more Fs a woman has, the more likely that she has gallstones. Agnes fit the four Fs to a T.

Sam Malecek, 62, was on 6LM, the cardiac rehab floor. He lived in a distant suburb of Milwaukee but traveled all the way to St. Luke's with his chest pain because he knew that Luke's was the place to be if you had a heart issue. The hospital was renowned for offering superb cardiac care, and performed an unusually high volume of cardiac bypass surgeries for heart disease. He was like so many of the cardiac patients I had seen in medical school- short and overweight, very high cholesterol, with a strong family history for heart disease. His heart attack didn't come as much of a surprise to him. But prior to the actual event, he lived his life in denial and continued to eat the wrong foods, avoid exercise, and smoke cigarettes.

Sam had spent a week in the coronary ICU with an inferior wall myocardial infarction, and his recovery was proceeding uneventfully. He told me proudly that he'd been free of chest pain for five days, and he thought he was ready to try walking the hallways. He looked at me pleadingly. I decided to stall, since I had no idea of what an appropriate cardiac rehab protocol was. Who was I to make that kind of decision on my first day? I told him I'd think about it and get back to him.

Chester Polinski, 67, was not happy to see me. As I entered him room I sensed that his mood was dismal. He looked gaunt, and withdrawn. He hung his head as I introduced myself. He was admitted a week earlier with lower back pain, but a routine X-ray showed suspicious lesions in his spine which turned out to be multiple myeloma, a bone disease much like cancer, and he was justifiably depressed and hardly looked at me when I talked with him.

Julia Meyer, 71, was morbidly obese. There seemed to be a lot of this weight problem going around. She had congestive heart failure which necessitated restricting the amount of fluid she could drink daily. This upset her because she was an avid water drinker. Since her admission three days earlier, she'd lost nine pounds – most of it from massively swollen lower legs – it was all water that had accumulated due to her failing heart, an affliction common to many older people, especially in the hot summer months.

Teresa Olson, 69, was senile and disabled with emphysema. She was sitting up on the side of her bed gasping as she tried to eat a piece of toast, connected to her oxygen tank by a long rubber tube leading to prongs sticking in her nose. She was extremely thin, a stark contrast to my previous patient. Her lungs were so poor that she couldn't eat without struggling to breathe. Her children had railroaded the ER intern into admitting her until they could find a nursing home for her. The admission wasn't justified because her condition hadn't changed for years – it was just that her kids were tired of caring for her as their search for appropriate nursing homes was delayed longer than they'd anticipated. Now that she was here, we were stuck with her until a nursing home could be found. Fortunately, she didn't require much attention on my part.

At 1400, I high-tailed it to the sixth floor conference room for rounds with Dr. Parent. He was late, so I had a chance to organize the notes I had scribbled concerning each patient on those little index cards. Without the cards, I had no idea who was who – I was completely helpless to remember anything about these people. As I admitted new patients and followed their hospital courses from start to finish, remembering them would be much easier.

The conference room was nothing more than a private patient room that had been converted to a place for the residents to meet. It had a small table to fit six or eight people, and a blackboard and two X-ray reading lights on the wall. I looked out the window for a moment and saw two dozen pigeons congregating in the shade on the east face of the eighth floor. Oh, what I wouldn't give to live such a simple life right now! I thought to myself. Their picture of freedom reminded me that I was $70,000 in debt, and obligated to survive this training ordeal or else spend the rest of my life paying off this debt. The thought ended abruptly as Jill Harmon, my senior resident, entered the room.

"How's it going so far? Anybody having problems we need to talk about before Jerry Parent gets here?" At that moment, she seemed as nonchalant as a waitress asking us if the food was okay. It set us at ease, and I vowed to someday be that relaxed and command the same air of confidence that she exuded.

"Sorry I'm late Jill." It was Dr. Parent. He entered the room briskly with a harried look on his face and two Styrofoam cups of coffee in his hands. "Do we have much business today?" he asked.

"Three admits to staff, but no consults," she replied.

"OK, let's get to it. I'm Jerry Parent. Nice to meet all of you. Why don't you each tell me where you're from before we begin our rounds."

I noticed that Jerry Parent bore a striking resemblance to Steve Martin, with similar facial features and silvery hair.

Jill told us he'd been out of his cardiology fellowship for four years, and he was in his mid-thirties. He was now in private practice as a cardiologist, but supervised the medicine ward for the family practice residents four afternoons a week.

As Dr. Parent listened to us tell of our backgrounds, I noticed that he was an intent listener, and he seemed genuinely interested in who we were as people. That surprised me because all Jill had told us about the man was that he was very well read, an excellent clinician, and extremely practical when it came to decision making. I didn't think a doctor as smart as that could be a good people-oriented person as well.

Konrad Krawczyk was first. He hailed from Northwestern in Chicago. Dr. Parent had lived there during cardiology fellowship, so they chatted about that briefly. I noticed that Dr. Parent spoke quietly, as if he expected everyone to focus on what he said without raising his voice.

Konrad was bearded, overweight, but obviously intelligent, and very likeable; he and I hit it off well from the beginning of the day even though he had more patients than I did. Konrad Krawczyk – the nurses had just as difficult a time with his last name as they did with mine. Hence, the nicknames Con-man and Caddy-chak – easier to handle.

Doug Landers was a radiology resident. He was married, which set him apart from the rest of us. He had an athletic, boyish look about him that girls are usually drawn to, but seemed not to notice his own good looks or be spoiled by that fact. He was easy-going and the rest of us took to him immediately. All of the X-ray boys were required to do a month on the medicine wards to round out their educations. Doug was glad he was getting his over with while the rest of us were as green around the wards as he was. Doug seemed confident in himself, as did Konrad. He spoke with a southern accent.

Josephina Ramirez was much more awkward. She was short, thin, and seemed uncomfortable in her own skin. She'd graduated from a foreign medical school, and as soon as she mentioned that, I noticed Dr. Parent scrutinize her more thoroughly. She had a noticeable problem speaking English, but it was too early to fully assess her command of medical knowledge . Dr. Parent gave Jill a look that said, "keep an eye on her."

65

Then it was my turn to speak. I informed Dr. Parent that I began med school for two years in Duluth, and graduated from the University of Minnesota in Minneapolis. He seemed impressed. Apparently, it was ranked one of the top twenty schools in the country, unbeknownst to me. I told him that I was the oldest of 13 kids, and that John Holtan and I had been roommates and best friends since college.

"Oh, so you'll be at John's wedding next Saturday?" he asked. "I'd say so. I'm the best man!"

"My wife Katie and I will be there too. Sounds like it'll be pretty fancy. Okay, Jill, time to run the list."

Jill Harman picked up the master patient list and began calling off names. "Sam Malecek."

Pause. She looked around the room then said it again.

"Doesn't anybody have Sam Malecek?"

Another pause. Suddenly, I realized that he was mine. I blushed and cleared my throat.

"Oh, that's me! Sorry about that. He's doing okay – proceeding with rehab."

Dr. Parent interrupted. "Rich, for the benefit of the rest of the interns, I like to hear a capsule summary of every patient before you say anything about them, okay?"

"Oh. Uh, Sam is a late fiftyish, no let me see, I guess he's 62. He's here with, he came in for, uh, he had an MI about a week ago, an inferior wall MI. Now he's on 6LM and not having any problems."

"How high did his CPK go?" Dr. Parent asked. "Ummm... I'm not sure."

"It peaked at 485," Jill interrupted. Thanks, Jill, I thought.

"When is he scheduled for a submax stress test and gated wall motion study?"

"Ahhh... I'll have to check." Boy, was I looking bad! "Next week for both – right before discharge," Jill added.

"Fine, Jill. Now, Rich, what's the most important complication you'll be watching for with a patient who's had an inferior MI?"

"Hmmm... a rhythm disturbance?" I was stabbing in the dark. "Right! Why?"

"Ummm..."

Konrad cleared his throat and spoke apologetically, "It's because the sinoatrial node is supplied by the right coronary artery, which becomes occluded in inferior MIs."

*

Dr. Parent seemed pleased. "Right, Konrad. Okay let's continue."

The next patient we discussed was a 59-year-old female with a bloody cough and weight loss. Dr. Parent asked Konrad to list some of the possible diagnoses that could cause a bloody cough and weight loss. He listed bronchitis, pneumonia, gastrointestinal bleeding, and cancer. Dr. Parent then instructed all of us that he wanted each problem to be considered within the framework of the following eleven categories. If we could remember the categories, we could arrive at many more diagnostic possibilities. Before he listed them, he told us how to remember each category on the list:

Congenitally Infected Nude Virgins May Frequently Take Toxic Douches If Necessary.

He then explained that "Congenitally" was for conditions that occurred at birth.

"Infected" was obvious – any infectious causes of the problem.

"Nude" was for nutritional causes, such as lacking B12 vitamin in one's diet.

"Virgins" was for vascular causes.

"May" was for metabolic disorders.

"Frequently" was for factitious, or fake causes.

"Take" was for traumatic causes, such a motor vehicle accident.

"Toxic" was for toxic causes, such as a carbon dioxide overdose.

"Douches" was for degenerative causes, such as osteoarthritis.

"If" was for inflammatory causes, such as lupus erythematosus.

"Necessary" was for neoplastic, such as lung cancer/

It changed my entire approach to thinking about a differential diagnosis, and within no time I was thinking, "congenitally infected nude virgins may frequently take toxic douches if necessary". I said it over and over in my mind.

Dr. Parent went down the list of patients systematically and I discovered that I knew very little of the kinds of things I was supposed to pay attention to regarding my patients. By the time we finished, I felt pretty stupid. No one else looked that smart either, though, except for maybe Konrad. I took consolation in the fact that Dr. Parent didn't seem bent on "pimping" us – asking questions merely to embarrass us – he asked them in a manner that was educational to all, even if it was a little embarrassing not to know the answers.

Finally, we were done with the list, and it was time to staff the new admissions from the night before. We went to their rooms one by one and the intern responsible for their care presented their cases. Josephina had the first one, a 26-year-old guy with severe asthma.

We stood in the hallway outside of Josephina's asthmatic patient. The three other interns, and Jill our senior resident, and Dr. Parent huddled together in a small circle as we listened to Josephina's presentation of the patient. She began to speak when Jerry Parent interrupted:

"Now, before you start, let me tell you what I want to hear," Dr. Parent began. "I want to know his name, what he does for a living, and his social history first, followed by his past medical history, so I can put this man into perspective before hearing why he's here with us today."

I was really impressed with Dr. Parent from that moment on. Anyone who could look at a patient as a person first, and then a disease, had my vote of confidence and respect.

Josephina fumbled through the presentation of the history and physical. We then entered the patient's room, and Dr. Parent approached the young man and started his own exam. He began by examining his hands, looking at the fingernails, and checking the pulses in his wrists. As he listened to the chest, he informed us that the guy had obvious rales and rhonchi, which was a sign that his lungs were really struggling.

Josephina Ramirez hadn't heard them – she had informed Dr. Parent that the patient's chest was normal, and now she had major egg on her face. We all listened to his chest and the findings were clear as day, even for novices such as I was. Then as we discussed her treatment, she told Dr. Parent how much aminophylline this guy was getting to help open up his lungs. Jerry Parent looked at our senior, Jill, with disdain. The dosage was only a tenth as much as he was supposed to be getting.

*

Out in the hallway, on the way to see our next patient, Dr. Parent pulled Jill aside and I heard him tell her in a low voice, "Watch her real close, Jill, please."

During the staffing of the other three new patients, we were constantly besieged by pages from nurses who wanted to clear up details, questions about orders, etc. before their shifts ended at 15:30. I was on call, so most of my pages came from the ER, where there were already several patients waiting to be seen. I hadn't even finished taking care of the patients I already had, and here were more on the way. I started to panic once again.

My First Night On Call

Finally, rounds with Dr. Parent ended and I could start the rat race of trying to get my morning work done before the phone calls and ER patients and new admissions put me further behind. I started by seeing the two people waiting in the ER, a little girl with an ear infection, and a man with sawdust in his eye that caused an abrasion to his cornea. I was in and out of their rooms in record time, and I'm sure they were indignant about how little time I spent with them, especially considering how much the hospital was going to charge them, but I really didn't care. I was way behind. I came first.

I no sooner made it back upstairs when I was called to the phone. It was Dr. Saul Wally.

"Hi, Dr. Mayerchak. There's a lady I'd like you to see for me. She's very interesting, and we can go over her exam in the morning. In the meantime, take care of the orders, okay?" Dr. Wally hung up abruptly.

Basically, the interns get admissions from two sources. One source is from the ER, usually from patients without doctors. We then become their docs, and they see us at our family practice clinic when they're discharged from the hospital. The other type of patients we care for on the wards are the "privates", patients admitted already having personal physicians who have agreed to work with us and teach us in exchange for our doing their initial history, physical exam, and orders. That saves the private docs from getting out of bed in the middle of the night to attend to the details of emergency hospital admissions. Some of the docs come in anyway, but we still get stuck with the paperwork.

The lady Dr. Wally referred to was Judith Warff, aged 57. She was on 6JK, and I was right down the hall from there, so I saw her right away. Her case was interesting. She had been to his office today, complaining of cold hands and feet. Her extremities turned purple, but the rest of her skin was a normal color. She had what is known as "Raynaud's phenomenon", a syndrome where the arteries in the extreme periphery of the circulation

69

clamp down and don't let enough blood through. It is associated with many different diseases, especially arthritis and collagen vascular diseases, and Dr. Wally had her admitted to do some tests to find out what else she might have underlying it all.

Dr. Wally sounded pretty sharp from what little I heard from him on the phone – I was looking forward to meeting the guy.

19.30

By the time I finished working her up, I had three more admissions stacked up waiting for me. The nurses were paging me for orders on them because they couldn't do anything until they had them. Several of the patients hadn't eaten supper (well, I_hadn't eaten lunch or_supper, lady) –the nurses wondered what kind of diet did I want to order for them? My reply to them was: how did I know? Maybe they were diabetic or had special fat or fluid restrictions or something. I thought it was pretty unfair to ask – but I told them all to order general diets for them – anything to get them off my back for a while.

I was decompensating. A good patient workup required an hour and a half, and it was already after 8 p.m., and it didn't look like I was going to eat again today. These workups would take until midnight. Hey, the coffee shop! How late would that stay open? I had renewed hope. Maybe if I hurried, I could catch a bite later on.

I hoped the ER would stay quiet. Of course it didn't. Before I had a chance to see my next admission, the ER called with a stat message – a man with chest pain down there – come quick.

When I got there, I saw a man in his mid-fifties, of Mediterranean appearance, complaining of squeezing chest pain. An elephant was sitting on him, he said. He spoke very broken English. He was short, olive complexion, sporting a thick crop of graying hair. His face was thick and rough. He was muscular but also had a round potbelly. The nurse told me his name was Constantine Marcos, from a Greek ship that was in port for the weekend. He was the first mate on board.

His electrocardiogram showed changes consistent with an anterior wall myocardial infarction – a heart attack – and his initial enzymes indicated that it was a fairly large one. I admitted him to the coronary intensive care unit, and Laurie Woodard, my senior resident on call for the evening, made

70

her first appearance of the evening. Laurie hailed form Vermont and had an erudite air of refinement that I detected instantly. Laurie was dark-haired, thin like Jill, and short, and so her white coat appeared to flirt with touching the floor. What she lacked in height she made up for in self-confidence and aptitude. She had a swagger that reminded me of Jill, as if they were fellow generals in command of their troops. I was so envious of their confidence and ease. Laurie was intending for me to try to manage most of the on-call matters on my own, but something like this obviously needed more supervision.

Laurie began her coaching.

"What do you want to give him for pain, Rich?"

"Well, how about nitroglycerin?" I was groping.

"Well, not bad, but there's something better – he needs morphine. He needs enough to keep him free of pain. If he's having pain, his heart attack is still worsening."

Laurie went over all the medications and orders with me in a nurturing way that forced me to think out loud and remember logically why certain modalities were indicated. I really appreciated her teaching. After we bedded down Mr. Marcos, I went back upstairs to tackle the other admissions. Laurie Woodard retreated once again to the safety and isolation of the ninth-floor call rooms.

Jerome Stark, aged 47, was admitted from the ER when the doc down there decided that he was at risk for DTs. He thought this guy might already have the early signs. As I began to take his history, I was astounded at what I heard. This man drank over a case of beer every day, and two-quart bottles of vodka! When he arrived in the ER, his blood alcohol was .47, which would kill more than half of all people with a level that high. Not only that, but this guy was seeing bugs, and trembling, having fevers and showing most of the classic signs of DTs, delirium tremens, which only came when the blood alcohol level was <u>dropping</u> precipitously. That implied that his normal level was much higher than .47, and that was hard to swallow, excuse the pun. I put the guy on generous doses of Librium, at the prodding of the ER doc, who was coaching me through the management. I leaned on everybody I could at this early incompetent stage of my training. I had to keep this guy sedated and safe from the dangers of DTs – about 1/3 of all cases <u>die</u> without treatment. They have seizures and then they die.

I next went to John Thompson, aged 60, another boozer with a swollen

71

leg that was infected from a bump on his heel that he'd neglected. It wasn't the only part of his body that he'd neglected – the stench served notice of that – my first order in the chart was to allow him to take a shower with supervision.

His right leg was twice as large as the left, and cherry red, with mounded up skin toward the center of the wound where pus was emanating out of several holes like little volcanoes. When I saw it, I immediately did a flashback to med school, at Hennepin County Hospital in Minneapolis, where I'd seen Mathilde, a bag lady who hadn't taken her boots off for two months. Back then when we took off her boots in the ER, she had maggots all over her rotten necrotic legs, which were a mixture of red, black and white skin. What a stench it had made!

I got halfway through the orders for Mr. Thompson, the man with the swollen leg, when the ER called again. Two people for me to see – a man with a swollen ankle, and a little boy with a cut finger that probably needed stitches. I went down immediately to look at the finger. It was such a lousy feeling having unfinished business – I hated to get interrupted – I had six index cards loaded with little details I had to be sure to not forget to finish.

Before I sewed the finger, I looked at the man's ankle, and ordered some X-rays. Better to have them cooking while I was sewing the boy, I thought. I was learning efficiency. I finished the cut, which only took three stitches, long before the guy with the swollen ankle returned from X-ray, so I headed back to finish Mr. Thomas, with the swollen, red leg.

Finally, I got around to Fred Kukowski, Fred is 76, wiry, and – surprise – he was a longtime drinker. He was admitted with profound ascites, which is an abdomen full of fluid, something that's usually termed a "beer belly". I observed that his entire body is skin and bones except for the giant pot belly sticking out from his chest. I estimated that he had sixty pounds of fluid in his belly – he looked fifteen months pregnant. The problem was that we couldn't just stick a needle in there and pull it out; that fluid was tied intimately with the circulatory system. It would have to be drained very slowly over months to prevent any chance of shock. I realized sadly as I went through his orders that this guy would probably be here at least a month, and would probably get out and go back to his massive salt and alcohol intake that got him here in the first place. Oh well, at least he was civil – seemed quite pleasant, in fact. The guy obviously realized that he was a train wreck with self-destructive behavior, but he didn't try to make excuses for it. He just smiled and joked about his grossly swollen belly. I took an instant liking to him, even if he did eat up an hour of my time.

23.55

Just before midnight, I walked down to the coffee shop. It was closed until midnight. Just my luck! I frowned. Rather than wait the few minutes until it opened, I went back up to the ER to review the ankle X-rays. The ankle wasn't broken, but the sprain was bad enough that he would need a cast. He would have to wait a day for the swelling to abate, so I sent him home with an ace wrap and crutches.

I jumped back into the stairwell and headed back to the coffee shop when the seventh floor paged me to pronounce someone dead. At this point I was still fresh enough to take the stairs all the way up the seven flights. On my way up there, I thought to myself, I don't know the first thing about pronouncing someone dead. Is there a protocol of things to look for, a certain way of stating it in the chart – what if I make a mistake and the guy isn't really dead?

When I walked into the patient's room, my fears were put to rest. The guy was obviously dead – he had cancer written all over him. His eyes were sunken, his skin very pale, his bones jutted out everywhere because he had no meat on him. I listened for a heartbeat, but there was none. His pupils were fixed and dilated. He wasn't breathing. Those were objective enough signs for me to be certain. Fortunately, there was no family around for me to talk to – I felt awkward enough without having to bungle my way through this with them present. I made the sign of the cross on his head and left the room to find his chart.

His chart had the diagnosis written on the first page; cancer of the pancreas. No wonder he was so wasted, I thought. That was one of the worst ones to have. I wrote a quick note and left the floor before any family members arrived. I didn't really have time to contemplate the profundity of what I had just done. I had pronounced a man dead!! I had written a note in his chart, attesting to my observation that his pupils were fixed and dilated, and that he had no heartbeat or pulse, and respirations were not observed. I therefore pronounced him dead, at 23.59 hours. If he had lived another minute he would have lived another day. I could have made that happen with one stroke of a pen, changing his time of death by a minute. That thought amused me for a moment. I was surprised to see that my chart note certifying his death was sufficient documentation for all authorities to start the cascade sequence of what transpires from the moment a death is pronounced. The nurse removes the IV, oximeter and any other life support. The ventilator might be turned off, or other support device removed. The morgue is contacted, the body removed, and housekeeping is notified that there is a room that needs cleaning. The process is strangely similar to what one might expect when a guest leaves a hotel room. However, renting a room at St. Luke's Hospital was one very expensive hotel room, indeed.

In the year 1799, a century before the era of antibiotics, ex- President George Washington developed a tonsillar abscess and it progressed to a severe infection. The best-known treatment of that era was "bloodletting", to intentionally remove blood from a seriously infected patient. He had almost four liters of his blood removed in a single day, which constituted about 80% of his total blood volume. He was so exhausted from the treatment that he realized then that he was not going to survive his infection, so he vetoed any more bloodletting by his doctors, and accepted his fate. He instructed his wife Martha to leave him lying in state for three full days because he wanted to be absolutely sure that he was really dead. He was afraid of being entombed and yet alive to some degree. I am sure there are people even now who have that same fear, and I have read stories of people who were pronounced dead, but actually still alive in some comatose state that closely mimicked death. In this particular case of the man with pancreatic cancer, the death was obvious, and there was no concern that I had blown the diagnosis. I did briefly pause to consider the amazing power my words carried: I could now pronounce someone dead.

As I headed back to the coffee shop with my stomach growling, I realized that there were going to be many times when I would be unsure of myself in the same way, and I would either have to use common sense and hope for the best, or get the kind of guidance I needed and review as many of my actions as possible with the senior resident.

I stopped in the bathroom on first floor on the way to the coffee shop.

I was right in the middle of a well-deserved dump when I heard:

"CODE 4, CODE 4, sixth floor, Knisely Building, Room M6502, M6502".

When a code is called on the overhead loudspeaker, it is an emergency alert that assembles doctors, nurses and lab and other support personnel to a patient's room to resuscitate them back to life.

What timing! I pulled up my scrub pants and didn't even bother to completely wipe myself – man was that an uncomfortable feeling. Even more uncomfortable was the apprehension of what this code was about – I'd never run a code, even though I'd been at a few. I wasn't sure how many other docs were in the house, or how many would respond – would my senior resident Laurie come down for it, or did she think I knew what to do?

When I got to the room, Laurie Woodard was already calling out orders. There was no mistaking her authority, and she commanded the attention of everybody in the room. "His rhythm is V-fib – charge the defibrillator, please. Have some lidocaine ready and some bicarb, please."

Laurie was calm, almost quiet, and obviously relaxed, kind of detached from the scene. It reminded me of that saying I had seen in an old book: "When it gets dark enough, the stars come out." Here was a dark situation, and Laurie Woodard was clearly a star. I remembered my first code, as a third year medical student. I was in the patient's room when the patient had fainted, and his nurse pushed the code button which is located in each patient's room, and I immediately snuck out of the room and pretended I wasn't involved. I quietly sneaked down the hallway away from his room. For weeks afterwards, I was deeply ashamed. But I knew nothing about codes, and I was scared. Fast forward to now. My senior resident Laurie was in charge, so I could breathe easier about this situation. The victim was an older-looking man on 6LM, the cardiac rehab floor. He was one room away from Sam Stuckey, the patient I had inherited who was recovering from a heart attack. This was not a private room. The guy we were now resuscitating was in a two-person room. His roommate had been wheeled out into the hallway, and was obviously distraught at what was happening.

After shocking the patient twice, his heart rhythm reverted back to a normal sinus rhythm, and he came around. I was really impressed. Not only did Laurie save the man, but she was able to take charge without shouting or seeming the least bit frazzled.

Afterwards, she thanked all the nurses and techs, and retreated to the ninth-floor call rooms again.

Before she retreated, she looked over at me. "Everything going okay, Rich?"

"Yeah, so far. Laurie, have you looked over the people I worked up yet?"

Laurie nodded. "Uh huh. Looks fine. Be sure to check on Constantine Marcos in CCU before going to bed. Let me know if you have <u>any</u> problems, okay?"

"Okay."

Before I went to bed??? Who was she kidding? At this rate, I knew I wasn't going to bed. It was 2 a.m. and I still had a million details to tidy up. But finally, I had a break; I dashed to the tiny little coffee shop on the first floor. It was darkly lit out of respect for the hour. I was the only one there.

While I ate my "Big Luke" burger and chocolate malt, I pulled out my little red manual with code meds and orders and reviewed it all. Someday, I would have to do what Laurie had just done-save someone's life- and the realization was most unsettling. I noticed that no other doctors had shown up for the code. I had no excuse, though, because I was supposed to be covering the whole "house" until 8 a.m.

After the "meal", I went to check on Constantine Marcos. He was the first mate on the Greek vessel in the Milwaukee harbor who had come in with chest pain. He was doing well – no problems. His chest pain was responding to the morphine Laurie had suggested. While I was in the CCU the cardiac care unit- the ER called – the bar rush was making their usual stampede of casualties. I sighed. Would I make it through this night?

My first customer was an American Indian named Felix who had been cut with a broken whiskey bottle in a barroom brawl. He had a gash on his face that sliced deep into the cheek, about five inches across. Before I made it into his room, the doc in charge of the ER pulled me into the back room where the doctors dictate their ER reports. He opened a cabinet door and showed me a sign taped to the inside of the door. In big bold letters it read:

YOU CAN'T FIX STUPID.

Then he smiled knowingly and said; "every so often I walk in here and look at this sign to remind myself not to get wigged out when I take care of these low-life's doing stupid things to themselves."

I nodded, and then I walked into room 4 to assess that face laceration on the drunk. As I reached for the needle to anesthetize his face, the thought occurred to me – this guy was so drunk that he didn't need anesthesia. I was right. As I put the sutures in, he lay there docile as a sheep being shorn, paralyzed to reality, and saying "patch me up, doc."

I went back upstairs to finish writing orders on my admits, and finished everything at 3:45 a.m. I realized then that I should have taken a nap rather than spending that twenty minutes in the coffee shop, hungry or not – now I was really wasted. I found the call room reserved for the house intern on the 9th floor, started to take off my socks, and collapsed on the bed halfway through the process. When a person is dead tired to this extent, sleep arrives almost instantly, and with it comes weird dreams. The dreams are bizarre and rapid-fire. I was in the middle of a nonsensical dream when, only ten minutes later, I heard my beeper. I had just drifted into that wonderful fog of twilight sleep when that beeper jolted me back to reality. It was my first taste of the helpless lunacy that overtakes an exhausted mind that suddenly is forced to reawaken against its will.

I looked at the number – the ER-Damn!! The ER nurse who answered my return call immediately detected the disgust in my voice.

"No time for that now," she rebuked harshly. "Get down here right away, doctor. We have a bad one…"

It still felt weird to hear someone call me "doctor." It was still my first day of internship, technically, although I was now 21 hours into this call shift. I swung my legs over the call room bed. I was so tired that I felt sick, nauseated, as if I might vomit. This pace is inhuman, I thought. Seriously? It can't be legal to work someone this hard when I am this exhausted! I noticed that I hadn't even disturbed the bedsheets – I had just plopped down on the mattress 10 minutes ago, and it remained neatly made. I eased myself off the bed slowly and ambled out the door.

At 4 o'clock in the morning the hospital hallways are dark. Hospitals dim the lights so that the patients sleep. I stumbled out of the call room with my shoes still untied and my scrubs not quite up to my waist.

There was nobody in the hallway to see me so it was irrelevant. Earlier in the call shift I was bounding up and down the stairwells because it was more expedient; now I decided to take the elevator so I could wake up while I waited for it to reach the 9th floor call rooms. I took one hand and made my fingers into a comb to brush my disheveled hair, and cinched up the drawstring on my scrubs. In the elevator I stooped over to tie my shoelaces. I smelled my armpits. My sweaty body stunk from running up and down the stairs all evening. I heard the overhead speaker playing Kim Carnes' latest hit song…" she's got Bette Davis eyes…" I briefly pondered what that meant. Then the elevator door opened and I was in the ER.

At ground level where the ER was located the first thing that hit me was the bright lights.

The ER never sleeps. My eyes made the painful adjustment to the intense light and I met the nurse at the control desk. See saw my frown and waved it off with a disapproving nod.

"Room 3 – head laceration – bleeding quite a bit. She's a black woman age 56. Deloris Bafta. The story is that her son's best friend rang her doorbell at 3:00 a.m. and she let him in. Turns out he was mad at her son and the first thing he did was hit her over the head with a tire iron. I think she has a skull fracture."

That story woke me right up again. Funny how you can be dead tired and jerked awake suddenly to fix someone's life-changing trauma. The nurse led me into room 3 and tried to introduce me to the patient Deloris. I tuned out the introduction. I was completely focused on her head wound. All I saw was that the once pristine white bedsheets on her gurney were now all red and soaked with blood. I lifted the pile of large gauze taped loosely on the center of her head. The gauzes were soaked through as well. Then I saw the enormous laceration of her scalp. It was as if someone had decided to peel off her scalp to expose the brain. The laceration extended from the back of the head, directly down the midline to her forehead. It was deep – I surmised that the skull was fractured as well.

Then I suddenly felt sick again. This time it wasn't from lack of sleep. It was the nausea of seeing gross amounts of blood on a patient writhing in pain. She was moaning and jerking. I knew I had to leave the room. This patient was depending upon my help to save her life but I knew I wouldn't be able to do it. I headed for the door of her room and told the nurse I had to leave for a moment.

I had no intention of returning. I nonchalantly strolled past the ER control desk so as to avoid drawing attention to myself, and made my way out the front entrance as if I had a purpose in mind. Then as soon as I was out of their sight I bolted down the long hallway leading from the ER. I was queasy. I sprinted to the main hospital entrance and through the double doors to the circle driveway in front of the parking lot. There was no one outside – it was just after 4 a.m. on a hot summer night. I sat on the curb of the driveway circle and put my head in between my knees to restore the blood flow. I was faint.

Once the blood returned to my brain, my head was flooded with thoughts. Thoughts of guilt, of panic, of self-preservation. I was done with medicine. I realized that I would not be able to take another day of this kind of stress. My apartment was only a few blocks down the street. As I stood up from the curb and headed in that direction, I felt the immense sadness of failure. I would have to find another way to pay back med school loans, I decided, as I walked off the hospital grounds.

As I walked, I flashed back to medical school. What would Dr. Griesy think of me now?

*

I deliberated. The guilt was getting to me. It wasn't that I was unfamiliar with sleepless shifts, but how did one ever get used to them? I remembered back to my first time on a 40-hour call shift as a med student, on a surgery rotation. We were doing our eighth consecutive operation – it was a weekend night on a busy orthopedic service – and I was assisting the resident with his suturing. All of a sudden there was a lull, as he was busy cutting some dead tissue. I'd been up already for 30 some odd hours, and, as I stared down at all the blood on the operating room floor, I saw lots of weird pictures – it was like looking at clouds. I started to drift off into a dream, and then I awoke and took my sterile suture scissors and began to draw pictures on the floor with the blood as my ink. The resident was too busy sewing to notice. Then the scrub nurse returned to the room just as the resident asked me to cut his stitch. She shrieked "NO!" and then he looked down at me and noticed that I'd been drawing pictures in the blood on the OR floor, in my sleepless stupor. Her shriek snapped me back into reality, and I felt foolish and ashamed, but the admonition only kept me awake for 45 minutes, before I began to feel the craving for sleep again.

To top it off, (on that infamous night several years ago) the surgeon/resident got his turn on our next case an hour later, when he wrapped up a whole foot thinking he'd already sewed it up when the wound was still gaping and bleeding. I had to remind him that we still had to sew up the open wound. And, a week later, we discovered that we'd made a major mistake on one of the operations, because we'd removed the wrong toe – the man came in still complaining of the pain, and the resident realized, after looking at an X-ray, that the wrong toe had been removed. Sleeplessness – it does wonders to change a perspective and affect judgement. That was when I was a medical student- I had someone else in charge of me back then.

Now, I was the man in the hot seat. And now, once again, I was in that

79

warped frame of mind where sleep seemed to be my only god. If I could only arrange for a two-hour nap... that would fix it, I was sure of it. Everything about the outside of this parking lot stood in stark contrast to what lay right inside those hospital doors. I had too much common sense to go back.

Heck, nobody had a right to keep us awake for that long! I had always wanted to be a musician anyway. I went through every rationalization in the book, hoping for one valid argument to tip me over the edge and justify my walking away right then and there. I was already 90% convinced that I should leave for good. I only had to talk myself into the last 10 %. Just when I thought I would actually quit, I remembered that $70,000 medical school debt I owed; no way would I pay that back unless I stuck this thing out.

There was another major thought haunting me at that moment. This was my SECOND residency attempt. I had originally been accepted through the residency match system to start my training at Broadlawns Hospital in Des Moines, Iowa. Then, in June, one month before we were to start, I was training for a marathon and had wrenched my back violently. I had called the director of the program and asked for an easy rotation to start the residency because of my sore back. Then the next day I received a telegram from the director of the program. He informed me that my position had been rescinded. They had fired me before I even began!! My dad then reminded me that life was not fair. I had to adapt or die. Which was it to be? After several weeks of soul-searching and wallowing in self-pity, I reached out to find another spot somewhere. My college roommate John Holtan then found me this position in Milwaukee. It turns out that my interview here at St.

Luke's had impressed the program so much that, even though they had their full complement of interns for the year, they found some extra money and added a spot for me in their program.

And now I was going to walk away from a second chance at residency, on the very first night on call. At that moment of truth in my young medical career, something crawled out of me that was buried deep in my soul- a burst of surprising courage-and I realized that the ER needed someone in there right now. I was the one they were counting on – who was I to selfishly think of my fatigue, when this lady had a huge hole in her head?

In that moment of courage, I became a doctor. I assumed my responsibility as I saw it in spite of my warped, sleepless perspective, and I walked back into her room and started to work on her wound. Laurie Woodard, my senior for the evening, came down to offer some pointers, but allowed me to muddle through the surgery. We had to feel her skull with our gloved fingers to decide if the bone was broken. From what we could tell, it was ok. Now it was just a matter of piecing together the scalp and stopping the bleeding. An hour later, about halfway through the repair, it was looking pretty good.

My former college roommate John Holtan walked in. "What you got here, Richie?"

"Johnnie – is it that late already? What are you doing here?"

"I'm scrubbing with Andy Owsiak the general surgeon this morning. Laurie told me you were down here. How's it going?"

"Okay, now, Johnnie. Looked hairy for a while. What do you think?" It was probably the first time I ever acknowledged to John that he knew more than I did, because he was now a year ahead of me in his training, and I really wanted his advice and experience. He examined the wound, put on a pair of sterile gloves so he could feel the skull for any cracks, and put a stitch in to show me how to snug up the scalp better. It seemed as if we were college roommates again, only now we'd made the big time – doctors! Life and death! Guts and glory! The drama and pressure evolved into a sudden rush of omnipotence. Who needed sleep?! That was for the wimps.

As I rode the elevator to 6JK to begin morning work rounds, my watch said 07.00. I'd been here 24 hours already. I had a full day ahead of me – no time for breakfast today; I'd have to try to squeeze in lunch. I prayed that the ER would stay quiet until 08.00 – that's when my "call" shift ended, and after that I wouldn't be responsible for any more ER patients or admissions. I ruminated briefly about that person I'd pronounced dead last night. What a power bestowed onto me! I could decide if someone were dead! It overwhelmed me with awe. The elevator opened and destroyed the moment. My head was swelling. I was still riding the high of my recent triumph in the ER with that severe head laceration – a triumph mostly against myself, and against my close call with quitting. I remembered that moment of doubt where I'd almost given in to the overwhelming temptation to walk away from it all. Dr. Griesy would be proud, I thought. He would approve of how I repaired that head laceration. I harkened back to the time in the Two Harbors ER when he showed me how to place my first suture on a patient with a chain saw laceration. Also, he would be proud that I

81

didn't walk away when I was dog-tired and beaten down. I reminded myself that this would be a marathon, and I had to pace myself- to take it one mile at a time. And I had to adapt, or I would die. It was abundantly clear that I would need to get more sleep when I wasn't on call. Those three strategies would be critical to my success or failure.

6JK signified the 6th floor, J and K wings. This hospital was indeed massive. Laurie Kuehn, the head nurse who had flustered me yesterday with Mr. Olson's insulin order, handed me the phone. On the line was Dr. Saul Wally.

"What kind of a fly-by-night doctor are you, Mayerchak? You didn't do a damned rectal exam! I should have come in myself last night!!"

He was fuming. He didn't even say hello. He was on 2EF. I was glad I'd missed him – I'd been in the ER when he'd seen his patient Judith Warff, the lady with Raynaud's syndrome, giving her the blue/white fingers and toes. Now he was on his way out the door.

"But Dr. Wally, I really did plan to do a rectal exam – she told me that you'd done one on her in the office yesterday, so she refused to have me do another one."

Dr. Wally wasn't buying my excuse. "Get one thing straight here – you're the boss, not the patient. I asked you to examine her and I expected a full exam." He hung up abruptly before I could reply.

"Great." I thought. I'm in big trouble already. I took a deep breath and headed down to the CCU (cardiac care unit) to see Constantine Marcos, the Greek sailor I had admitted yesterday with a major heart attack.

Fortunately for me (and for Constantine), Laurie had walked me through his management because of the severity of his deficit.

When I arrived, the nurses were changing shifts, so the place was a bit chaotic. I walked into his room to talk to him. To my surprise, he told me he wanted to leave. He said he was the first mate on a Greek vessel which was leaving port today, heading home to Greece. If he wasn't on board, he would forfeit his year's salary and all his possessions would probably be stolen. As if that wasn't reason enough, he had only 6 months to go before retirement.

If he stayed behind at this hospital, he would forfeit his pension. He had a wife and two kids in college to support – he <u>HAD</u> to leave.

I reviewed his chart. The lab results back from the morning run showed even more convincing evidence that his heart attack was a big one. He wasn't in any pain right now because we had him pretty well snowed with morphine and confined to strict bedrest. To travel back to the ship would be unthinkable.

*

I explained the severity of his condition to him. It didn't seem to matter. The welfare of his children and wife seemed much more important – he told me he'd rather die than forfeit the pension that he had coming. His wife would get the money if he didn't live, but he had to be on that ship. It was leaving the port of Milwaukee in two hours.

I called Dr. Johnson, the cardiologist on his case. He discussed it with Constantine but was unable to impress upon him how serious the heart attack was. Finally, we both realized that this man was leaving, with or without our help. Johnson decided to load him up with as much medication as possible to help keep him pain free for the cab ride to the ship, and from there on in, he'd have to pray for an easy trip home.

He thanked us for our help, and left. I wondered if he would even make it back to the ship, let alone back to Greece.

I headed upstairs to meet with Mr. Kukowski's children. Fred, the man with the 60 pounds of fluid in his belly, was going to need a long stay here, I informed them. I spent about twenty minutes explaining the details of what needed to be done and, as I left the room, I noticed it was already 10:30. I went to 6LM to see Sam Malecek, my other patient who was recovering from his heart attack.

As I was glossing through his chart at the nursing station, I listened to the nurses conversing. This was just another day on the job for them. I envied their casual talk, and also the fact that they had merely an 8-hour shift to work through, and then they were out of the hospital. I was already 26 hours into my marathon shift. One of the nurses mentioned that she was going to a Milwaukee Brewers game this evening. The Brewers were in first place in the pennant race. Another nurse was discussing the upcoming Sommerfest. Each weekend there was a different festival-Italian fest, Polish fest, etc – to celebrate the rich ethnic diversity of this major city.

As I sat there listening to their stories while I reviewed Sam's chart, a physician in his mid-forties, with gray hair and no tie, walked up to the table and looked at my name tag.

"So, you're Mayerchak. I'm Dr. Wally. Why weren't you at my ten o'clock conference on 6JK? You were the only one that didn't make it."

83

Oh, darn it all, I thought. I'd forgotten all about it. I started to explain: "Well, I had a problem with my patient in CCU – he wanted to leave, and…"

"Cut the crap, Mayerchak." Dr. Wally took a chair and sat down across the table and intently stared me right in the face. In that sudden silence I was painfully aware that all eyes were on me – the hustle and bustle of the station ceased, and everybody listened. Dr. Wally continued his accusations.

"I know damn well why you weren't there. You just can't handle the pressure, can you? It's too much for you – you didn't do that rectal exam on my patient for the same reason. I know what's going on. You don't have what it takes to be a good doctor..."

His invectives had reduced me to quiet tears. I didn't know what to say. I couldn't look away, because everybody was watching me.

I mustered the courage for a reply. "No, that's not it. I was tied up in the CCU. It won't happen again." As I retreated from the station, I could feel every eye in the room still trained upon my back.

Halfway down the hall, I felt a hand on the back of my white coat. "Don't worry about him, Caddychak. He was way out of line."

It was Konrad. He'd watched the whole thing. I hadn't noticed him, in my embarrassment. He told me he was going to say something to Dr. Laufenburg, the head of the family practice residency program. Apparently this wasn't the first time Dr. Wally had done something inappropriate like this. The guy was well respected for his superb clinical skills, and the residents liked the fact that he always seemed to have interesting patients, but his interpersonal skills were definitely deficient. That's why he'd recently been canned as head of the family practice medicine wards; Dr. Parent had taken his place. Maybe that's why Saul Wally was upset that I'd skipped his lecture, I consoled myself.

I looked in on Virginia, the lady with the skull laceration I'd repaired in the ER after coming oh-so-close to bailing residency for a saner life. Now that the euphoria of my early morning triumph had passed, I realized that my repair of her head laceration was passable at best, definitely not something to brag about. I still had a lot to learn in the realm of practical surgical skills such as repairing serious lacerations. Still, I was elated that I had gutted out the shock of seeing all of the blood on her sheets. Now she was resting comfortably. It was such a good feeling to see her and realize that I had prevailed in my moment of sheer panic – the trip to her room was well worth the effort.

I sped through morning rounds and was able to see most of my patients in half the time that it had taken yesterday. I was almost through my list when I got a page from 6 LM.

"Dr. Mayerchak, call 6LM <u>stat</u>. Please call 6LM stat."

It was Sam Malecek, the guy with the MI (myocardial infarction-heart attack). His monitor was showing third degree heart block. He needed an emergency pacemaker put in, because his heartbeat had fallen into the thirties and forties. Dr. Johnson the cardiologist was still in the house, so I asked him to come up urgently, and he had him stabilized with a temporary pacer in less than half an hour. Dr. Parent's words of wisdom rang true as I headed for the caf for some lunch: watch for rhythm disturbances in patients with inferior MIs.

Dr. Parent was late for 2 o'clock rounds again. Jill said we could count on that happening quite often. He had a busy practice in addition to the three hours he spent with us each afternoon. He arrived at 2:15.

"Lot of work today, Jill?" It was Dr. Parent. "Yeah, Rich was busy last night."

We flew through the list of stable patients and headed quickly to staff the new ones. On our way to present our first patient, I noticed that Josie Ramirez wasn't with us.

"Jill, shouldn't we leave a message for Josie?" I asked. Jill frowned.

"Josie quit today. Dr. Wally chewed her out this morning about something and she quit. We're gonna have to change the call schedule to cover her days – Rich, you'll be on again Sunday instead of Monday, and every three days until we find another intern – <u>if</u> we do."

Doug and Konrad and I looked at each other and sighed. Terrible news. The last thing any of us wanted to hear. If nothing else, Josie had been an extra body to make the call schedule reasonably tolerable.

Jerry Parent broke in. "I hear you had some trouble with Dr. Wally today, Rich. Sounds like the way he doled out his criticism was uncalled for. I think the team ought to write a letter to Dr. Laufenburg to document the incident."

At that moment, I felt really accepted as a part of "the team," as Dr. Parent liked to refer to us. It was so characteristic of him to use words like "team". He seemed to be a team player. Dr. Wally appeared to be a prima donna, perhaps a star in his own right, but unto himself.

My presentations went well, considering my state of fatigue. The rush of omnipotence had long ago worn off, and now I was stuck smelling my stinky body in dirty scrub clothes and feeling my unshaven face, and I felt like a total pig. Again, Dr. Parent asked me questions that I couldn't answer, but I didn't mind, considering the comparison between Dr. Wally and him. I could take Jerry Parent's way of teaching any day –even his badgering. I hated to imagine what Jill had gone through as an intern under Dr. Wally. I now had a new role model, just as Dr. Griesy had been for me in medical school: I was going to imitate Dr. Parent.

After Jerry Parent left us that afternoon Jill told us what it had been like working as an intern with Dr. Wally leading the medicine rounds with the residents. The biggest difference was that Saul Wally never saw the patients, instead relying upon the senior residents to verify that the interns' exams were validated. The rounds were conducted solely in that conference room on 6JK so that he could speed through his day. There was little accountability or verification of what the residents had done.

As Jill regaled us with the story of Dr. Parent's first several months supervising the medicine service, I noticed that she, like Laurie Woodard, was very relaxed and comfortable in her role as a senior resident. I noticed her ring. Was it because she was married? Having someone to come home to each day must be very nice, I thought. How I envied her calm. She told us that when Dr. Parent took over, he immediately insisted that the residents travel to each patient's room and make their presentations at the bedside of the patient. Jill said they soon discovered that most of the interns hadn't taken a past medical history, or a social history on their patients. Most of the time there were gross errors in the physical exam findings. They missed obvious congestive heart failure, pneumonia, and many other overt physical findings. Jill observed that Dr. Parent never got angry, but he wouldn't stand for shoddy work. He insisted on a standard way of presenting each patient, beginning with the description of their social history, some background with which he could frame them as people. After the intern presented the patient, Dr. Parent would examine the patient at the bedside and verify the resident's findings. Jill said that the quality of presentations steadily improved because Dr. Parent expected no less. He soon instilled a sense of pride in the residents because much more was expected from them.

After Jill gave us the low-down on Jerry Parent, I finished rounds, then

I tidied up several orders, checked a couple of lab results, and headed out the door at 6:30 pm. I had been awake for over 35 hours at that point. What an exhilarating feeling! I felt as if school had just let out for the summer.

Never mind the fact that I was coming back in twelve hours. I was FREE. The air never smelled so sweet. It was summer, and I had the evening off. The options for others on this beautiful warm evening might have been numerous, but I knew of only one. The most important thing this call shift had taught me was that getting adequate sleep would be the absolute key to my survival. I made a beeline home, didn't bother to eat, unplugged the phone, and plopped on the bed. I was soon dead to reality.

Saturday, Day #3

Summer in Milwaukee was magical. The Brewers were on fire, and that seemed to buoy the spirits of the entire city. I walked through the main entrance to the hospital with less trepidation and a sense of relief because I knew I was going home later this afternoon. All I had to do was get through this day. It would be a piece of cake after what I'd been through yesterday. I met Konrad in the hallway.

"How was the night, Con-Man?" It was 07.00, but my body was still in shock from my previous call shift, despite twelve hours of sleep.

"Lousy, Caddy-chalk. Dr. Noonan dumped on me pretty bad. He admitted two old ladies with back pain and someone with mild abdominal pain that I think just has the flu. That guy really pisses me off."

Dr. Noonan was one of the private physicians whose patients we cared for. He and his group had a reputation for admitting people to the hospital much more frequently than some of the other docs. Jill said it was because that's where the money's really at in medicine. Having a dozen people in the hospital to round on daily, as they did, really contributed strongly to their incomes. Of course, from the perspectives of Doug, Konrad, and me, we looked at the practice as abusive, since we had to do most of their dirty work – H&Ps (history and physical exam), discharge summaries, and numerous beeps from nurses. It wouldn't have been a sore spot if the admissions were justifiable, but most of them seemed unnecessary, according to Jill. She'd already warned us of the problem. I hadn't gotten any of their admissions on my first call night, but Konrad had been hit hard – five admissions from them alone – the three I already mentioned, and two which were seemingly legit.

Just then Doug Landers showed up.

"Hey, you guys, what are we gonna do with Josie's patients?"

"I'll take care of 'em. It was Jill, combing her hair as she arrived. Must be nice to be married, I thought to myself.

"Jill, any luck finding another intern?"

"Not yet. You're still on again tomorrow, Rich, unless some miracle happens today. Herb Laufenburg is working on it."

We parted for work rounds. I noticed a camaraderie developing between Konrad, Doug, and me. Even though Doug was the radiology resident, and as such he would have no future interest in managing medical patients, to Konrad and me, he was a teammate. Our team chemistry was the one bright spot in a sea of challenges that never seemed to let up. If I was to be on call again tomorrow, I knew I had to get rid of a few of my "players", or drown in extra work. Just the rounds alone were eating up hours.

Since it was a weekend, our 2 p.m. rounds with Dr. Parent would be replaced by rounds with Dr. Laufenburg, the director of the program, at 10 a.m. Saturday. On Sunday, we wouldn't have rounds at all, except on our own. If anybody really needed to be seen by a staff doc, Jill could call one in, but otherwise we would wait until Monday to staff Saturday night's admits – as well as Sunday's. Mondays promised to be busy days, when the staff docs finally reviewed all that we had done on the weekend.

I first stopped to see Agnes Jones, the lady with the gallbladder disease. She was ready for discharge, so I wrote her orders. It occurred to me that if I really did discharge as many people as I wanted to, I would have a mountain of paperwork to catch up on – they all required discharge summaries to be dictated, as well as discharge orders and notes in the chart.

Next, I sent Julia Meyer, the lady with the congestive heart failure, packing. Her legs were normal size now, except for small traces of fluid; she'd lost fifteen pounds, almost all of compromised of the fluid she had accumulated in her legs.

Jack Larson, the drinker with the pancreatitis, was now stable enough to transfer to the DePaul rehab hospital where he'd promised to dry out for good. I thought to myself that it wasn't likely to happen.

Chester Polinski, the man with back pain that was diagnosed to have multiple myeloma, was leaving AMA – against medical advice. He'd been withdrawn all week, depressed about his diagnosis – now he wanted a second opinion and was leaving to find one. I was relieved – and hoping that all of my patients would leave AMA. At this point I didn't really want any extra work. I was not yet interested in learning. All I wanted from this month was to survive.

Fred Kukowski, the man with the ascites, the belly full of at least 60 pounds of fluid, was his jolly old self. He was telling me all sorts of trivia about the Milwaukee Brewers. He asked me to stop by on my next evening on call and watch a few innings of a game with him. He'd lost five pounds since being admitted 36 hours ago, so I had to back off a little from my aggressive use of diuretics-water pills to rid him of extra fluid.

Judith Warff, Dr. Wally's patient, had tests that led nowhere, so he was planning to discharge her today. He chalked up her Raynaud's syndrome to "idiopathic"– reason unknown – and decided to concentrate on how to treat it, but that could be handled as an outpatient. I had to hand it to Saul Wally – he had no interpersonal skills, but he was a conscientious physician. If Judith had been Dr. Noonan's patient, she might be here another week.

Viola Anderson, the lady with the stroke, was unchanged. Her stroke could get worse or better at any time, but the likelihood diminished with each day if no improvement took place. I had forgotten to discontinue her lidocaine, which I was using for the ominous bout of V tach-rapid heartbeat – she'd experienced two days ago. Two days was a long time to keep someone on lidocaine, I'd been told. They could develop neurologic complications from it – just what Viola needed. I switched her to an oral drug and stopped her IV. Fortunately, this mistake did not injure her, but it could have. The realization of that error was very disquieting. I shrugged my shoulders as if to apologize to her, and moved on.

John Thompson, the man with the swollen, infected cherry red leg, was benefitting from the enforced bed rest and elevation of his leg. Already the swelling was starting to diminish. His weight had dropped two pounds. Once we'd removed the extra fluid from that leg, the healing would proceed more easily.

Jerome Stark, the alcoholic man seeing bugs and threatening to go over the edge into DTs, was stable. I still had a hard time believing the story he told me of the case of beer and two quarts of hard stuff he drank daily. I continued to snow him with massive amounts of Librium, which seemed to validate his drinking tale. That much Librium would have killed most people, but a dyed-in-the-wool alcoholic has a liver that will chew up almost anything you throw at it, no matter how strong. Sooner or later, though, that liver becomes sick, and then it won't work. People cannot survive without a liver. It is a fact too often ignored. When people overdose on Tylenol in a suicide attempt, they often regret their action and present to the ER in a state of remorse. Even if the Tylenol(acetaminophen) is neutralized, the effect on the liver may be to permanent destroy it, and then they die an inglorious death a week after their suicide gesture-from liver failure. The alcoholics like Jerry Stark are basically committing a form of suicide, just much more slowly.

Sam Malecek in the cardiac care unit was doing well – Dr. Johnson had put a permanent pacer in him this morning, and he remained in CCU for a day of observation.

Virginia Brown, my lady with the head laceration, inflicted by her son's best friend, was still feeling a small headache, but otherwise she thought she was well enough to leave. She had several small kids at home to care for. I gave her a list of warning signs of what to watch for that would signal internal bleeding or pressure buildup, then sent her on her way. She would see me at the family practice clinic in a week to have her stitches out.

I was back on 6JK, which was our home base for the family practice/internal medicine service. I glanced at the nursing station bulletin board. On it was tacked pictures of all the residents, from a hospital bulletin that had just come out. Underneath the names corresponding to each picture were little marks. I asked Laurie Kuehn, the head nurse, what the marks meant.

"The 'S' is for single, the 'M' for married," she said.

"You're kidding! They actually pay attention to that kind of stuff around here, Laurie?"

"Rich, you wouldn't believe it. Some floors have little dossiers on every one of you – especially you single ones – there are so few of you that are eligible."

"How do they all know who's single so fast?"

"Oh, word travels fast here. Believe me, they all know. The head nurse on 7GH married a resident rotating through here from County Hospital last year. Ever since that, everybody's had the same idea. Up there, she's got her ears open for any info to pass on to her single girls."

I didn't believe the fuss, but then again, I'd been too preoccupied with

90

merely surviving my job up until now. Maybe for the nurses who'd been here awhile, it was easier to notice us without worrying about handling their jobs at the same time. I did notice that I was becoming more interested in the nurses, especially Laurie Kuehn; I wondered whether she was dating anyone.

I went up to seventh to write an order I'd forgotten, and noticed that the nurse's station on 7GH had circles around the pictures of the single residents. Laurie was right – we were noticed.

By the time I got finished with rounds, it was 10:45 a.m.. I decided to call Konrad and ask him about Dr. Noonan, and then realized in horror that rounds had started at 10:00 with Dr. Laufenburg. Man, was I in for it now! I ran down to the conference room and saw everyone seated at the table.

"Sorry I'm late, Jill. I forgot today's rounds were changed."

"That's okay – it's still the first week – we figured you were busy with something important. If that happens again, though, let me know so I know where you are and what's up." Jill seemed understanding. Then I remembered that she'd gone through it once herself. The biggest problem for me was keeping my days straight – they all blended into each other. We'd started on a Thursday, and now it was Saturday, but even the weekend days were just regular old work days. All I knew was that it was day #3, with 28 left to go before I could graduate from this miserable service. Konrad had two months on the service, and one later on in the year – I had it the other way around; one month now, and two in a row later on.

After we walked to the rooms to staff Konrad's admissions, it was 1:15 p.m. and I had nothing else to do – my patients were all bedded down or discharged. Since I was on call again tomorrow, I headed for the door after signing out to Doug, who was on call. Sign-outs were merely a matter of giving our patient lists to whomever was on call, with any instructions for special problems that might arise overnight.

As I rounded the corner on 2EF, I passed a group of nurses heading in the opposite direction. As they turned the corner out of my sight, I heard one of them say "six" and then another one replied, "no, I'd say seven, but I didn't see the face."

So Laurie was right, I thought. This place was a meat market and, for the first time in my life, I was the shoppee, not the shopper.

That afternoon, I decided to get to know my neighbors. Arne Celinski was an auto mechanic who owned two adjacent lots next to the house where

I rented a room. Arne owned a garage in the neighborhood where he fixed up cars and sold gas. His son Dale was his business partner.

Arne used the vacant lot next to my house to plant a large very colorful garden. It was in full bloom. I spent part of the afternoon visiting with him, and the rest of it talking to my college roommate John Holtan about his wedding plans. John had met a nurse from the CCU during his third week as an intern here last year. Now, after a year of dating, they were getting married on Saturday. Eileen, his betrothed, was talking of setting me up with some of her friends. I looked forward to it.

In the meantime, there was the matter of this free afternoon facing me. I went for a long run and pondered what had transpired in the first three days of internship. I had turned the corner from a medical student wearing a short white coat, to becoming an actual doctor in a long white coat, signifying the power I possessed to write orders and pronounce people dead. With that power came an awesome increase in responsibility for keeping those patients alive. I was feeling the heavy weight of that burden as I ran down the suburban Polish streets of South Milwaukee. I remembered that I had panicked on the first night and nearly walked away from residency for good. That thought was still quite unsettling. I feared that it might happen again. I decided to run five extra miles to rid me of that fear. Our medical school dean, Dr. Leppi, had been right all along: running was still doing more for my head than what it did for my physical health. In addition to getting enough sleep, I was going to need to keep running, for my sanity.

Sunday, Day #4 On Call Again

On my way into work this morning, I stopped to take a good look at St. Luke's from several blocks away. It was a massive hospital, even by modern standards. Its footprint occupied most of a block in two directions, including the parking space provided for employees. It stood nine stories tall, most of it comprised of modern materials, walls with thin layers of marble to give the appearance of a solid building. The original building was much smaller, and still stood intact, but was concealed on two sides by all of the additions which more than doubled the bed capacity of the original facility.

As I entered the long hallway leading from the lobby, I noticed for the first time the red and green and blue lines painted on the floor.

"What are they for?" I motioned to the lobby desk clerk. "They point to the ER, the two sets of elevators, the outpatient department, and X-ray, you know, like the yellow brick road."

I took the red line to the JK elevators and headed for the sixth. We wouldn't be staffing today, as I recalled, because it was Sunday. The docs merely had to do their rounds and get the hell out of there, except for me, stuck here until tomorrow after 2 p.m. rounds with Dr. Parent, which usually persisted into the evening.

On 6JK, I met Laurie Kuehn, the head nurse. We were rapidly becoming friends.

I greeted her with a smile.

"Hi! What's with the can, Laurie – that stuff you're spraying really stinks."

Laurie contorted her face.

"It's air freshener. If you think this is bad, it's ten times better than what we've been smelling up 'til now. Monica, our nurse's aide, just had an ileal bypass to help her lose weight. Now, she's got terrible flatus – she's farting every five minutes – it's unbelievable."

I caught my first whiff of what she was describing. "Remind me to do rounds somewhere else from now on."

In the middle of my morning rounds, I ran into Doug Landers, the X-ray resident on our team this month. I asked him about his evening on call.

"Unbelievable, Rich. I slept like a baby from midnight until 6:30. I didn't get a single admission after 9:30 last night."

I was flabbergasted. Why him? Admittedly, it couldn't have happened to a nicer guy, but I couldn't help feeling his luck meant my misfortune; maybe twice as many would come in tonight.

I razzed him: "You dog! Hope it continues for one more night – I could use it!"

Just then I then got a page from 4EF. They needed help putting an IV in one of their patients. I walked over to investigate.

The patient was Joe Slater, a massive 420-pound man of 5-foot height. The guy was grotesque to look at. He was here to have surgery tomorrow – a jejuno-ileal bypass; if successful, it would mean that the major part of the fats he eats will be poorly absorbed from the diet because of removal of certain segments of the small intestines. I was reminded about the gassy smell on 6JK from the lady who had just recovered from the same surgery this guy was about to have. I wondered if he knew there would be side effects from his surgery- including the gassiness.

I was getting to be an expert in finding veins in impossible cases even like his, so I continued to look even though nothing obvious presented itself. The veins were probably two inches below all of that flab, I guessed. As I searched, I talked with him. He told me that he'd been eating steaks and spaghetti and getting drunk, and really piling on the extra calories ever since he'd heard he could get this operation, because he knew that afterward he wouldn't be able to eat in the same fashion. In the last three weeks, he'd gained over 30 pounds.

Finally, I gave up and called the surgery team to do a cut-down. The procedure is simple: to make an incision in the skin, usually the wrist or the ankle, and then to find a vein by digging around under the skin once the arteries and veins are exposed. In this case, the surgeons decided to put a central line in, a subclavian line, and I left the room as they were preparing to stick a big needle under his clavicle (collar bone). The guy was a pig, and I was sure they'd have trouble, and I didn't want to hang around wasting time.

Rounds went easy on me today. Sam Stuckey, the guy with the heart attack, had graduated from the CCU again and was back on 6LM starting all over with his cardiac rehab. Fred Kukowski, with the belly full of fluid, had gained half a pound since yesterday, so once again I got more aggressive with his diuretics-water pills. As I passed 6JK, I caught another whiff of what Laurie had alluded to – the foul smell of large amounts of flatus (gas) mixed with but not hidden by air freshener.

I went to lunch by myself. So far, the ER had been a real gem – not a single call from them. I sat at the end of a long table and proceeded to read my newspaper and eat my lunch. At the other end of the table was a group of ICU nurses. I didn't really pay any attention to them at first, until I heard one of them mention one of the internal medicine residents. It was a guy who was rotating here for a month from Milwaukee County Hospital. My ears perked up as she began to describe what happened on a date with him last night.

"…and then he said, let's go to the bedroom, we'll be more comfortable in there… he's got a hairy chest… you guys thought he's so quiet and harmless… well, not in there he wasn't! Then we…"

At that point, I had put my paper down and was listening so intently that the nurses looked over and noticed me. Then the story stopped in mid-sentence and I didn't stick around for it to resume. As I headed back to the call rooms, I resolved to NEVER date a nurse from this hospital – NEVER! Did they all talk about their dates that way, that explicitly? I was really shocked. Since when was it fashionable to do a play-by-play of your intimate moments with someone in such vivid detail?

On my way upstairs, the ER paged me, so I swung over there. The man they wanted me to see was complaining of butt pain – and he was a real pain in the butt. I could feel something lodged in his rectum, as I did an exam with my finger, but I couldn't ascertain what it was. I obtained an anoscope to get a better look.

"My God, there's a long stick in here! Did you put something up inside your rectum, sir?"

"It's a carrot." He looked at me sheepishly, and said nothing more. I didn't ask anything more, either. I sent him to a proctologist – I wasn't going to mess with that one.

The ER nurses were laughing with me about it as he was leaving, and they told me that his case was not the first such incident they'd had at Luke's. They'd had a man with an eggplant in his rectum, and one with a glass funnel with the large side inserted first that had broken in his rectum.

Somehow, their stories were believable, after what I'd seen today. After hearing their story, I walked to the back dictation room in the ER and once again opened the cupboard where the sign was taped inside the cupboard door: YOU CAN'T FIX STUPID.

The afternoon remained relatively quiet. I was very surprised. I had one admission from Noonan's partner, Dr. Weber, but it seemed justified – a man with atrial fibrillation and subsequent congestive heart failure – Charles Anton, 63, a retired foundry worker.

After bedding him down, I made it up to the ninth floor on-call bedrooms for a look at what goes on there for the lucky dogs who don't work as hard when on call. For instance, there was Mark, a flexible intern. He was only called when the nurses needed an IV started or had trouble drawing blood or something similar. He didn't have to cover the ER or admit patients. I really envied him. Then again, the responsibility I had was really teaching me medicine the hard way – at crash course speed. A

Milwaukee Brewers game was on TV. I watched a few minutes, then remembered Fred Kukowski was a Brewers fan, and ran downstairs to watch some of the game with him. I loved baseball anyway, but this year the Brewers were making baseball fans out of everybody.

I sat in the corner of Fred's room watching the baseball game. Rollie Fingers, sporting his signature handlebar mustache, was on the mound for the Brewers. For a few glorious minutes I forgot that I was on call. Then the ER paged me. They were busy. They wanted me to come quickly.

I bounded down the six flights of stairs to the ER – I was still full of energy. When I arrived, I saw the reason for their call. A sixtyish-year-old man was lying on a cart complaining of profound difficulty breathing. He'd been brought in from a brothel. He asked me not to tell his wife where the ambulance had picked him up.

"What's your name, sir?"

"Harold Wilmann."

"I'm Dr. Mayerchak. What do you do for a living?"

"I'm laid off – from the foundry. You gotta help me, doc – I can hardly breathe."

I decided it was time to lay off the chatter. I took a step back and tried to decide what to do first. He had a nasal cannula giving him oxygen already. His monitor showed normal cardiac rhythm. I ordered a chest X-ray and arterial blood gases. With the lab tests cooking, I decided to ask a few more questions and get my workup over with – I knew he'd be admitted to me.

"Have you taken any medications in the past, Mr. Wilmann?" "Yeah, dyazide, for high blo…"

All of a sudden, he slumped over and stopped breathing. Then it hit me like a Mack truck – this guy was in respiratory arrest! Why had I waited so long to intubate him? Even though he was breathing on his own, he should have been on a ventilator – he had no reserve left, no strength to keep up the rapid rate of breathing he was doing – over 40 times a minute. Now he was out cold, and I was all alone in the room with him.

I ran over to the wall and punched the button that indicated a code 4 was going on in here. Inside of ten seconds, there were three nurses and the ER staff doc down there to help me code him. The staff doc intubated him and called the orders.

"Get those gases, stat! Where's the monitor? What's his rhythm? Get

96

EKG over here for a 12-lead right now! Give him some bicarb – two amps, and... he's in asystole – get some epi for me – I want him to have an amp of epi right now. Where's the respiratory techs – this guy needs to be bagged!!"

The staff doc spoke in one fluid motion, and just kept calling orders one after another. Now there were ten people clustered around, setting up IV lines, handing tubes for blood samples, and doing CPR and giving medications. It was amazing just how synchronized everything was.

I looked at Mr. Wilmann, lying there oblivious to everything that was happening. His skin was pale now. Twenty minutes had elapsed since he'd gone out in mid-sentence. Then the staff doc spoke:

"Time to reassess. Do we have a pulse?"

"No."

"Rhythm is asystole. Let's call it – that's it."

As if someone had pulled a giant plug somewhere, all motion ceased at that instant. Everyone stood there for a brief instant to pay homage to the man that didn't make it, and then, just as abruptly, everybody went their own ways, carrying their machines and instruments with them.

I stayed behind to sit with him for a minute. I was angry with myself for not thinking to intubate him sooner – why didn't I recognize how bad off he was? Boy, that line between life and death was so fine. I remembered back to organic chemistry at Luther College with Dr. Koeltzow, my advisor, who told us time and again that the line between life and death is so fine that we treaded it every day without knowing it. He graced us with that philosophy on several occasions after becoming deathly ill from influenza one year.

Now I really appreciated his point. This guy had been sitting up, talking to me one minute, and bang, he's gone forever. It was too profound for words.

As I was leaving the ER, I saw some commotion off in the distance.

The staff doc motioned me over to take a look.

"Look at her – what a mess, huh?"

It was a seventeen-year-old girl, unconscious, with chopped up legs and arms, and a squashed-in head. The story unfolded that her fifteen-year-old sister was mad at her for going out with her boyfriend, so she'd chopped her with an axe. Everything was hanging together, but pretty badly gashed. I was glad I didn't have to manage this one. I put on a pair of gloves to examine her skull: it was bashed in like a pumpkin. I put my finger right through to her brain – what a gruesome experience. Fortunately for everyone, she didn't live long.

When I got upstairs, I had an admission waiting. Selwood Bannon, 42, was here with chest pain, admitted directly by one of the docs who hadn't ever seen him. He was on 6LM being monitored until I could see him.

Selwood had a very interesting story. He'd had 13 operations in the past. He'd had every disposable organ taken out already, from appendix to gallbladder to spleen to part of his stomach. He'd had four cardiac catheterizations to look for heart disease in his coronaries, all of which were normal. Now he was in complaining of chest pain and wanting another catheterization. Something smelled fishy about him.

Jack Robbins was the senior on call today. I walked up to his ninth-floor call room to discuss this guy with Jack.

"Sounds to me like you've got a Munchhausen's on your hands."

"A munch what?"

"Munchhausen's syndrome. It's a person who come in with all kinds of complaints, just so he can have unnecessary surgeries and procedures and stay in the hospital. These folks get sympathy and secondary gain from doing it. Why else would the guy have FOUR negative cardiac caths? Did you ask him if they were all done in the same place? Bet you money they weren't."

I went down to get some more history from this Mr. Selwood Bannon. When I asked him for the specifics, he hesitated. He told me the first cardiac cath was done in Cleveland, but the others were in Detroit – oh, and the last one was in Pittsburgh. He couldn't remember the names of the hospitals, though. Then he added:

"The only thing I remember is that the last time I had this chest pain, it took 12 milligrams of morphine to take care of it. That's what I need now."

So that was his game. Morphine. Well, I had a plan of my own. I asked the nurse to draw up an IV with normal saline in it, just plain old salt water. Since this guy had a normal EKG, I doubted that his chest pain was for real.

We gave him the IV, and injected some saline into the line which I told him was morphine. He smiled in relief. Two minutes later, I returned to ask him about his pain.

"Much much better, doctor. Thank you."

Half an hour later, Mr. Munchhausen, I mean, Bannon, was on the warpath.

"That's not very strong morphine, doc – it doesn't have the usual kick. My pain seems to be getting worse again."

"Mr. Bannon, I've got news for you. I did some calling around town. You've been to Columbia Hospital recently – why didn't you mention that to me? They said you left there AMA (against medical advice) two weeks ago after you couldn't get the medications you wanted, even though there was no need for you to have them."

He looked me in the eye indignantly.

"You guys call yourselves doctors? I'm in real pain here, but it's obvious that I'm not getting any help from you."

"Well, what're you going to do about it?" I prodded him in hopes that he would take the bait.

"I'll be damned if I'm staying here," he replied, just as I had hoped.

At that, he ripped off the nasal cannula of oxygen and jumped out of his bed and tore the monitor leads off his chest. In three minutes, his room was vacant. I felt guilty for a moment for having facilitated his sudden outburst, but only for a moment. Then I was glad to have him out of my hair. That turkey would have kept me up all night with his complaints. Thank God for patients who leave AMA, I thought.

By this time I'd missed supper, so I had a hot dog and fries in the coffee shop and started for the call room. On the way, 3CD called me to pronounce someone dead.

When I arrived, the room was full of family members, the newly widowed wife of the deceased, his sons and daughters, and two of his brothers. He'd had an aneurysm of his aorta repaired, and was doing well until earlier this evening when he suddenly stopped breathing. Because of his age, he'd talked about not doing a code on him if anything should happen, so the nurse had let him quietly slip away. It appeared that he'd had a pulmonary embolism, a clot from his legs which travelled to his lungs and stopped his breathing.

I asked the family to leave the room for a minute so I could assess him.

I went through my routine of listening to the heart, lungs, examining the eyes, and pinching him to see if he reacted. Nothing. Then I called the family back to the room.

I looked at his wife. "I'm sorry, he's dead."

She began to cry, and instinctively I put my hand on her shoulder. I had to think of something else to say. They were expecting me to make it easier, I could tell. I continued.

"I've seen many people die. Often times it's a slow, labored process, very painful to experience. It appears that Joe went quickly, without any pain whatsoever. The nurse tells me you were with him earlier today. I think you should count yourselves very lucky to have had that opportunity. Many people don't get to be with their loved ones close to the time they die. You were with him. When you think about his passing in the next several months, remember how fortunate all of us are that he went quickly and peacefully. I can see that he's at peace now – look at the calm on his face.

None of us can ever predict or try to scrutinize the will of God, but we can be thankful for his granting Joe a merciful death."

I was surprising myself at how easy that flowed out of me. I realized that it had been brewing for a while now, ever since I'd pronounced that man dead three days ago. Even though some of it was obviously hype, I sensed that to them I represented all of medicine at that moment. I was the man in white, the final word on this man's final hour. Even though I didn't consider myself important to his case – I'd never seen him before in my life – it was obvious that they were hanging on my words, looking for some wisdom or consolation. I asked them if they had any other questions. Then I left so that they could have some time alone.

After that, the night went without a hitch until 11:45 p.m., when I decided to hit the sack. The ER was quiet, the admissions were all bedded down, and there was nothing to do that wouldn't wait until the morning.

At 2:45 a.m., the ER called. Dr. Stolp, our kidney specialist, had a patient down there that he wanted me to see for him. I crawled out of bed, thankful for the little sleep I had gotten, and wondered if this was the last of my sleep for the night.

Agnes Kinsey, 67, was complaining of abdominal pain. She looked old for only 67, probably from the cigarettes and what the smoking had done to wrinkle her skin. I did a cursory exam and decided it was probably indigestion. I heard only faint bowel sounds, but figured she hadn't eaten in quite a while. I ordered a chest X-ray, glanced at it quickly, had a bowel film done and it too looked fine, so I bedded her down and crawled back to my own bed. It was now 4.00 a.m.

At 7:00 a.m. the operator woke me as I had requested. I wanted to get an early start on rounds so I could make it out of the house(hospital) as soon as 2:00 rounds with Jerry Parent ended – which was typically at 5 p.m. or 6 pm.. I only had two admissions to staff with him, since Mr. Bannon, the Munchhausen's guy with fake chest pain which had ruled out for heart attack, had left AMA. Also, Mr. Wilmann, whom I'd seen briefly in the ER, had died suddenly after an unsuccessful code 4. Hell of a way to get rid of patients, I thought quietly.

I saw Mr. Kukowski first. Fred had the belly full of fluid, which was slowly leaving his body through his kidneys, day by painfully slow day.

"Fred, who won yesterday?"

Fred smiled victoriously. "Brewers kicked 'em. They're gonna go all the way this year."

"Well, don't count on it. I'll believe it when I see it. How's your weight today – down two pounds – not bad, Fred! That tummy of yours is disappearing. Keep up the good work – see you tomorrow."

"Okay, doc. Take it easy on the nurses."

That didn't seem to be a problem. By now, rumors were swirling that I was dating multiple nurses, and the nurses were avoiding me as a result.

Viola Anderson, the lady with the large stroke, was unchanged. I called the social worker on her case, and we discussed the possibility of transferring her to Sacred Heart Rehab Hospital. There was nothing more for us to do with her.

At 10:30, Dr. Stolp asked me to meet him down to 4EF, where Agnes Kinsey was. Agnes was the gal I had seen in ER with the abdominal pain in the middle of last night.

When I arrived, I saw Dr. Stolp sitting in his oversized suit coat which still couldn't button over his short stocky tummy. His tie was loosened to accommodate his meaty neck. He wore shiny black Florsheim shoes and half-moon reading glasses that made him look like the serious doctor that he was. He was THE kidney specialist for these parts- very well-respected for his medical acumen. He was staring intently at the chest X-ray I had ordered at 3 in the morning.

I was nonchalant as I announced: "I already looked at it, Dr. Stolp. It's normal."

He was frowning. He spoke with a low, ominous tone. "Do you see this? It's free air under the diaphragm. It looks like she's ruptured a viscus. I think she's got peritonitis."

He then peered at me by looking over his reading glasses and directly into my eyes.

He didn't say anything derogatory, but I could palpably feel the lesson he was pounding into me. I'd SCREWED UP big time. This lady had a life-threatening problem that I could have picked up on hours ago if I'd taken a closer look at that chest X-ray. There was air under the diaphragm where there shouldn't be any air at all, and as I inspected the X-ray closely I saw it clearly.

Dr. Stolp called in a surgeon who immediately took her to the operating room. I waited anxiously for the result, but at 12:30 I decided to go down and get some lunch. Agnes Kinsey was still in surgery.

The caf was bustling like a typical weekday. I found my college roomie John Holtan sitting with Doug and Konrad.

John spoke. "Richie, guess what? Remember that guy you tried to put the IV in yesterday – the fat one? I scrubbed in on his case today."

"Really John? I didn't know you were with Farrell today."

He continued. "Guess what? He died on the table – had a massive MI. The guy was in his forties – two kids, a wife – we coded him but it went nowhere. Must have been a massive clot."

"Wow! He told me he'd gained 30 pounds in the last three weeks piggin' out – he must have clogged his coronaries good by doing that. Can you imagine. Wow."

We laughed. Then Doug and Konrad left, and John and I were alone.

John sighed. "We've sure come a long way from those times at Luther College, eh' Rich?"

I thought back on those days at Luther, when my dream of making it into medical school seemed so out of reach at times, even though I had a 4.0 average. I knew of many students who never made it into medical school.

"You can say that again. Man, those days studying for organic chemistry and physics – how trivial they seem now! The real pressure now seems to be whether or not I'll stay awake – or screw up big like I did with one of Stolp's patients last night. I missed some free air on her chest film and now she's in surgery with Kumar with peritonitis." I sighed and John could see my embarrassment and disappointment.

"You can't know everything, Rich. Everybody makes mistakes – I'm sure Stolp wasn't too hard on you – he knows what it's like – he was there once too, you know."

"Yeah, maybe you're right. If I were him, I'd have chewed me out good, but he didn't. He just looked at me, and we both knew, and that was all that was said."

As John attempted to cheer me up I realized that he was right- mistakes happened all the time and I would make more. I would have to accept that fact and live with my errors, but learn from them too.

John changed the subject. "I'm worried about this Saturday, Rich. Think I should go through with it? What do you think of Eileen?"

John was getting married to Eileen, one of the ICU nurses. The wedding was five days away.

"She's nice, John. I envy you in a lot of ways. Heck, I often wish I had someone to help me through these difficult times. I don't know – you two seem to be pretty happy. No one's perfect, anyway."

"Yeah, but Eileen isn't like Kris, or Terry, or some of the other girls we knew in college. They were dreamers, true romantics, into music and the arts.

Eileen's more practical. I wonder if those other areas of my life will suffer."

Now I was the one musing wistfully. "Life sure changes, Johnnie. Milestones are coming here – you're through with internship, now you're getting married, next you'll be thinking about kids. Man! Did you ever think we'd get this far?"

"Nope. Hey, I hear you're going out with multiple nurses."

I was mad. Even my best friend from college was hearing the rumors about me supposedly asking all the nurses out. I hadn't asked anyone out yet. I sighed and got up from the table.

*

I stopped on 4th floor to see how Agnes Kinsey, the gal I'd missed the free air on, was doing after her surgery. Dr. Stolp was up there dictating a summary. He looked up at me. "She died on the table – massive peritonitis." At that moment I felt like a total jerk, lower than dirt. He looked at me in a knowing way and just said, "well, I think it was just her time." Then he left.

How does one adjust to the realization that you have just caused a death? When I was a nursing home orderly years earlier, I was pushing a large dish cart down the hallway and an old lady darted out of her room into the hallway and I ran her over with the cart. She died of a hip fracture the following week. The head nurse told me it wasn't my fault; the lady was demented and was supposed to be restrained in her bed. The guilt stayed with me though.

Now I had guilt of a much higher order of magnitude. This lady had depended upon my reading that x ray properly and determining that she needed immediate surgery. I had failed her. Dr. Stolp knew it and I knew it. It was a guilt I would have to bear for the rest of my life. It was the first skeleton in my medical training closet. I wondered how many more I would accumulate.

I made my way to 6JK to start 2 p.m. rounds. I was smelly, unshaven, and feeling pretty guilty for having slept at all after seeing what my greed for sleep had caused – a death. But no one upstairs knew about it – it was between Dr. Stolp and me. I resolved to never sleep again when there was work to be done – medicine was serious, I was learning.

In the conference room, the head nurse Laurie Kuehn was talking to Jill Harman, my senior resident.

"Laurie, what are you doing here?" I asked.

"Every week I try to get to one staffing, to keep up on my patients." I nodded. "Oh. Neat."

Doug Landers broke in. "Did you guys hear the news? I'm gonna be the best man – Joe Stockman on 8GH is getting married tomorrow."

Joe was a patient admitted with pneumonia last week. Doug was taking care of him. The guy was 75, and his girlfriend was 72. She told us that Joe was a slippery devil, and now that she had him trapped in the hospital, she was gonna get him hitched. Joe asked Doug to be the best man, and the ceremony was to take place tomorrow morning, just before Joe's discharge.

Jerry Parent made his characteristic entrance. "Hi everyone, sorry I'm late. How much business, Jill? Laurie, nice to see you again. Okay, let's run the list, folks. Sam Malecek."

I started. "62-year-old white male, 10 days status post inferior MI, two days ago had permanent pacer put in for third degree block. Back on 6LM, rehab going smoothly." I was becoming more organized.

"Very nice, Rich. Next. Ahh… Joe Stockman."

Doug cleared his throat. "Joe's the 75-year-old on eighth floor who came in for pneumonia last week. He's a febrile times 36-hours. Plan is to discharge him in the a.m. after he gets married – I'm his best man!" He smiled, as did everybody else.

"Good, Doug. What are you going to send him out on?"

"I thought we'd give him an IM shot of procaine penicillin that would last him for ten days. He's not too reliable with taking meds by himself."

"Not a bad thought, Doug, but be sure you watch him after giving the shot. When I was just out a year out in practice, I had a guy in the clinic one day. I had diagnosed a strep throat and gave him an IM shot of penicillin and left the room for a minute. I came back two minutes later and he was on the floor – dead. Anaphylaxis – can happen to anyone. Make sure you're with him to watch for reactions."

Dr. Parent seemed pretty serious right then. I realized that every one of us had skeletons in our closets – Agnes Kinsey wasn't the last one for me. The point was, I had to resolve to learn from my mistakes, and those medical experiences of others, like Jerry Parent's penicillin episode. If I could at least avoid the mistakes I had made once, then future patients would benefit. Again I was reminded of the saying: "Good judgment comes from experience. Experience comes from bad judgment."

After rounds, it was time for home. I signed out to Konrad, who was already busy in the ER. Then it was off to the hinterland of my blankets and sheets. I was fast becoming a guru of sleep hygiene. Because of my attention to adequate sleep before call and after, I'd survived my second call night – it was beginning to look like I could actually survive the whole residency.

In the middle of blackness, the phone rang. I was in such a deep fog that I let it ring for about ten times before I knew what it was. I turned on a light. The alarm showed 1:10 a.m.

"Hello?"

A mysterious voice answered back "Hello."

"Who is this?"

The mystery continued. "Who do you want it to be, honey?"

"What do you want?"

"I'm lonely. I need a maaaaann…"

I could hear a little child crying in the background. Who was this? Did she have a pimp? How did she get my number? Worse yet, did she know where I lived? I told her we all have to deal with loneliness in our own fashion, and hung up the phone. I was still in a daze when I flipped off the light, checked my alarm, unplugged my phone cord, and fell back asleep.
Tuesday, Day #6

Morning came too suddenly. I woke at 7:30, thirty minutes late to start work rounds. I called Jill and told her I'd overslept. I dashed into my car parked in front of Arne's empty lot where his garden stood. My nose embraced the smell of summer: it was warm, and humid, and Arne's lilacs were in bloom. As I scurried down the hallway to my first patient, I realized that most of my patients were on autopilot. Viola Anderson, unchanged from her stroke, had been accepted at Sacred Heart Rehab hospital, so she was on her way as soon as they had a bed for her. Fred Kukowski was losing 1–2 pounds daily. This morning's weight was a pound lighter than yesterday. Sam Stuckey up in cardiac rehab was looking at discharge in a few days. It was time for me to use the spare time I had to hi-tail it to the medical records department. I had at least six charts stacked up waiting for me to do discharge summaries. I noticed on my way in that there was a list of doctors with delinquent records. They were docs who had more than twenty charts with histories and physicals or summaries that needed dictating. These doctors were on suspension until their charts were caught up – they couldn't admit people to the hospital until they'd finished their delinquent records.

On the top of the list – Dr. Stolp! He had 43 charts overdue. I wondered if they really enforced their temporary suspension.

Not only did I have seven summaries to dictate, but I had a mass of charts to sign – anytime I called an order over the phone, they eventually needed my signature on the chart. I'd called a lot of orders during my two evenings on call, and now all of those orders needed signatures. I had to make 26 signatures in six charts.

On the way out of the department, I ran into Dr. Stolp. I was feeling bad about Agnes Kinsey, and was about to apologize, when he interrupted me by asking,

"How would you like to earn some spare cash?"

"Sure." I was startled.

"I have a few charts that need summaries. I'll give you $15 a summary."

I eagerly accepted the job. I decided I would stay here late at night until I got them done – he had about fifteen for me to do. I was so elated that he trusted me to do his summaries – all I had to do was page through the notes and summarize the hospital course – but after Agnes Kinsey, it was a welcome relief to know that he wasn't miffed.

106

At noon, I met my college roommate John outside of the auditorium. The weekly lecture was to begin in twenty minutes, and we were eating the free sandwiches they put out beforehand.

John pointed to a guy by the door. "See him?"

I saw an elderly man with a leisure suit on, gray hair, sitting by himself, and looking around sort of nervously.

"Yeah, what about him?"

"He's a retired staff doc. Watch what he does with his sandwich."

We both watched as he looked around, then suddenly stuffed his sandwich in his coat pocket.

"Now, watch where he goes." John seemed to know this guy's routine. I watched as the elderly gentleman got up and walked into the bathroom. Then he came out, looked around, and walked back into the food line for a couple of sandwiches. He stuffed them in his pocket again and headed for the bathroom.

"Nobody knows what he does with the sandwiches, but they're always gone when he comes back out of the John."

"Why don't we look for them, Johnnie? He's gotta hide 'em somewhere."

"Okay, let's do it."

The man was walking toward the bathroom, but he stopped when he saw us walk in ahead of him. We searched the bathroom, but no sandwiches in sight. On the way out, I washed my hands and threw away my paper towel. The garbage! Of course! I rummaged around through all the wet hand towels and, down at the bottom of the pail, sure enough, were 6 neatly wrapped sandwiches.

"The mystery's solved!"

"Not quite, Rich. We still don't know why he hides 'em. He sneaks out early from the conference – I suppose he picks up his sandwiches and takes 'em home. But, can he be that destitute?"

"We'll have to ask around about this guy."

During the lecture, I noticed the old man walk out about ten minutes before the end. I'd left a note on one of his sandwiches – "we're onto you"– now I was wondering if that had been a good idea. Maybe the poor guy really did need the food – who would miss a few sandwiches? I decided to ignore him from here on in.

Dr. Parent was off today, so Dr. Laufenburg was staffing rounds. At

1:45, Konrad and Doug and I were watching the TV in the lounge while waiting for rounds, when Konrad had an idea. The hospital was playing bingo on TV, and anyone with the winning card had to call the lady that was shown on TV with a phone next to her. We decided to page Jill, our senior resident, and told her to call the number for bingo – we said, "Jill, call 6854. Call 6854 stat." Then we hung up. 6854 was the number to call if you thought you had a bingo. We watched the TV as the lady's phone rang. We could hear her voice over the TV – "Hi, this is Jill. Who is this?"

"Hello, this is bingo. Jill, do you have a winning card?"

"Hello? I was paged stat to this number. Who are you?" "This is bingo. Are you a winner?"

"This is <u>Doctor</u> Harmon. Who are you?"

"Oh dear, we must have some mistake."

At this point, we were rolling on the floor. It was a bit rude, but the levity was well-timed. A little comic relief never hurt anybody. Our folly was interrupted by an overhead announcement.

CODE 44LMCODE 44LMRoom 4502 bed A4502 bed A. We instantly ran out of the lounge and down the stairs to 4th floor. By the time we arrived, the room was packed. I noticed many of the staff docs in the vicinity turning the other way, as if not to notice what was going on. It seemed as if these codes were a disease that they wanted no part of. There were obviously enough docs and helpers, so we walked back upstairs. Jill was waiting for us.

"You guys know anything about my bingo prank page?" We looked at each other and then burst out laughing.

"You should have heard yourself, Jill. You were classic." Doug was giving her a hard time.

"Well, don't do it again. A stat page is like crying wolf – nothing to mess with. Someone else won't take it as easily as I just did."

Rounds ended, and I signed out to Doug. I stayed late to work on the summaries for Dr. Stolp, but surprisingly, I got all fifteen done by 7:30 pm. I left the hospital knowing I was $225 richer. That was quite an improvement on my bottom line. I earned just about $21,000 as a resident, which was barely enough to pay my rent, my food, and my college and med school loans.

Wednesday, Day #7

It dawned on me that I hadn't even been here for a week, yet the place was as familiar as any place I'd ever known. I started my morning rounds with the lightest load ever – only three patients. After seeing Viola Anderson, the stroke lady who was to leave for Sacred Heart Rehab today, I saw Sam Malecek, rehabbing from his myocardial infarction. I'd be sending him home in another two days. He was doing very well. Then came Fred Kukowski, the guy with all the fluid in his belly and legs, who would be here long after I left the service.

After I left Fred's room, I bumped into Dr. Stolp in the hall.

"I've got something for you." He handed me 10 twenty-dollar bills and 5 five-dollar bills. I felt quite wealthy. This work had its rewards after all.

It was a lazy morning, and I had a nice leisurely lunch. I noticed a piano at the end of the cafeteria, and since I was itching to play, I strolled over and started plinking, and then before I knew it, I was immersed in all of my favorite songs. I was oblivious to the swarm in the cafeteria, but I noticed that someone turned off the overhead music so that they could hear what I was playing. After 45 minutes, a nurse handed me a request for New York, New York. I played it and the whole table applauded. It was a thrill for me. Why couldn't I do this for a living, instead of being wakened by overly cheerful night nurses, I thought. In the middle of my next song, my beeper went off. It was Jill.

"You're late for rounds. Rounds at 2:00. Where are you?"

I'd become so engrossed in my piano, and work had been so light, that I'd forgotten briefly that I was a resident. Now I was back in the real world.

"Hi Rich, glad you could join us." Jill was a bit sarcastic.

"Sorry I'm late everybody."

Jerry Parent chimed in. "I hear you put on a concert in the cafeteria, Rich. The nurses on the cardiac rehab wing were asking me all about you."

"Really, Doctor Parent?" I was amazed, and kind of flattered. "Yeah, really."

Dr. Parent was obviously in a casual, less frantic mood, so Jill broke in. "Dr. Parent, did you hear about the guy who almost drowned in Lake Michigan that they brought into ICU today? He's alive after 25 minutes under water."

"That's interesting, Jill," Jerry commented. "You know, when I was a cardiology fellow in Chicago, Katie and I were walking along Lake

Michigan one day when we heard a swimmer crying for help. A man pulled off his clothes and ran out to help him, and the water was so cold that he soon got into trouble, so now there were two swimmers calling for help. A third man swam out to save them, and got into trouble also. Before long, the two men that had swam out to help had gone down, and only the original man was left calling for help. A squad car pulled up, and two officers got out, looked the situation over, and got in their squad and left. By this time, the third guy had gone down. Ten minutes later, the squad returned with a lifeguard – big, strong, husky guy. He swam out to the approximate location where the last guy had submerged, and pulled him up. After dragging him ashore, there was a crowd of 50–100 people gathered to watch – and they were all black. Kate and I were the only white people. I told them I was a physician, so they let me do CPR on the guy. I did CPR until I was blue in the face, but it didn't seem to help."

We were all spellbound. "What did you do then?"

"What could I do? I was the only white guy there – do you think I was going to stop? Finally, after another twenty minutes, an ambulance came and they took the guy to a hospital. Then he started breathing again on his own and seemed to be making a comeback. A few days later he was still alive, but in a coma. He never did come out of the coma though."

Quite a story. It topped anything else that was said at rounds that day.

After staffing the new hits, Dr. Parent took us all to see one of his private patients, a 52-year-old man with the "locked-in syndrome." It's what results when you have a stroke that's so complete that you can't talk, write, or use any part of your body except the muscles in your head to communicate. He could hear us and understood what Dr. Parent said to him, but he could only blink or nod at a board with letters on it to spell out words. It was so frustrating being in the room with him – we all wanted to leave right away so that we could deny that such an existence could actually be a reality for someone. Dr. Parent patiently communicated with the man, and then put his hand on the man's shoulder, gave him a compassionate glance, and left the room.

The evening on call was benign. I went to bed at 11:30 p.m., and the next thing I knew, the operator was calling to wake me up at 7:00 the next morning. A whole night without a single call! No admissions, no hassles. Wow – I felt as if someone had sent me an expensive gift.

While I was doing rounds on Fred Kukowski, Doug came over to me.

"Fantastic news, Caddychak! We've got another intern to help us out with the call schedule. Bill Weatherspoon – an ENT man from County."

"Dy-no-mite!!" My whole day was made.

We met Bill during rounds at 2:00. He seemed nice, easy to talk to, eager to create a good impression and get along with everybody. It was obvious that he didn't really relish the thought of doing medicine wards, but boy were we glad to see him!

During rounds, we staffed one of Doug's patients that we hadn't gotten to yesterday. It was a man who was complaining of a headache and stiff neck, and fever, who had signs of meningitis. Doug had seen him in the ER, but after sticking him three times in the back, was unable to get the spinal tap done correctly. He'd asked the staff ER doc to help, and the staff guy had tried two times unsuccessfully, and finally another staff doc had come along and done it successfully. I felt sorry for the poor man – six holes in his back.

– one was usually bad enough!

"That's the good news," Doug continued.

"The bad news is, the lab tech took the spinal fluid and added formaldehyde to it, and ruined it all by mistake. So, now we're back to square one with him. He needs another spinal tap."

Dr. Parent was disappointed. "What's the problem with the lab tech?"

Jill answered. "It's been rectified. I called the head pathologist and she was fired on the spot early this morning."

"Well, I don't think I want to ask him for another tap, Doug. Let's just sit tight and watch him, okay?"

Doug was happy to hear Dr. Parent's words of wisdom. We were all happy for the man – no one wanted to see him suffer through that again.

After rounds, I signed out, and was passing seventh floor on my way to the elevator when I overheard one of the nurses talking about me.

"Yeah, that's the one that is going out with all the nurses – he's single. He's made the rounds. You wouldn't catch me gettin' burned by him."

I felt very self-conscious at that moment. From here on out, no more piano playing in the caf. Keep a low profile. Rumors were getting out of hand.

That evening, I had lots of energy despite having been at St. Luke's for 33 hours straight. I was trying to decide what to do, when Peggy, a girl from the computer department, saw me in the hallway. We'd talked a few times before that, just casual conversation.

"Have you eaten yet?"

"No, I…"

"Good, 'cause I baked a lasagna dinner and two special desserts… can you come over in half an hour?"

"Uh… I guess so. But I really can't stay, okay? But, since you made the supper, well, I guess I can come over and visit for a while…"

I drove over to visit Peggy and was quite surprised at what I found. She lived in a very fancy apartment, penthouse style, with VCR, color TV, every modern appliance and comfort a person could want. Her furniture appeared expensive, as did everything else in the apartment.

On the dining room table, she'd set out her finest China and silver, and the wine glasses sparkled.

"Hi! You're just in time. The lasagna is ready. What do you want to drink? Is Rhine wine okay?"

"Sure. Listen Peggy, I…"

"Sit down and hush up."

"But I didn't expect you to go to so much trouble…"

"It was easy. Wait'll you see what I made for dessert – a seven layered cake, and a cream pie."

As I watched her carry the lasagna, she was the picture of domestic fulfillment. She was obviously no stranger to the kitchen. Yet, there was something strangely seductive about her as well, as if to hint that there were other rooms she enjoyed as much or more. She cut a beautiful figure, with red hair topping her tall, thin frame, and there was something devilish in her eyes that made me curious, even though I was reluctant to be here. I was reluctant mostly because she was so aggressive that it made me want to instinctively shy away from her.

She poured me a glass of wine. I downed it before she'd finished pouring one for herself.

"My, that was quick. Want another?"

"Sure. Yeah, it's good wine."

I took a bite of the lasagna. It was excellent. Then, I had another glass of wine – in one straight dose. Before I knew it, I'd polished off the entire bottle. This was very unusual for me; I was a real lightweight when it came to alcohol. I made a fatal mistake by not eating more than that first bite of lasagna, and an even bigger mistake by drinking the bottle of wine.

"Boy, Peggy, that was the best wine I ever had.

It didn't take me long to feel the effects of the wine. I noticed that my words were beginning to twist somewhat. She was smiling at me in obvious comprehension of what was taking place. Then I reached a point where I no longer could talk in sentences; only one or two-word thoughts came across without mistakes. Then I looked at her and realized that the room around her was turning dark, and that I no longer cared to see anything. I dropped my head.

"Uh… Peggy, I think I need to lie down for a while."

At that, I rolled off my chair and crawled over to the linoleum of the kitchen floor so, in case I had to vomit, I wouldn't mess up her expensive rug. She came over to where I was lying, and knelt down by my side and began to loosen my shirt. Fine, I thought. I don't need this on anyway. It's too hot in here. Then my shirt was off, and she turned to me and kissed me. Oh no, definitely not a good place to be right now, I thought. And, to be honest, it sounded like a good idea, but I was sick. Then I became really sick. I slept on her kitchen floor all night.

I woke up on the floor in her kitchen. Then it dawned on me – I was late for rounds.

"Oh my God, Jill's going to kill me! Sorry, I gotta go Peggy. Thanks for supper – too bad I didn't eat more of the lasagna. Sorry I got sick on you."

"I'll save it for another time, okay?"

"Sure."

I left, and knew that I would never return. Peggy was nice, but I knew I needed something more than a good homemaker for a companion, and I'd recognized from the beginning that she would never fill that need. I sped home with a huge headache, and vowed that never again as long as I lived would I ever have more than two glasses of wine.

Friday, Day #9

When I got to St. Luke's, I realized that today was my clinic day, which meant that I had to finish rounds by 9:45 so that I could be in clinic from 10:00 'til noon. It was already 8:30, but fortunately my patient load was still down, thanks to an incredibly easy night on call last time. Fred Kukowski was unchanged in weight, otherwise in good spirits, and Sam

Stuckey was anxiously awaiting his discharge tomorrow.

At 9:30, I decided to hit the caf for a quick breakfast before clinic. My head was still pounding. After grabbing some OJ and toast and eggs, I sat down at an empty table and noticed a newspaper. It was open to an article about Oneida Wheeler, a publisher from Delavan, Wisconsin. The article stated that she was writing a book about single men in Wisconsin, entitled, *A Single Woman's Guide to the 100 Most Eligible Men in Wisconsin.* She listed a number to call for information. I scribbled it on my hand, and left for the clinic.

It was my first day at the St. Luke's Family Practice Center. The center was formerly a nursing home that had been converted to a clinic. The seven first-year, second-year, and third-year residents all used the clinic to learn the skills that would be most applicable to their day-to-day practice once they graduated from the residency. It seemed ironic to me that most of the residency training was spent in the hospital, when most of what we would do as doctors happened in the clinic setting. Then I remembered that the third-year residents actually did spend most of their time in the clinic – four half days a week, as compared to the one half day a week I would spend during my first year. That explained why Jill was never around to help us on the wards when we needed her – four mornings each week were spent here at the clinic.

I only had one patient scheduled for me this day, since it was my first day. I was given an orientation to the clinic by the office manager, and finally it was time to see my first and only patient, Emily Vance. Emily was 55 years old, quite obese, short, with dark hair, and very jolly. She was here complaining of a breast lump that she was worried about. I did a complete history and physical on her, and discovered that she was the mother of eleven children, and lived within walking distance of the clinic.

My exam revealed a lump in her right breast. I decided to have Dr. Laufenburg, our family practice residency director, confirm my findings. After his exam, we left the room to talk in the hall.

Dr. Laufenburg concurred with my impression. "Yes – I feel it too. What do you think should be done?"

"Well, how about a needle aspiration?" I was groping, not sure at all. "Ordinarily, I'd agree with you, Rich. But, this lady is obese, with very generous breasts. It might be very difficult to get the needle in the area you want. Open biopsy would be better."

114

I nodded. "Okay, where – at St. Luke's outpatient, or should she be admitted?"

"Outpatient is fine – it's an easy procedure."

I went in to discuss the procedure with Emily. We set it up for early next week, at the hospital outpatient surgery department. She left, with a concerned look on her face. I made it back to the hospital in time for lunch.

"Hey Doug, Konrad, what do you guys think of this Oneida Wheeler's idea to publish *A Single Woman's Guide to the 100 Most Eligible Men in Wisconsin?*"

"What are you babbling about?" Konrad seemed confused.

I explained the article I'd read this morning at breakfast. They seemed skeptical. I decided to call her sometime to find out about it – I wanted to find a way to have safe dates –away from the hospital nurses – maybe this was the answer.

Just then the overhead PA flashed this announcement.

"Your attention please. The paging system will be inactive for a short while. Please refrain from using the paging system until further notice."

"What's that all about?" Doug asked.

"Who knows? Maybe they're mad at you for pulling that bingo joke, Konman!"

"Whatya talkin' about, Caddychak? You were the one who thought of it."

On the way to 2 p.m. rounds, I passed the switchboard room.

I introduced myself to the ladies in the small cubbyhole where the operators sat. "Hi everybody. I'm Dr. Mayerchak."

"Oh, so you're the one we talk to – you know, you have a very pleasant voice – and you're not rude like a lot of the doctors. We notice those things down here, so don't change, okay?"

"Don't worry – I'm not planning to. By the way, what's with the pagers being turned off?"

"Somebody phoned in a bomb threat. Whenever they do that, we can't risk the radio signals from the beepers – they might set off the bomb. These bomb threats happen every so often – nothing to worry about, I hope – we've never had a real one."

So that was it. I walked upstairs for 2:00 rounds. The elevators were busy for the longest time, it seemed. As I passed the 'vators on sixth, I saw Doug getting out.

115

"Whew – I made it."

"What're you talking about, Douggie?"

"There's a guy in ER that we're getting. He's on his way up here, so I've been tying up the elevators for 15 minutes so I wouldn't get stuck with him. If he's not on the floor, I can't get him, right? Now it's 2:00, so I'm safe – Konrad gets all the hits now – his call has started."

So that was the way the game was played, I realized. Doug was on call until 2 pm, so he had tied up the elevators for 15 minutes by pushing all of the buttons for all nine floors, so the ER patient couldn't arrive on the ward until after his call responsibility had elapsed, and now it was Konrad's responsibility.

*

"I don't know, Doug… pretty shaky. But, I guess I'd do the same thing at 1:45 – it is a heck of a time to get a hit."

I told everybody about the bomb threat. Jill didn't seem too surprised, but everyone else was. Dr. Parent was late.

Jill continued: "Konrad, you'll be getting an admission. The ER called me to say they have someone waiting – should be coming upstairs any time now. I thought he might make it up before rounds in time for Doug to take him – I guess not though."

"Okay, Jill." Konrad was not thrilled, I could tell. I looked at Doug. His elevator trick had worked, and he was free to leave after rounds, because his work was finished. The person on call for the day got all the admissions that made it to the floor after 2 p.m. until the following 8 a.m., except on the weekends, when the person on call got all the hits for the entire day starting at 8 a.m.

After rounds, which lasted until 6:00 p.m. because Jerry Parent was an hour late, I headed home. Tonight was the dress rehearsal for my college roommate John's wedding in the morning. As I was changing out of my scrub clothes, I looked at the number I had written on my hand, and decided to call Oneida Wheeler, the woman who was publishing the book on eligible bachelors in Wisconsin. She answered the phone with a cheerful voice.

"This is a pleasant surprise. Yes, of course you would qualify for my book. It will be patterned after the bestseller done about the eligible bachelors in Chicago last year. I've talked to many of the men in that book, and they're all happy they were a part of it."

She sounded very energetic. I decided to fill out an application, and

116

sent her some of the info right then while I was thinking about it. As I drove to John's wedding rehearsal, I realized that the whole idea of the bachelor's book was ludicrous; I decided to call Oneida and back out of my commitment to be included in her book. I felt relieved that I had passed on it, and drove to the wedding rehearsal.

John was in a festive mood. His entire family of 8 siblings and parents were there at the rehearsal dinner. After the dinner was finished, they brought out the cake. He motioned to the waitress, who brought a special piece for me, since I was his best man.

Seeing John just then brought me back to a day in my third year of medical school. I was staying in Minneapolis, in an area called "Dinkytown", near the University of Minnesota Hospitals where I spent most of my time.

John had driven up from Iowa City medical school to spend the weekend with me. We had been watching a movie, and he made me a hamburger with all the fixings. I ate it with delight, but twenty minutes later I was in the bathroom, peeing like a racehorse. The worst part was that my urine was bright red and orange, and I couldn't stop urinating. I was scared that I had something seriously wrong with me. I returned to the room where we were watching the movie with several other people. My face was ashen. They all noticed my look of fright, and then after another 20 seconds passed, they all burst into laughter. It was all a joke!! John had laced my hamburger with Lasix, which is a diuretic, something that makes you urinate a lot. Also he had mixed pyridium dye with the ketchup, to make my urine red and orange.

As I was remembering this past misery he had caused me, it dawned on me that tomorrow was his wedding, and I could finally get even with him.

The following morning was Saturday, John's wedding day. I put 40 mg of Lasix in his coffee just one hour before the wedding. Throughout the ceremony he looked at me in obvious pain from a swollen bladder.

He whispered, "Richie, I gotta go, <u>bad</u>"– and by then I was feeling guilty for messing up his wedding.

After the ceremony, we made a truce and decided to avoid using medications on each other from that day forward.

After the wedding, I returned home to find my neighbor Arnie watering his humongous garden that occupied the spare lot next to his house. He called out to me.

"Hi-ya, doc!!" My roommates at the house I rented next to Arnie informed me that Arnie was bragging to the whole neighborhood that a doctor lived next door to him. He didn't seem to understand that I was merely a lowly intern, not a full-fledged out-in-practice doctor, but one in the first month of residency training. At that matter to Arnie was that I was a doctor, and we were becoming friends.

"Anytime you need your car fixed, doc, you come to me, OK?"

I promised him I would bring my car to his garage for an oil change one of these days.

The weeks passed, and finally I was in the final week of the medicine rotation. After this I would be headed to pediatrics, at Milwaukee Children's Hospital in downtown Milwaukee. It would be a culture shock for sure, to transition from a lucrative private hospital to a county hospital full of screaming little sick kids.

Today was my last day of call on medicine, and as luck would have it, I was on call it with Jill Harmon as my senior resident for the evening. I reflected on the past month on medicine service. I was beginning to see a change in my attitude toward the residency. Instead of merely trying to survive, as I had done for the first few weeks, I was now developing a hunger to actually learn the medicine. My love life sucked, but after the wine fiasco with Peggy I had sworn off dating, and it allowed me to focus exclusively on learning my trade.

The only patient still with me from my first day on the service was Fred Kukowski. He was down 55 pounds – all of it fluid – and now his belly was reduced to flabby redundant skin folds that hung off his rib cage like fins. I was actually sad to think that Fred was leaving me. I enjoyed sitting in his room each day for a few minutes when the Brewers were playing. That third baseman Paul Molitor could really run; he had a knack for turning singles into doubles by scrambling. The Brewers were creating quite a buzz in town; people were speculating about a World Series run.

In addition to Fred, I had eight other patients to manage, which kept me hopping. However, I had now figured out how to get them all seen and taken care of before the 2 p.m. rounds with Jerry Parent. After rounds concluded, I was called to the ER to officially start my last night on call.

Marie Vickers, a 42-year-old, had been talking to her sister on the phone, when she suddenly felt very funny, and told her sister something was wrong. Then her speech had become garbled, and she had dropped the phone. Her sister had rushed over to her house and found her unconscious.

Now she was in the ER, conscious again, but a little confused. I did an exam, but couldn't really ascertain what was wrong. I decided to let her lab results come back, and headed upstairs. On the way, I met Jill Harmon. I told her about Marie Vickers.

"I'd better take a look now," she stated. She looked worried. It caused me to wonder what I was missing.

I went back down with her. Jill spent an inordinate amount of time looking in Marie's eyes with her ophthalmoscope. Then, in the middle of her exam, Marie began to lose consciousness again.

"I think she's got papilledema, Rich. She needs mannitol, and a neurosurgeon – NOW."

I noted the urgency in her voice. She helped me write the orders, then called in Dr. Frazin. He told her to alert the OR, and he'd be there in 30 minutes.

"He thinks she might need surgery – or at least a burr hole. He's coming in."

I was awfully glad Jill had popped up when she did – I knew I'd made a major error by assuming I could wait with Marie. It was the same type of error I'd made with Harold Wilmann and Agnes Kinsey – thinking that their conditions were less serious than they really were – and now they were both six feet under. They were the first skeletons in my closet. At least Marie had a chance – because of Jill's seasoned judgment.

It reminded me of my inadequacy as a neophyte doctor. At that moment I realized how fortunate I was to have the guidance of the experienced hand of Jill Harmon.

Marie Vickers, with the evolving stroke, was taken to CAT scan and we were on our way to read it with the radiologist.

The ER called me, so Jill went with Marie to CAT scan, and I went back to ER. They had a 35-year-old man for me to see. He'd been cleaning his mower, and decided to drain it of gas. Rather than simply pour out the gas, which he hadn't thought of, he ran his mower hoping it would use up all the gas. After twenty minutes, he got impatient for the gas tank to empty, so he turned the mower upside down to empty it out – while it was still running.

The next thing he knew, he'd chopped off part of his thumb – at least the top fourth of it. Now he was here with a bleeding thumb, which had ground in grass and dirt from the mower blade.

It was a squeamish thing to look at, with all that grass and dirt mixed in. I paged Nancy Petro, the surgical resident on call, for some help. She showed me how to anesthetize the entire thumb so we could clean it without him hurting. It is very difficult to work on someone who is in obvious pain. It makes me even more squeamish. Nancy then she guided me through a skin graft. We shaved skin off from his wrist with a razor blade – a very thin layer – and sewed it to the top of his thumb to form a stump. I was excited at what I'd learned. We sent him home an hour later, and I told him to follow up in my clinic next week.

The next patient waiting was a 4-year-old who'd been eating a sundae and had poked the plastic spoon through the roof of his mouth. He wasn't bleeding or complaining, but he had a big hole in the soft palate – I could put my finger through it.

Not knowing what to do, I called Dr. Kidder, the ENT man, at home.

He advised me to do nothing – he insisted to me that they healed fine by themselves. I was relieved – the thought of trying to put stitches in this 4-year-old's mouth was disturbing. I reassured the parents and sent him home.

As I was leaving the ER, I noticed the cops handcuffing a man.

"What's that all about?" I asked Jean, the ward clerk.

"He was caught stealing a couple of the paintings from the lobby." It takes all kinds, I thought. Never a dull moment on the weekends.

I looked at my watch. It was 2:45 p.m., and I'd missed lunch. I headed for the coffee shop. While I was eating my hot dog, when I heard CODE 46508 Knisely Building, CODE 46508 Bed A.

I'd resolved to be a code authority, and tried to be at every code I could, even if the room was packed. I usually wormed my way to the front of the action and tried to help the senior resident in charge of the code by drawing blood gases or sticking in a line or intubating. Already I was gaining valuable experience with these tasks, and a reputation as "Mr. Code."

I slept with my shoes on every night to be ready to run at the first announcement from the overhead PA.

I arrived in the room before any other doctors, to my surprise. For once, my policy of taking the stairs, instead of waiting for the elevators, had worked. I reasoned that everyone responding to the code probably rode the same 'vator, and waited for it to stop on each of their floors. I was alone in the stairwells each time.

There were only two nurses in the room, and me. They were doing CPR. I was quite out of breath from running the stairs, and gasped out some questions. For the moment, it seemed that I would be in charge.

"What's the diagnosis here? Who was here to call the code?"

The patient's nurse replied in a high-pitched, nervous voice: "He's status post MI 8 days ago. We saw him go into V tach at the desk on his monitor, and now he's in V fib."

My adrenaline was running over. Where was Jill Harmon? Maybe she had scrubbed in with Frazin for the neurosurgery on Marie Vickers.

Then the sickening thought – maybe she wouldn't be here. No time to worry about it. I began to call out directions as people began to arrive.

"Have you got a pulse with CPR? Good. Stop CPR for a minute.

Check for a pulse or breathing."

At that moment, everything stopped. It was the first signal that everybody in the room regarded me as the boss. They checked for a pulse. None.

"Resume CPR, please," I stated in a shaky voice. In the past, I'd noticed that I always talked louder and more rapidly when I was nervous, and I was doing so now.

"What's his rhythm – still V fib? Okay, please charge the defibrillator. Somebody please draw blood gases and a potassium, and get some lidocaine ready – 75 milligram bolus with 2 milligram drip to follow."

The defibrillator was across the bed from me, but nobody knew how to charge it up. I'd learned by watching Laurie, so I punched it and set the current. Then it was ready.

"Okay, everybody clear the bed. Stop CPR."

With the bed clear, I zapped him with 300 watt-seconds.

ZZZZLLLAACKK!! I knew the sound instantly. I hadn't made good enough contact with the paddles, and a big arc of current had burned the hair on his chest. I charged up the paddles again and delivered a second charge.

This time I held the paddles firmly against his chest. His chest and entire body jumped from the sudden delivery of current. The nurse was about to resume CPR when I shouted.

"No, hold for a moment. Let's see if we have a rhythm." His rhythm stayed at ventricular fibrillation.

"Resume CPR, please." I was getting more comfortable at taking charge.

A tech ran into the room. "Blood gases are back."

I looked at the gases. pH - 7.24, HCO3 – 21, pCO2 – 58, pO2 – 60.

"We're not ventilating him well enough – please over bag him, okay?" I wanted the respiratory tech who was breathing for him to deliver more breaths with his ventilation bag.

"Also, give him an amp of bicarb, please." I realized then that I should have done that earlier, but it certainly wouldn't hurt now.

Nothing was working. It was time to try a new approach. I thought back to the red book I always crammed from to be ready for this. What was next? Oh yeah – bretylium.

"Draw up 5 milligrams per kilogram of bretylium – let's see, this guy is about 80 kilos – give him a 400 milligram bolus IV, please."

While they were preparing that, I charged up the defibrillator to 400 wattseconds, or joules, which was the maximum energy level it could deliver.

"Okay, everybody clear the bed."

I zapped him again, making sure to hold the paddles firmly to the chest. Still no change in his rhythm. Then suddenly, he was in asystole, an ominous sign. It's when the heart stops beating altogether.

"Okay, I want an amp of epi and an amp of calcium – give them both now, and follow that by another amp of bicarb, please. Somebody draw some more gases. How long has this code been going?"

"Twenty minutes."

I looked around the room. It was packed – about 30 people.

"Why don't about twenty of you people leave, so we have more room to operate here?" I shooed them out of the room. All we had left was a skeleton crew of a dozen people to carry on with.

The nurse doing CPR was tiring, and as I felt the man's pulse, I realized that she wasn't pushing down hard enough to pump blood from the heart to the man's vital organs. I took over for her. I pushed much harder than she'd been doing, and another nurse confirmed that she was getting a pulse with my actions. Then, all of a sudden, I heard a loud CRRRRAAACKKKK! I'd cracked his ribs. Occupational hazard. It was necessary to the survival of this man. I didn't let it bother me. After showing her how hard I wanted the

122

compressions to be, I let another nurse spell me. Jill still hadn't showed, and it was obvious that she wouldn't.

"How many minutes has this been going?"

"Thirty-three. mg."

"Okay, try bretylium again – this time <u>ten</u> milligrams per kilo – 800."

Then I surprised myself. "Somebody find me an intracardiac needle, please." I remembered that, when all else fails, intracardiac epinephrine sometimes works. The nurse handed me a syringe with epi in it attached to a long needle, about 6 inches long.

"Stop CPR please." I looked at the monitor. Still asystole – flat line.

I took the needle and positioned it underneath the left nipple and drove the long needle into where I presumed the heart to be. I was pulling back on the syringe. As soon as the syringe began to fill with blood, I knew I was in the center of the heart. I quickly discharged the contents of the syringe – epinephrine – into his heart and pulled the needle out in one swift motion.

Then I watched the monitor. Nothing.

"Resume CPR."

Sometimes CPR helped to mix the epi so that it would excite the heart again. Epinephrine is known in lay terms as adrenaline.

"Wait – stop CPR – is that a rhythm?" I was excited. Yes, something a spike, then a couple more…

"He's in sinus! Does he have a pulse with it?"

"Yes, we have a pulse."

"Somebody please get a pressure. I want some more gases now." I was really surprised, and very pleased. For the moment, I was a hero. I've never felt so overwhelmed with a sense of accomplishment as I felt at that moment.

"How far are we into this code?"

"46 minutes."

I left the room to call his private doc and write a note in the chart. He wasn't alert yet, but he was alive! I'd survived the role as director – my first time ever in that role – and I'd managed some heroics besides. Intracardiac epinephrine was not too highly touted these days. I'd taken the risk of looking bad if it hadn't worked, or looking good if I hit the heart successfully without puncturing the lung. I was lucky.

An hour later, I stopped back to see how he was doing. He was still unconscious – the nurses were transferring him to the ICU. I realized then that I hadn't saved anything, but instead had created a problem. This man was brain dead, it appeared. What had I done? Maybe a more seasoned code director would have called the code off after twenty minutes without any signs of response on the man's part.

It was with mixed elation and disappointment that I walked away from the station. I was initiated now – the first step on the long road to maintaining my cool in pressure situations. I hoped I could learn to be as cold and detached as Laurie Woodard and Jill Harmon were in these situations – as impersonal as it might be misconstrued to be, it was the ultimate level of control based on years of experience, which enabled objective decisions to be made definitively.

At 9:30 p.m., the ER called. Gene Simmons, a 51-year-old, was complaining of chest pain. I admitted him to the CCU with a diagnosis of probable myocardial infarction. It seemed to involve the anterior leads of his

EKG, and I was impressed that it might be evolving, because the CPK was very high. I paged Jill.

"How's Marie Vickers doing?" Marie was the lady who might be having a stroke.

Jill responded quickly. "She had a berry aneurysm that bled.

Frazin put a clip on it. How did the code go?"

"Fine – except the guy isn't with the program. I think he's brain dead."

I asked Jill to come down to see Mr. Simmons, the guy with the possible large heart attack.

She declined. "You know what to do now. I'll be down in a bit." I was glad to see that she trusted me, but it was an uncomfortable feeling at the same time. I was still greener than green. I consulted Dr. Johnson as my cardiologist.

I looked at my watch. It was 10:48 p.m. I still hadn't eaten supper. Time to hit the coffee shop before it closed from eleven 'til midnight.

I got there at 10:53.

"Sorry, we're closed until midnight."

"But, my watch says seven minutes to eleven. Please? I was running that code you heard earlier, and I'm starved…"

"Well, okay… what will it be?"

"A hot dog and a large shake… and fries, please." My diet was getting to be pretty consistent, much to my dismay. I decided that I had to keep the little kid inside of me happy on these call nights – anything he wanted to eat, he got. They told us on my first day here that interns usually gained twelve to fifteen pounds during their first year of training. It wasn't too hard to understand why.

At midnight, I went to my call room. No sooner had my head touched the pillow when the ER paged me. It is a God-awful feeling to get so incredibly close to the edge of slumber, only to be jerked back to reality like a lure on a fishing line. They had two patients for me to see. The nurse on the phone call seemed so cheerful. I realized that she had begun her shift at 11 pm, and this was the beginning of her day. I resented her for that pleasant voice, and I reminded myself on my way to the ER that I had to keep my resentment in check or it would land me in trouble.

After three hours in the ER, I was headed back upstairs, and they called me back at 3:30 a.m. to see a patient with presumed diverticulitis who needed antibiotics before she was admitted to the surgical service. I was placing her on ampicillin, gentamicin and clindamycin, a three drug combination to treat the various different bugs that could cause an abscess in the abdomen. When it came to calculating the dose of the gentamicin, it had to been done in milligrams per kilogram of the lady's body weight. I realized at that moment that my brain refused to do the calculation. I stared at the numbers but couldn't' seem to do the math, even though it was relatively simple. I loved math, but my brain was too fried to finish a simple computation. It was scary to realize that. I tried it three times before I was comfortable that I had the right numbers. Gentamicin was nothing to trifle with: too large a dose could have significant side effects and cause permanent kidney damage, but too little a dose would not help her. It was then that I realized that my brain cannot perform math without adequate sleep. I wrote the orders and then headed to the call room for a quick nap. It was 4:47 a.m. I drifted off to sleep.

CODE 4 !!CICU!!CODE 4!!CICU!! The announcement was loud and crisp in the stillness of the predawn hour.

My shoes were still on and I was up like a flash. It was instinct now.

Andre Agassi the tennis player had a coach Nick Bollettieri who would remind him that it wasn't usually the better player who won the match, but the player who wanted it more.

I looked at my watch as I flew down the stairs at a gallop. I, "wanted it more". I figured that even if there were better docs at the code, if I arrived first, they would let me run the code or play an integral part, and I would become proficient. There was something about these life and death moments that gave me an adrenaline rush and I was hooked on it. It was 5:30 a.m. I was the first one to arrive at the CCU except for the patient's nurse. Then I recognized him – it was Mr. Simmons, the man I had admitted with a probable large myocardial infarction.

"What's his rhythm – what's the probl…" I was out of breath. I collected myself.

The nurse replied: "He suddenly dropped his pressure and now he's in EMD – he's got a sinus rhythm, but we can't get a pulse or a pressure."

*

"Open up the IV on him, please. Give him some calcium chloride."

Some other people arrived, and Jill Harmon with them. They must have taken the elevator together, I guessed. Jill calmly walked to the front of the bed and asked what the story was.

"Looks like EMD. Sinus rhythm, but no pulse or pressure."

Then Jill took over directing the code. EMD is electromechanical dissociation, where the heart is beating with the normal electrical impulses, but the heart muscle isn't contracting to pump out blood. Usually it's due to a heart attack that has weakened the wall of the left ventricle so that an aneurysm, or very weakened segment, has formed. The aneurysm usually bulges out and fills with blood instead of pushing the blood out into the circulation. If the aneurysm ruptures, it's all over.

With Jill at the helm, I resumed my more comfortable function of drawing blood gases and helping out with the more mundane chores. As I watched him, I noticed for the first time the number of tattoos he had covering most of his body. It shocked me that I could have done a history and physical on him without noticing all of those tattoos.

They told a story. There was one of his mother, and one of a girl named Laurie. Another one showed the US Marines with the logo of the USMC. There was another of a bottle of vodka. For an instant, I drifted off to imagine what it must have been like having those tattoos put on – what possessed a person to do that? Were these all put on at once, or on different occasions?

We coded him for 25 minutes, but to no avail. Jill called it off, and everybody left except for his nurse, who was left to clean up the mess we'd made.

"Probably had a big aneurysm, Rich. Nothing we could have done would have made a difference."

I knew Jill was right, but still, it was hard to take. Like Harold Wilmann, this was a man I had known before coding him. He was real to me, another reminder that you can be here one minute and gone the next. When I admitted him, I hadn't the slightest thought that he wouldn't make it out of here alive. I'd been used to thinking that these intensive care units kept everybody alive. That thin line between life and death. That thin line.

It was 6:45 a.m. I decided to have a small breakfast before rounds.

The ER called me. A 17-year-old boy had fallen out of bed and dislocated his shoulder. I examined him and got an X-ray. It appeared to be a posterior dislocation. Since it had just occurred less than 20 minutes earlier, I decided to attempt to reduce it. I warned his parents that it might look funny to them. I then hopped up alongside him on his ER gurney and placed my left foot in his left armpit. I had taken my shoe off. Then I pulled on his left arm as hard as I could while pushing my foot in his armpit. We heard a sudden loud "clunk!" and he let out a wail as his arm was back in the shoulder socket where it belonged. His parents were noticeably relieved. Just then, I spied an orthopedic surgeon in the ER, so I asked him to take a look.

He perused the X-rays.

"That's not a posterior, that's an anterior dislocation," he said.

"What?" I was embarrassed and confused. I had made the wrong diagnosis about what part of the shoulder was dislocated.

He pointed out why. Then he asked what I did to reduce it. I told him and he laughed. Despite what I thought had been the problem, I had serendipitously done what was supposed to be done for anterior dislocations, which is what he actually had. My ignorance had saved me – or rather, saved the patient – and me. I vowed to defer any future dislocations to the orthopedists – I was obviously on thin ice in this area, as in many others.

I headed down to the switchboard to complain about my beeper. It was dying. Every third page or so would fade out or crackle. The switchboard operator looked up the service record.

She then reported, "You're supposed to throw this one away– it's been serviced too many times already."

She took my beeper and tossed it in the garbage, and handed me a brand-new shiny replacement. As I left her office, I was hit with a flash of brilliance. I ran back into the room, asked if I could take the old beeper for sentimental reasons, and the operator gave it to me. Then I went to 6JK and let my good friend Laurie Kuehn, the head nurse, in on my plan. I would fake an emotional outburst in the middle of rounds, and someone would page me, and I would get mad and destroy my beeper.

Laurie Kuehn thought it was a great idea. She agreed to page me at exactly 2:20 p.m. Dr. Parent should be going down the list by then. He wouldn't expect me to hurt my beeper, since they cost $280 each; the hospital administrator had warned us several times that we would have to pay the full amount for lost or damaged beepers.

Rounds at 2 p.m. began on time for a change. Jerry Parent was early.

I started the conversation by acting grouchy, saying that I'd had an awful call shift, and that I was close to decompensating.

I huffed. "If I get any more damn pages, I'm gonna kick somebody!!!"

Jill and the others were a little startled by my mood, as was Dr. Parent. We continued with the list, and then my old beeper went off. Instantly, in a fit of rage, I swore and grabbed the beeper and flung it against the wall. It hit the blackboard squarely and burst into many very small pieces. The battery whined through the speaker as it lay on the floor in chunks.

Jerry Parent did a double-take. He was noticeably concerned. "Time out. Rich, are you okay?"

I stood there and didn't say anything. For about twenty seconds I could see that Dr. Parent was quite unsure about what to make of the situation.

Then Laurie Kuehn walked in. She was grinning. "Did you get my page?"

We both smiled, and then I walked over to the file cabinet and brought out a cake with a gravestone sticking up which said: "Here lies Rich's beeper. RIP."

Jerry Parent was grinning. I could see that he was relieved that I wasn't really unhinged after all. It was all a ruse.

We took a break to dish out the cake, then finished the patient list. It was one of my finest hours.

After presenting Marie Vickers, the lady with the stroke, I was done for the day. I signed out to Konrad Krawczyk, the Kon-Man, and headed home. As I parked my car on the street, I saw Arne watering his garden as usual. I waved. Milwaukee was growing on me. I liked my neighbors. This

128

was starting to feel like a job, something I could handle. But I was tired. I would sleep well tonight. On this call shift, I'd learned some valuable skills, not the least of which was the ability to direct a code 4.

The following morning was my last day on the medicine service.

I looked at my little pocket notebook as I walked in the lobby doors and noticed that Emily Vance, my clinic patient, was scheduled to have her breast biopsy this morning at 7:45. I walked up to the outpatient department and asked Dr. Wengelewski if I could watch him.

"Sure, no problem. Put on a pair of gloves and a gown."

I was glad he had invited me to participate. This was my patient, and I had grown attached to her. I could see that she was relieved to see me there. Dr. Wengelewski took the biopsy, and Emily waited anxiously while the frozen specimen was evaluated by the pathologists. Finally, after 45 minutes, a runner from the department came in. "It's malignant," he told us in hushed tones.

Dr. Wengelewski informed Emily of the news, and I watched her face turn into a full frown, consumed with worry. He asked her to stay in the hospital now so that definitive surgery and treatment could be started as soon as possible. She consented, and we wheeled her to a room. I did an H&P on her, since she would be my patient.

I began my rounds on my nine "players" with Fred Kukowski. He was now down 58 pounds, and ready for discharge. I arranged for him to see me once each month at my clinic, and then we bid farewell. I was going to miss him. Marie Vickers, the stroke lady, was doing well – relatively. She was still unconscious much of the time, but came into consciousness enough of the time for there to be hope for a complete recovery.

Rounds were held early today. Dr. Laufenburg had meetings in the afternoon, so we had rounds at 11:30 a.m. Dr. Parent had the day off.

After rounds, I went to spend some time with Emily Vance, my clinic patient with the newly diagnosed breast cancer. She was pretty worried about her surgery and what was to come. I tried to be as supportive as I could. I stayed with her for 25 minutes, then signed out to Doug, who was on call. As I was about to leave the hospital,

I got a page from Jean, the secretary to Dr. Palese, the Chief of Staff of the hospital. He wanted to see me today. I told her I'd be right there.

I knocked on the door to Dr. Palese's office. "You wanted to see me, Dr. Palese?"

"Yes, come in. Sit down."

"Did I do something wrong?" I was nervous.

"Well… there's been some talk, and I wanted to hear it straight from you. Rumor has it that you're making an effort to go to bed with as many nurses from this hospital as you can lay your hands on. I've talked with several of the nursing supervisors who have expressed concerns to me."

"WHAAAT? Me? Where do these rumors come from? I've only been here four weeks!"

*

"Word travels fast in a community such as the one here at St. Luke's. You're in a highly visible position, Doctor. Remember that from now on. I believe you, but do your best to squelch these rumors by keeping a low profile."

I walked out of his office feeling like I'd just been reprimanded and absolved from the confessional of Father Palese. "Go and sin no more."

As I drove home from the hospital, I was still reeling from the meeting with Dr. Palese. The CHIEF of STAFF was watching me!! I was feeling very down in the dumps, not sure how to handle the accusations. I arrived home several minutes later.

My next-door neighbor, Arne Celinski, was in his garden as usual. "Hey, doc! Nice to see you out on time for a change."

"You too, Arne. Home from the garage early today, huh? By the way, Arne, my muffler is loose. Can I take my car to your garage sometime to have it looked at?"

"Anytime, doc. Dale will take care of it for you."

Dale was Arne's son. Together they ran their own auto repair shop.

As I stood there in front of my house, talking with Arne, I realized that this city was now my home. It was growing on me. It had been a rough month, but happy-go-lucky Arne was picking me right up from my doldrums.

I stood there and made trivial, nonsensical conversation with Arne while my mind whirred at another deeper level. I thought about all that I had endured during this past month. I had made several critical mistakes that had cost patients their lives. I could still see Dr. Stolp peering at me over his reading glasses as he realized that I had misread his patient's X-ray. I was still smarting over the rebuke I got from Dr. Palese, the chief of staff. I thought about what my dad would say in this situation: "no sailor ever learned anything in calm seas".

But on the bright side, I had learned how to run a CODE 4 without losing my cool. I had made a smart decision to decline the offer to be in Oneida Wheeler's book on eligible Wisconsin bachelors, and to avoid dating. And best of all, I had survived MYSELF, my worst inner temptations to quit when I was the most exhausted. I had refused to succumb to fatigue, and fear, and self-doubt.

I reminded myself that this marathon was going to be long and difficult. This was only mile one. But I was still in the race, and that was enough for now.

SECOND YEAR RESIDENT

Finally, the urge came to push, and Steve guided the baby out slowly. I wanted so much to do it myself, but I fought back the urge to interfere, much as Dr. Griesy must have had to do with me way back when. The baby – a boy – came out looking healthy as can be, and I breathed a huge sigh of relief. Steve then checked the uterus and cervix for tears, a routine procedure, and we proceeded to sew up her episiotomy. I supervised while he sewed, and when it was done twenty minutes later, the placenta delivered. He delivered that as well, and I did an exam of her uterus then to check one last time.

Right then, my heart dropped. Her uterus was still unusually large, given that the baby and placenta were already delivered. Why was the uterus still this big? I could feel a large bulge in her uterus. The it hit he like a brick – it was another baby. My God, it was dead. The realization broke me into a cold sweat and I felt faint. We had killed the second baby by giving the pitocin, the drug that contracted the uterus down after the delivery was over.

I had left the intern Steve to do the first check, so I wasn't immediately aware of the extra bulge – now it was big and plain as day. (*Editor's note:* back in those days, we didn't yet have ultrasounds readily available for pregnancy care; in fact most of my OB patients never had an ultrasound during pregnancy. Therefore, it was not uncommon to discover twins or other unusual findings immediately at the time of delivery.)

In that moment, I lived a thousand lives, atoned for a thousand sins, and died a thousand deaths. It's the moment of truth that every doctor secretly fears: the moment when all responsibility rests on you and you alone, that moment when you know you must act or lose your patient to catastrophe, yet you don't know what to do. I felt really, really sick inside. This was one mistake that would stigmatize me for life. The error was squarely on my shoulders as the supervising physician. And it was too late to erase…

*

The minute my first 12 months had passed, my internship was officially over, and I was eligible to apply for a real medical license. Before that point, I could only write orders and practice within the scope of a residency program. Now I could obtain a real license, and if I chose, I could go out into a practice. Of course that made no sense, because most hospitals required the completion of a full residency before allowing a doctor to admit patients. I took an oral exam in Madison Wisconsin so that I could officially be licensed to practice medicine, and I received my Wisconsin medical license. I could now call in prescriptions for family members, and friends. It reminded me that I was evolving into a more experienced physician.

The second year of residency was basically more of the same type of rotations, such as the Internal Medicine rotation I had done with Dr. Parent. I would again rotate through General Surgery, Pathology, Radiology, etc. The main difference was that now I was seasoned enough to take a crack at managing the Medical Respiratory Intensive Care Unit (MRICU) St Luke's had many ICU units, because it was a large cardiac hospital. There were two ICUs for recovering coronary artery bypass patients. St Luke's was renowned for bypass surgery. There was a surgical ICU and cardiac ICU – the CCU. We residents covered all of the units to some degree when we were on call; we acted as the first responders to the codes, and put in the IVs and other lines that were needed at night. However, to be the chief person running the ICU was a definite step up the ladder of responsibility, and that key was handed to us only in the MRICU. Here is my account of my first opportunity to manage that unit.

St. Luke's Hospital Medical Respiratory ICU March 1983
Milwaukee, Wisconsin

Friday, Day #1

07.00 I met the Con-Man in the hallway outside of the "unit". Konrad Krawczyk was through with his month of hell on MRICU and was handing the reins to me.

I envied him. "Hey Con Man, I'll bet you're happy to be done with this hellhole. What you got next?"

"I've got dermatology, Caddychak. It's cake time for me, buddy... Are you ready? Let's do sign outs so I can dump this mess on you already..."

It was my first day in the unit. It is considered the unit even though there are five intensive care units at St. Luke's, because it is the only ICU that the family practice residents are required to take a month's rotation through. The setup is such that the resident "mans" the unit for the entire month and takes call every night by him or herself, coming in for every admission and answering all the nurses' calls every night. Even though the MRICU resident can sleep at home each night, he or she is usually called in and ends up sleeping here at the hospital or staying awake all night. For my first nineteen months as a resident, I'd been hearing nothing but horror stories of how bad this rotation is. Now it was my baby. I felt as apprehensive as I did on my first day of internship.

From the moment I walked into the unit, which had 10 beds, I noticed the noise and bustle. It was restless, unceasing. I knew that it didn't start beeping and buzzing and humming just when I walked in, but nevertheless it was a striking contrast to the relative calm in the hallway just outside the ICU doors.

Konrad started the sign-out process. The unit was relatively empty at this moment, with only five patients, compared to the normal near-capacity load of eight or nine.

"This is Harry Sutton, 56. He's the editor of the 6 o'clock news for channel 5 – a Milwaukee television station. He was admitted with a stroke 4 days ago, started on heparin and bled into his brain. Now he's pretty well vegged out – we're going through the process of declaring him brain dead according to the new hospital protocol.

He's a candidate for the organ donor program."

I looked at Mr. Sutton; gray hair, distinguished face, handsome and rugged looking – he could be anyone's father. He lay there with a tube in his mouth, connected to a respirator, which droned its constant 'oooooooohhhhh' and 'aaaaaaaaaahhhhhh', pumping and sucking sounds. I

133

tuned out what Konrad was saying for a moment to listen to the variety of other sounds I heard in addition to the ventilator in each room. It was as if we were immersed in a South American rainforest. I heard the steady high pitched beep, beep, beep of the IV in the next room signaling to the nurse that the bag was running out of fluid. I heard the buzzing of the phones at the desk of the ward clerk. I heard the clunk of an X-ray being snapped, and the hum of a dialysis machine and the gurgle of a chest tube suction pump. I heard the shuffling of many feet and the worried voices of family members asking questions of the infectious disease doctor doing a consultation one room away from us. I heard a medical student asking a question of the pulmonary docs doing their rounds at the other end of the unit. I wondered what adverse effects this unsolicited cacophony had on patients – and especially on their nurses – after long periods of time.

I perused the unit, a long, rectangular room that resembled a miniature zoo, with eight rooms along one wall, side by side, and two along the opposite wall, with the remainder of space taken up by a nursing station which consisted of a NASA style control desk with cardiac monitor screens, and a desk for the ward clerk. There were phones mounted all along the wall and eight X-ray reading lights behind the desk panel of monitors. The unit was quite small considering all that was packed within its confines. (*Editor's note:* keep in mind that back in this era there were no cell phones, and the need for communicating with lab and X-ray as well as medical consultants was continual. Hence, all of the individual rooms had phones mounted outside on the glass doorway for easy physician or nursing access. (Considering how often the doctors were paged, it was essential to have a plethora of easily accessible wall and desk phones.)

The row of patient rooms resembled cages, barely bigger than the size of one bed, with curtains that could be drawn to allow for privacy, and glass doors that could be closed in the event of serious infections that required isolation. Outside the opening of each room stood a small table where the charts and lab results for that room's patient were kept.

Konrad continued. "That's all you need to know about him. Now let's go to Walter Gould. He's 67. This is his fourteenth day in here. He's a real mess, Rich. He's an alcoholic with hepatitis, kidney failure requiring daily dialysis, and sepsis – he was admitted primarily for the pneumonia which apparently was limited to his left lower lung. It got steadily worse each day and now it's his biggest problem. Now both lungs are socked full of fluid, hence the respirator. He's got three different organisms growing from his sputum cultures – Klebsiella, Proteus, and Pseudomonas."

I frowned. "Oh, great. Pseudomonas. He's in big trouble. Any drugs working against it, Konrad?"

"Not so far. He's on amp and gent and mandol, but Brian Buggy is thinking of starting him on a fourth drug. That pseudomonas is a real problem – we're worried that if this guy stays alive any longer, he's gonna spread the bug to everybody else in here – then we're in mega-big trouble."

Dr. Brian Buggy was the infectious disease consultant I'd seen writing a note in his chart while we were with Harry Sutton. Konrad continued.

"Are you ready for his meds, Rich? How's this – ampicillin, gentamycin, mandol for the pseudomonas, then dopamine at 8 micrograms per kilo for the septic shock, which he's been in for the last day or so. Then he's on solu-cortef to protect his platelets, which have been getting chewed up probably from the sepsis. We're giving him four donor packets of platelets almost every day, but his numbers bottom out really quick. Several days he's bled from his gums and rectum and apparently from his stomach. We're not sure if the stomach bleeding is due to low platelets or a stress ulcer caused by the cortisone – the solu-cortef. So, we've got him on tagamet to cover the presumed stress ulcer, and antacids also. He's also getting multivitamins with iron in his hyperal line, which has freamine running for six hours a day and a piggyback line of intralipid running slowly over 18 hours a day. With me so far?"

"Yeah. Whew – what a mess. Keep goin'" I was getting worried – how would I keep all these meds straight? It was ten times worse than starting each monthly rotation and picking up new patients – these patients could easily keep me busy the whole day – individually – trying to learn their problems and keep up with their daily needs. I was glad the list was whittled to five.

"Okay, continuing with the meds; we've got thiamine daily because he's a boozer, and magnesium sulfate for the same reason. Now let's review his lines."

I looked in as Konrad pointed out the lines. The first thing I noticed was the patient's wife, about 70 years old, sitting at the side of his bed. She appeared to be exhausted. She wiped his brow lovingly and combed his thinning gray hair. It was difficult to tell that there existed a living human being in between all the tangled technologic wizardry surrounding Walter

Gould. Konrad pointed out the four IV lines, two stuck underneath his collar bones, one in his neck, and one in his arm, all with Ivac machines pumping fluids in and going 'beep beep' at a characteristic pitch that told the nurses that everything was working well. The nurses must have such exquisite hearing to be able to discern normal versus abnormal beeps from these machines, I thought.

Then Konrad pointed to the chest tubes – two in his left side, connected to a suction pump which created a vacuum in his chest to allow his collapsing lung to stay inflated, and to drain the pus from his serious pneumonia. He then pointed to the arterial line in his other arm. An arterial line is inserted to measure blood pressure; since he was in shock, pressure needed to be measured in an ongoing manner, minute to minute. The arterial line was connected to a monitor on the wall which showed the rise and fall of the pressure wave with each heartbeat.

Then he pointed to his endotracheal tube, which jutted out the side of his mouth almost as if he were smoking a large pipe. It was taped to his chin and nose to keep it from moving. It was connected to the ventilator, which was set for continuous breaths, since he was no longer able to breathe at all on his own. Konrad explained the settings on the respirator.

"You have tidal volume, which needs to be set generally at 10 ccs per kilo of lean body weight, which for him is 750 cc. Then you have to decide what mode you want, either "assist", where each breath he attempts to make on his own is assisted with a kick of air to help inflate the lungs, or "IMV –intermittent mandatory ventilation", which gives him X number of breaths per minute even if he doesn't breathe of his own volition. You can set a minimum number of breaths on assist, also. Rate is also dependent on his arterial blood gases – you'll have to follow them closely so that you don't over or under breathe him."

I was becoming overwhelmed, inundated with the details of just this guy alone. If the others were this complicated, I was never going to leave this place, that much was clear. The information was coming at me fast and furious; it was the equivalent of trying to take a sip of water from a fire hose.

Then he pointed out the nasogastric tube leading from the patient's nose into his stomach, which was also connected to a suction pump, placed on low, to drain the stomach contents in case there was bleeding, and to prevent aspiration of stomach contents into his lungs.

The Con-Man pointed out the special vibrating air bed underneath Mr. Gould. It filled up certain segments with puffs of air every twenty minutes or so, and each time new segments were filled and the previous ones deflated.

This prevented decubitus ulcers from forming on his buttocks and legs from the pressure of lying too long in one spot.

I introduced myself to Mrs. Gould, and informed her that I would be taking Konrad's place as the primary caretaker for her husband.

"He's a tough old buzzard. I know he's gonna make it – he's too stubborn a Polack to quit," she told me.

We moved on to the next patient, Mrs. Susan Grimes.

"Susan's here with myasthenia gravis. It has paralyzed her efforts to breathe, so she's on the respirator. Her progress has been weak – I think she's getting worse."

I looked at her. She was young, probably 25 at most. She was very attractive, but too thin, wasted from her disease. Myasthenia is a disease which affects the motor end plates of muscles in a way such that they are paralyzed because the normal chemical responsible for movement of the muscle is unavailable for use. These patients usually do well with medications to keep their supply of acetylcholine useable to their muscles. The only time they get into difficulty is when infections occur which require much higher than usual doses of their medications, and sometimes a serious infection can be fatal. In Susan's case, a simple pneumonia had caused so much grief with her respiratory muscles that they just tuckered out, and now she needed a respirator to help her take her twelve to twenty breaths each minute.

I looked in at her, then walked in to introduce myself. She looked up at me, but couldn't speak because of the tube in her mouth, connected to her respirator. She didn't exude much emotion from her face; Konrad explained that this was because any effort with her muscles was extremely fatiguing to her. She did blink at me a few times, to signal that she understood me and acknowledged my presence. I told her that I understood her needs, and I wouldn't require any other responses from her.

Konrad and I then stepped out of her room, and went over her meds, her IV lines, her respirator settings, and her special needs. The lists of details were as complex as with Mr. Gould. My head was really spinning now.

Richard Sink, 46, was next. "Richard has a very interesting story. First of all, let me warn you – we take care of him, but he's Dr. Wally's patient, and you know Saul Wally he has his hands in everything – he'll be in here every day writing new orders, crossing some of yours out – and adding things to your progress notes but he expects you to take the midnight phone calls and he expects you to be totally responsible for his patient's care. It's a catch 22 as usual.

"Anyway, back to the patient. He woke up one morning two weeks ago, and noticed blood on his toothbrush after breakfast, just before going to work. He's got a desk job – insurance, I think. He went to Wally a few days later because the bleeding got worse. Wally got a white count on him that was sky high. He's got leukemia. In a short week and a half later, he's here, a genuine FUBAR (resident lingo for Fucked Up Beyond All Recognition), and nobody knows why."

I looked at him – a real mess – Konrad was understating it. He had more ivacs and lines and machines around him than Gould – there was no contest. He fit the ivac rule, which states that the number of ivacs, or IV machines, and other machines in a patient's room, is inversely correlated to the patient's prognosis. More machines meant bad prognosis. It was similar to the consultant's rule; the more consultants you had on a case, the worse it was, and the worse the predicted outcome.

The Con-Man continued. "Mr. Sink is in heart failure, and has pneumonia, on a respirator for that, has kidney failure, so he's being dialyzed, has liver failure which might explain his bleeding from all available orifices, and, of course, he's in shock. I think he's got ischemic or dead bowel, but it's hard to tell – everything's so bad that we don't know what's causing what."

Dr. Wally seemed to think there was still hope for him, though, because surprisingly enough, Mr. Sink was looking better than a few days ago, on paper at least. As I looked in the room at him, he was a blob of bloated tissue being catered to by every modern device known to man – it was difficult for me to imagine that this man looked better than he had three days ago. His list of meds and problems again frazzled my mind. Mr. Gould's and the other patients' particulars were a distant fog now – I would have to go back to each of their charts with a notebook and find a system of keeping everything straight. Was it even possible? I wasn't sure.

Konrad brought me to the final room. "Lastly, we have Dr. Parent's patient, Teresa Sharp. She's got Parkinson's disease, and now it's so bad that she's on a respirator. Dr. Parent has had problems with the family, who wants to try to get her off the respirator. He's tried weaning her off several times, but she's gone into shock when he boosted her meds enough to take her off – he almost coded her the first time. Now the family wants to transfer her to another doc – someone out of County – 'cause this other guy says he can take her off the machine."

"Hi, guys, how's my lady doing today?" It was Jerry Parent. I always enjoyed seeing Dr. Parent. He was a doctors' doctor. He commanded respect from everyone, not just the residents. Since my three months rotating through his service as an intern the previous year, I had even more respect and admiration for his medical acumen and his classy demeanor on the wards.

"We're just going over her now," Konrad replied.

"Well, Konrad, I think she'll be going out to County. I wish her daughter would consent to unplugging her machine and giving poor Teresa a go at it – if she didn't make it, it would be better than living another year or more on the machine. They've spent $58,000 already in the past six weeks in here, and they're talking $5,000 a month for a respirator at home if she needs one. Add to that round-the-clock nursing care. I wish I could make them see the impracticality."

"When will she be going?" I asked Dr. Parent.

*

"Maybe today. You'll have to take care of any last-minute details, Rich, because I'm leaving for vacation. What's with the bowtie – a new look?" He was referring to my black bowtie. I'd decided to dress differently this month to keep me psyched up for the stress. I'd been emulating the style of Dr. Stolp, the kidney specialist. He always wore a suit and tie, and shiny black Florsheim shoes. Every day I wore the same pressed white long sleeved shirt and tie, and Dr. Stolp-style black Florsheim shoes, to set me apart from some of the other residents who chose to wear scrubs all day, every day.

Now I added a bowtie, to signify the intensity of this unit.

Dr. Parent then turned to the Con-Man. "Konrad, are you glad to be done with this rotation?"

Konrad smiled. "You'd better believe it. It's been a zoo – until almost everybody died last week and we cleaned house."

Jerry Parent frowned. "Keep up the good work. Rich, seen any good movies lately? My boys are wondering when you're going to take them to a movie again."

I laughed. "No. Too busy."

I thought about the past six months, and how well I'd gotten to know Dr. Parent and his family in that time. Right around the time my internship had ended, I began to take his two boys, 4 and 6, and his two girls, 8 and 10, to movies, roller skating, and fun things which somewhat reminded me of the things I used to do in Minneapolis with my own sisters and brothers. The Parents had become my home away from home.

*

Kate, Jerry's wife, was fast becoming a very good friend. She was a very good listener.

Dr. Parent paged through Teresa's chart. He was leaving later today for a vacation. "By the way, before I forget, here's the key to the house, Rich. Kate's explained everything to you, and you've house-sat there before, so I can't imagine you'll be having any problems."

They were allowing me to house-sit during their vacation. I commented to Dr. Parent: "I'm really looking forward to it – I only wish it wasn't happening now, during this ICU rotation – it's going to be a pain being here instead of enjoying your view," Their house was situated on a cliff overlooking Lake Michigan, a veritable mansion with all the trappings of an upperclass lifestyle.

"Have fun on your trip," I said as Dr. Parent left the unit.

Konrad was next to leave. "Well, that about covers it, Caddychak. I'm history."

I envied his departure.

"You <u>dog</u> – I can't imagine how good you must feel right now. You actually <u>survived</u> the unit!"

"Well, whatever you come up with, triple it, and then you'll know how good it is to leave – siyonara – good luck." He was out the door.

Now it was up to me to keep these hunks of living tissue alive, at least within the expectations of medical science, which, at that moment, struck me as having come an incredibly long way. The sounds, the relentless ocean of sounds, the individual noises I'd picked out of the rainforest earlier, were now blotted out by inner sounds, the ultra-rapid transit of hundreds of thoughts stimulated by what I'd seen so far. I had so many questions about

140

where to start, how to stay ahead of the incredible details, how to learn what I needed to know; Vic Waters was a good way to start, I decided.

Vic was the ICU fellow. A fellow is someone who's completed a residency and is doing additional training in a particular area of special interest. In Vic's case, this was the first of two years he'd be spending at St. Luke's to broaden his ICU skills. Presently he was doing a cardiology rotation, but he'd been in once a day to help out with questions and do some teaching.

Vic was an interesting guy. He was 40, and had been out in practice ten years as an ER doc before deciding to do the fellowship. He'd been making over $100,000 a year, and gave it up for a fellow's salary of $20,000. I'd met him a few times in the cafeteria, so I knew a little bit about him.

He'd been single all of those years, and just recently married for the first time. He had an interesting perspective on single life: "there's no reason to hurry into marriage. I'm very happy now that I am married, but I'm also very glad I waited. Medicine is hard on a relationship. Vic walked in just as I was sitting down to review Mr. Sutton's chart.

"Hi, Rich. Glad to see you made it earlier than I did. You know married life it agrees with me a little too well."

"Glad to hear it, Vic. I'm still trying to sort everybody out here."

Vic continued. "Take your time. Let me give you the rundown. I'll try to get here by nine every day to go over problems with you. You can call me any night – no matter what the hour – if you've got something you're uncomfortable doing by yourself – if I'm not around, then you can call Bottum."

Dr. Bottum was the staff doctor who oversaw the unit.

"Rounds with Bottum will be sporadic – he usually calls at the most awkward times and announces that he's on his way for rounds. It seems to be mostly around noon, but anytime from eleven to two."

"Okay." Vic and I then went over every patient the way Konrad and I had done, looking at their diagnoses, medications, and plans for the day. One of my biggest fears was that I would forget to do something vital to the patient's care, or add a medication that would interact with the ones already being given. And how would I have time to look up all the new meds that were used in the ICU – many of them had no application on the wards, so I was unfamiliar with them. I had to keep my head, that's all; as Dad was always telling me: "keep your wits about you".

141

I noticed that every room had the televisions going, but none of these five, except maybe Susan, was conscious to appreciate it. The nurses said that it helped keep the patients oriented and provided a familiar object to remind them of the outside world. Then again, each room was tuned to the favorite soap opera of the nurse attending the patient – could that be a motive for keeping the televisions on? I noticed that the programs played incessantly. Hospital scenes were frequently the setting; actors dressed in white coats portrayed doctors who lived glamorous lives and had oodles of time to worry about romantic affairs and intrigue. Did those actors – or the public they served – have any idea just how absorbing the actual nuts and bolts of medical practice really was? Where was all this extra time they seemed to have? And, why would patients want to watch hospital shows to orient themselves to the outside world? Well, no sense in arguing with the nurses on my first day – I needed them on MY side. I remembered Dr.

Warner's run-in with the nurses. Don Warner – a general surgeon who always treated the ICU nurses harshly had a reputation among the nurses as an arrogant jerk and was widely disliked. One of the ICU nurses had reached her boiling point with him a few months ago and had shouted out "Don, you're just a big pig-fucker!!" The entire ICU had heard it, and she was later regarded as a heroine. I decided that I wanted the nurses with me, not against me.

11.30

I ran down to the caf for a quick bite to eat, since it was beginning to look as if I wouldn't be leaving this place at all today. As I got to the cafeteria line, which was about 35 people long, I noticed Laurie Kuehn leaving the caf.

"Laurie! How goes?"

"Rich! Where've you been? Good to see you."

"Oh, I was on OB rotation at St. Francis for a couple months, and I did Pediatrics at Children's Hospital – yeah, I haven't been around much lately. Listen, you going back upstairs? I'll walk with you – this line's too long anyway."

As we walked back to 6JK, Laurie began in her usual way. "How's your love life, Rich?"

"Couldn't be worse. I don't think I'm ever going to find somebody I'm satisfied with. How about you?"

"Great news! I'm going out with a resident from Children's. I met him through my sister – the one who's a nurse there. You might know him – Doug Strothers?"

"Yeah, I do know him, Laurie – nice guy. I'm happy for you. I hope things work out for you."

I dropped her off at 6JK, and we chatted in her office for a few more minutes. I was just about to head downstairs again when I heard: CODE 4 CODE 4 Room 6508 Bed A Room 6508 Bed A

That was right where I was – I looked down the hallway and realized that the commotion was coming from the J wing. I ran into the room and saw a crowd already assembled. Dr. Parent and his family practice crew were commencing rounds early that day, and John Holtan was his senior resident for the month. The intern had been presenting the patient's history at the bedside, and the man had suddenly stopped breathing. John Holtan had grabbed the crash cart and intubated him. Now Dr. Parent was calling out orders. With seven physicians in the room, and four nurses, and two beds, and the patient lying on the floor between the beds, it was very, very, congested in there. I stepped out of the room and pulled some bodies with me. Then I helped the nurses pull the other bed and patient out of the room.

By this time, they had lifted the patient back onto his bed and were doing CPR. John's intubation was successful, so although he was still unconscious, he was being ventilated successfully. After some epinephrine given through his IV, his cardiac rhythm returned, and CPR was stopped. He would need to be transferred to an ICU for observation, and since I was standing there, I suggested the MRICU. I told Dr. Parent that we had five open beds. Never again would I be so eager to drum up business. But then again, it was Dr. Parent. Any of us would gladly do anything for him.

*

As we transferred Jerry Parent's man down to my MRICU, I walked alongside the bed to try to get some history on the guy. He was 62, was in for a minor back strain, and had been completely asymptomatic until he suddenly passed out and lost his pulse while Dr. Parent was staffing him with the family practice residents on rounds.

As we wheeled him out of the elevator onto the third floor in front of the medical respiratory ICU, he coded again. "I've lost the pulse!" the nurse shouted.

143

His blood pressure dropped to zero and his pulse was absent. A look at the portable monitor showed that he had a normal sinus rhythm, but was obviously not delivering blood to the tissues. Was this EMD – electromechanical dissociation? It sure looked that way. I directed the code as we did CPR in the hallway. Finally, we got it coordinated so that we could carry on CPR while we rolled his bed down the hall toward the ICU.

When arrived in the unit, where Dr. Parent was waiting with Vic Waters, who was reading another patient's chart. Both of them assisted in the code. We needed a second IV line, preferably a central line – a line put into one of the central veins either in the neck, which was the internal jugular vein, or in the chest underneath the clavicle, which would hit the subclavian vein. The central line had the advantage of being large enough to pour large quantities of fluid into the circulation very rapidly. The man had only a peripheral line – an IV in his hand – and we could only pour fluid in at 150 cc an hour, a relatively slow rate compared to what he needed now.

If this was truly EMD (electromechanical dissociation), he needed fluid, and lots of it. The first priority was to maintain CPR, but even with adequate chest compressions, we weren't getting a pulse in his legs, so I wondered if anything we did would be in time – this man was probably already a vegetable. It was Vic who tried to get a central line in him. He couldn't find a vein – Vic was pretty experienced with central lines – we were all surprised at how much difficulty he was having.

Dr. Parent seemed pretty distraught. It was Murphy's law: whenever a physician is leaving for vacation, all hell breaks loose. Jerry had arranged to round with the residents early so he could leave for vacation – and this poor patient of his was deep-sixing on us. Finally, I suggested calling off the code. Twenty-five minutes had elapsed. I was afraid that we might revive him and find a vegetable on our hands, as had happened so many times previously when the code had dragged on this long without a response. One thing I noticed was how smoothly things went with less people around. In the ICUs, codes are usually "silent", meaning that they are not broadcast over the PA system, because usually there are enough people on hand to run the code without outside help. This prevents swarms of people from flooding into the ICU for each code that is called.

Dr. Parent and Vic and I sat down afterwards and put our heads together about the code – why had it failed? Why didn't he have a pulse or pressure, even with CPR? Why couldn't we get a vein for a central line?

Something didn't fit. Parent sent him for autopsy to help find the answer. Then he left to finish rounds with the family practice team.

Meanwhile, I was swamped. I started with Mr. Sutton, since he was on the end closest to me. He was the editor of the 6 o'clock news on local television, who had stroked. What a bummer – a stroke at his young age.

Then to top it off, the heparin blood thinner they had given him had made it worse, causing a massive brain bleed, and now he was here marking time until the coroner takes him. There wasn't much to do with him except make a note in his chart about his exam, which was unchanged for the past few days, from what

Konrad's notes had indicated.

Then I went back to Walter Gould, the alcoholic his wife described as a stubborn Polack, with severe pneumonia growing multiple organisms from his blood. I thought to myself: Walter Gould, why won't you die for us?

Your lungs are incubating a lethal bug that could wipe out every patient in this unit. The worst tragedy would be if your next-door neighbor, Susan Grimes, picked it up. Poor Susan, with the energy-sapping myasthenia gravis. She was looking so tired; a bug like this would do her in for good.

I decided to take twenty minutes to review Walter Gould's chart. It was so thick that the first week of his stay had been removed and filed at the ward clerk's desk. Every day since then required six or seven pages worth of notes. I found notes from Brian Buggy, the infectious disease consultant.

There were notes from the pulmonary docs, the kidney doc, the surgeon who helped with the first chest tube, the staff note by Dr. Bottum, and Konrad's notes. It was very time-consuming to read through everything that had been written, so I scanned it briefly and decided to go on what Konrad and Vic had briefed me with, and if I omitted any major considerations, I would just have to hope the nurse caught them – how else was I going to assimilate that much background on five patients?

15.00

I got a call from County Hospital. The neurologist out there, a friend of Jerry Parent's from his days as a cardiology fellow in Chicago, would take Teresa Sharp off my hands today. Great – one less headache to worry about.

145

15.30

The ER called. They were sending a lady up for admission to the unit. Jennifer Lakein, 45 years old, kidney failure and diabetes, now had a fever and was shocky. Sounded like septic shock. The nurses were getting her bed ready when she rolled in through our doorway at the end of the unit, past the five patients already mentioned, to the room at the end of the unit. As she rolled by, I noticed that she was huge – 445 pounds – and she barely fit on the bed.

*

Vic Waters wasn't around, so I needed to wing this one unless I could find him in the house somewhere. Just then, Dr. Bottum showed up. "Are you ready to do rounds?" he asked.

What timing, I thought. I was happy to see him. "Sure, Dr. Bottum."

Dr. Bottum was an interesting man – I'd heard many stories about him.

The nurses liked him, but they had many anecdotes relating to his peculiarities, and their favorite one was the story about his left ear. He'd been injured in a car accident years ago and had lost his left ear. Since then, he wore a fake ear that looked so real that the only way people could remember which one was fake was to watch him answer the phone. One day during a code, he was doing CPR and his ear fell off, and scared the other people helping him with the code – it fell off onto the patient and he nonchalantly slapped it right back on the side of his head and kept going.

Until then, no one had known about his ear.

Dr. Bottum and I went room to room and I explained what I knew about the progress of the patients, which was essentially diddly squat. He didn't seem to mind, though. When we got to Jennifer Lakein, he told me to work her up and call him so we could review her together. That made me feel better – I wouldn't be totally unsupervised for my first admission.

Jennifer was a whale – there was no better way to describe her. She had so much fat oozing out from the sides of her hips that I didn't even try to find her anus to do a rectal exam. I would have needed two nurses to hold her cheeks apart while I did the exam.

Jay Grassell, the senior resident for the night, wandered in just then. "I worked her up in the ER, Rich – figured you were the best place for her."

"Thanks loads, Jay. I'll get you back for this." Then Jay pulled me

146

aside. "You think this is bad, Rich? I had a 475-pound lady in clinic last year who was complaining of abdominal pain. Her husband usually took care of her, but he was sick, so she had an ambulance carry her to the clinic.

I told her I needed her to take off her pants to do a pelvic exam. She couldn't pull 'em off by herself. She said her husband had to dress her every day because she was too big to pull her pants up. Anyway, when we got her pants down, the whole room began to reek – her pants were chock full of old and fresh stool! The lady had been soiling her pants every day, but since her husband was ill, she hadn't taken her pants off to clean herself! What a stench!"

Jay laughed. "Everyone must have a fat story or two in their files, I guess. Good luck with this one, Rich. If you're still around at suppertime, give me a call, okay?" Jay left. It was comforting to see the camaraderie that had grown between the family practice residents. It made every rotation bearable knowing that the other FP residents were there for support. Konrad, Jay, and the others got together once a month for a dinner or some activity just so we could bitch about guys like Dr. Wally and Dr. Noonan, the "dump king", and anything else that bothered us.

Jennifer Lakein promised to be trouble. She was alert, for the time being, but she had a fever of 103 degrees, which spelled trouble down the road. I understood now why she was diabetic; it was her extra weight putting a tremendous strain on her pancreas until it simply gave out, and stopped producing insulin in sufficient quantities. Her body was resistant to the insulin it did make.

Her major problems were infection and shock, which was evidenced by a lower blood pressure than was normal for her. Her diabetes and kidney failure were of secondary concern; dialysis would take care of those problems.

I completed my exam and immediately prepped her right arm for an arterial line. I inserted the IV into her radial artery at wrist level; after I hooked up the line to the IV, which had blood shooting out with each heartbeat, I watched the monitor as it showed the classic arterial pressure wave which told me I was indeed in the artery. This line could be used to draw her blood without us needing to stick her in the arm each time; also, it would give us a constant readout on her blood pressure. At present, her blood pressure was 90 over 60, which was acceptable but worrisome – it normally ran 160/100 for her. I got a chest X-ray which showed a small

147

haziness in her left lower lung base; I decided to culture her sputum and blood, and started her on antibiotics until the results were in. Cultures would take 24–48 hours, and she couldn't wait that long for treatment.

She needed a central line inserted; I opted for a subclavian, since I didn't know how to do the internal jugular neck line. I knew Vic would teach me eventually. I got her line in without difficulty, and sighed in relief; in fat people, lines are always a problem because the usual landmarks are obliterated. Now we had ready access to her circulation in case she needed large amounts of fluids, or blood, infused rapidly.

After going over her problem list with Dr. Bottum, and discussing treatment strategies, I went back to my rounds on the others. Teresa Schiff, who was Dr. Parent's patient with Parkinson's disease, would be going to County Hospital soon. Mr. Sutton, the editor with the devastatingly severe stroke, would probably be declared dead by tomorrow, but that still left major disasters in Susan Graves, the lady with myasthenia, and Richard Sink, Dr. Wally's FUBAR with leukemia, and, of course, Walter Gould, with the severe pneumonia.

18.30

I was just about ready to leave for home, when the pathologist came up with news on Dr. Parent's patient who had coded earlier in the day. The guy's autopsy showed that he'd had an aneurysm, or weak wall to his aorta, and it had blown a big hole out the side of it, close to where it originated at the heart. No wonder our CPR had been ineffective, and no wonder it was so difficult finding a central vein – they were all so collapsed from the lack of circulating blood. It was all leaking out the large hole in his aorta. Well, I took a small consolation in knowing that nothing we could have done would have made a difference – it was his time. Another incident to remind me of that fine line between life and death – one minute you're up and around and thinking about filing your income taxes, and the next minute is the future you'll never know. Death and taxes, the only two guarantees in life.

18.45

I decided to head home – to Dr. Parent's house – for whatever short time I might have before I had to be called in. Who could predict? Maybe I would

148

be lucky enough to stay away until morning.

19.30 (7:30 p.m.)

The unit called to report Jenny Lakein's SMA12 lab results. I wrote them on my scratch pad – they looked good. Her pressure was 100/75. She was alert and her temp was down to 100.

20.45

Call #2: Walter Gould's arterial gases are worse – the pO2 is falling. I decided to change his oxygen concentration to 75% – we normally breathe 21% in room air, and anything over 50% will be hazardous over any prolonged period, but his oxygen concentration was falling even on 45%. I wondered why – was he finally going to buy the farm, or was his pneumonia just spreading to the last ounce of normal lung?

21.10

Call #3: Richard Sink's platelet count is 24,000, which is dangerously low – and he's bleeding from his rectum and stomach again. He's the guy with leukemia – Dr. Wally's patient – I told his nurse to give him four donor units of platelets and get another count in two hours. With my luck Dr. Wally would call the nurse in 15 minutes and countermand all of my orders, but so be it. Jenny Lakein's pressure is holding at 100/75, but her temp is up to 102 again. I ordered more Tylenol. I thanked her nurse for pooling calls – I asked her to tell the other nurses to all get together instead of calling me individually each time someone had a report or a question. I wondered if it would work.

23.10

Call #4: Walter Gould was losing his pressure – now down to 80/40. I told his nurse to increase his dopamine to 12 micrograms per kilo.

23.40

Call #5: Gould's pressure was up to 90/50 now. His wife was right – he was too stubborn to die. Richard Sink's bleeding had slowed to an ooze now. Susan Grimes, the gal with myasthenia gravis, was spiking a fever, but she'd been given Tylenol and it was coming down.

00.56

Call #6: I was sound asleep for this one; it really knocked me for a loop to be aroused by a ringing phone after having heard ringing beeps and other alerts all day long. I was also startled to wake up in unfamiliar surroundings at Dr. Parent's mansion. It was Sue, the head nurse; they had an admission coming up from the ER, so I might as well get ready to come on in; I was twenty minutes away, so I wasted no time in throwing on some clothes and driving in. I sure hated to leave that beautiful home nestled up against the shore of Lake Michigan.

01.30

The girl in the ER had arrived at the MRICU by the time I did, and I was surprised at how much different the place seemed just by having the overhead lights turned off for the evening shift; the same noises were present, but somehow seemed less traumatic without the glare of those bright overhead lights.

Sandy Jonathan had been complaining to her girlfriend that she had a splitting headache two days ago. Her girlfriend had called her back this evening and couldn't reach her; finally she went over to investigate and found Sandy unconscious on the floor of her kitchen. Sandy was 26 years old, and had been in good health. Her husband was on his way to California to look for work, and had no idea of Sandy's condition. Her girlfriend was noticeably upset. I asked her to leave the unit for a few minutes until we could ascertain what was happening.

Sandy's exam was basically unremarkable except that her neurologic exam was abnormal. She looked to be bleeding in her head – she had the papilledema that I'd learned to recognize since those first days under the tutelage of my senior resident Jill Harmon. (My two favorite seniors, Jill and Laurie Woodard, were now graduated and out in practice) We got a CAT scan on her which confirmed my findings. I started her on mannitol,

150

an osmotic agent which sucks excess fluid from the swollen brain back into the blood stream where it can be removed by the kidneys. I called a neurosurgeon, Dr. Frazin, the same one that had worked on Marie Vickers, who had been fortunate enough to walk out of St. Luke's after six weeks of therapy. Frazin went over the results of the CAT scan, and told me it was too late for her; she was probably brain dead after bleeding for as long as she apparently had. I couldn't get ahold of her husband – I had no idea where to contact him; we would have to try to keep her alive until he called home.

Frazin opted not to drill a burr hole in her head to relieve the pressure; he thought that it was an unnecessary procedure under the circumstances. We opted to control her as best we could medically, and leave the rest to nature.

03.40

It was too late to consider going back to the Parent mansion. I drove over to my apartment and crashed. It was only five minutes away, in case I needed to come in again. It was psychologically good for me to get out of the hospital, even if only for half an hour.

05.30

Call #7: Walter Gould had a temp of 105 degrees. Did I want anything in addition to Tylenol? I ordered sponge baths and a cooling mattress. Why were we letting this guy live instead of killing him – and that nasty pseudomonas he harbored – while he was still the only one with it? It didn't make much sense to me, but that's the way his wife wanted it. She was right – he was a stubborn old Polack – anyone else with this bug, which was resistant to three antibiotics, would have succumbed to it within a couple of days. He was beginning his sixteenth day, and the eighth day of having this pseudomonas infection.

06.45

Call #8: Sandy Jonathan, the new arrival with the massive brain bleed, was having a seizure; did I want to treat it? I told the nurse yes, and ordered valium 10 mg IV and dilantin 100 mg IV; I would be in to do rounds in a few minutes, so they could hold any other calls until I got there.

What a night! EIGHT CALLS!!! I wondered to myself: would I get ANY nights of unbroken sleep this month?? How would I survive? I was on the board, so to speak. Psychologically it seemed a little easier knowing what I was up against, but would I hold out? In the past, after constant interruptions to my sleep, I was rewarded with a solid night's sleep after the call shift ended. I wouldn't be guaranteed any sleep all month – I would have to try to play catch up at every opportunity. Oh well, others had survived, and I would too – somehow.

Saturday, Day #2

07.15

I left the house where I rented a small bedroom on the main floor, and brushed the snow off my old Chevy station wagon. I noticed that Arne's garden in the vacant lot next to my house was completely blanketed with snow. My car was slow to start but finally turned over. The drive to St. Luke's was short, maybe five minutes. It took longer to clean the windshield than to drive there. On the radio Michael Jackson's new hit "Billie Jean" was playing.

I got in a little late, but nobody seemed to notice. Nurses were changing shifts and the frenetic bustle of activity and bright lights signified that another busy day was well under way. Just like the day before, the first thing I noticed was the noise, the constant chatter of IVs beeping as they ran out of fluid, and oximeters chirping if the oxygen level was too low, and the constant waxing and waning sounds the ventilators made to deliver their air to each patient. It dawned on me that this was very much like my trips to the Atlantic Ocean. Since I'd been born in New Jersey, our family had made several trips back to see relatives, and each time we had visited the Atlantic Ocean. The ocean waves produce a continual, never-ending waxing and waning sound as the waves first advance toward shore and then retreat back into the ocean. That ocean sound never stops, even when we drive away from it. In Minneapolis I would often remind myself that the ocean waves are still making that same sound, even though I am no longer there to hear it. And thus it was with this ICU. Even after I left each day, those peculiar sounds that fill a typical ICU continued, unceasingly, 24

152

hours of every day. One could count on the fact that the ICU would always be occupied with patients, and the noises would continue into perpetuity, just like the ocean waves.

I noticed that Harry Sutton, the editor with the stroke, was no longer with us; his organs had been harvested last night, the nurse informed me. Now he was truly dead, although after being brain dead for many days, it was only semantics, as Harry would have attested to, given the opportunity.

Teresa Sharp's room was empty also, which was nice to see. She was Jerry Parent's patient with Parkinson's. I wondered if she would ever make it off her respirator. She had been moved to County Hospital.

Sandy Jonathan with the brain bleed was lying peacefully in her bed, unaware of her predicament, with her respirator churning mindlessly away. She didn't need any real interventions from me, so I wrote a quick note and moved on to my real problem patients – the ones I could or at least should do something about.

Susan Grimes, the gal with myasthenia, who was actually aware of her surroundings despite the ventilator, was feeling better this morning. Her arterial blood gases were much improved over yesterday. I was quite surprised. I told her the news, and she mustered a smile for me. It was real work for her to do so, but the good news elicited that smile and somehow I didn't think she minded fatigue for a good cause. I was beginning to think there was hope for her yet; her fever had disappeared also, which possibly accounted for the improvement in lung function.

By the time I got to Walter Gould, with the antibiotic resistant severe pneumonia, Vic Waters showed up to go over my players with me. We tried to sort out the events of the evening prior: Walter had developed a new fever, an increasing need for oxygen, new hypotension – what was the primary etiology? His chest X-ray told the answer; it was completely whited out now. White patches on a chest X-ray indicate dense tissue, such as would be seen with consolidated lung in the case of pneumonia. Normal lung is a lighter shade of black. Mr. Gould had no more black on his film – the entire X-ray was solid white.

Vic wasn't convinced that pneumonia explained everything. He reasoned that the chest X-ray was not that much worse than yesterday, when only a small ditsel of black showed evidence of some normal lung. As we scrutinized today's film again, he pointed out a line along the right side about halfway up the lung – it was the edge of the lung itself. Of course!

He had a partial pneumothorax – collapse of the lung – and that's why he wasn't breathing as effectively. He would need a chest tube on the left side now, in addition to the two already in place on the right.

Vic and I donned gloves and gowns, and scrubbed his chest with what little room we had to work in between the other two chest tubes, the machines and lines and ever-present technology cluttering the room. I watched as Vic demonstrated his preferred method of placing the tube. He made an incision in the chest, spread the skin between the ribs, and suddenly we heard a pop as he'd penetrated the lung; I could hear the air whistling through the clear plastic chest tube, fluctuating with each breath, just like a kid blowing across the top of a soda bottle. Finally, he positioned the tube in the area that needed the suction, and we turned on the pump to suck the unwanted air out of the cavity between the lung, which had collapsed like a sponge, and the chest wall. The lung was sucked up firmly against the chest wall and consequently re-expanded, and a second X-ray showed the desired results. We could no longer trace the edge of the lung, because it had reinflated and was sitting in the normal position in the chest cavity.

When we got around to seeing Jennifer Lakein, the 445-pound diabetic, she was complaining of difficulty breathing. Vic and I discussed her pulmonary status; with her infection still unexplained, and her other problems, it was conceivable that she would be tiring out shortly. Her respiratory rate was already 35, compared to the normal rate of 12–20. We would have to consider intubating her, even though she was conscious, if she gave us any more indications of impending respiratory collapse.

11.30

Dr. Bottum came in to do rounds, just as Vic and I had finished going over everybody briefly. I decided that Bottum resembled Yoda, the character from Star Wars, with his unusual physiognomy and artificial ear.

13;30

I drove to my apartment, since it was Saturday, and the afternoon promised to be busy. I thought I would get in a quick nap.

13;50

The Unit called. Mr. Gould's arterial gases are better now – should I turn down his oxygen? I told them to back down to 45% and get more gases in 45 minutes. That would give me an hour before they'd be calling again.

15 30

I was napping in my bedroom. The Unit hadn't called back and I was in a total fog when Lee, one of the neighbors, came banging on my door in a frenzy. The shock jarred me into reality and, as I saw the look on his face, I knew he was in trouble.

Lee looked frantic. "Rich, it's Arne. Come quick."

I looked out my window and there was Arne, my next-door neighbor, the guy who owned the auto repair shop. He was face down on the ground in his vacant lot – in the snow – his snow blower purring on idle. I ran back into my bedroom to get my emergency kit. I threw tennis shoes over my bare feet, and ran outside in my flannel shirt and jeans, and made an assessment of Arne. I barely noticed the cold air and snowy ground. Arne wasn't breathing. He had no pulse. I asked Lee if he knew CPR – no – so I showed him how to do chest compressions. By then, Joe, one of the other guys from my house, had arrived, so I got him to work at breathing for Arne. Arne turned his head to the side and vomited a large amount of food and liquid which looked strange on the white snow. Joe was doing just a fair job of inflating his lungs, but with all that vomitus, I understood why. Arne's color was still pink, so that was encouraging.

I rolled up the four layers of flannel and polar shirts Arne was wearing on his right arm so that I could put an IV in and start some code meds. I got the IV in, then gave him some epinephrine. (I had "appropriated" some of these meds from the hospital because I always wanted to be prepared for emergencies – I was an ambulance chaser at heart) Still no pulse. By then, the paramedics had arrived.

They were very surprised at what they saw – two people doing CPR by the numbers, a third person holding up an IV bag, an IV sticking in his arm, and me giving him meds with a syringe, all the while the patient is lying on the snowy ground in his backyard.

"Hi, I'm Doctor Mayerchak. I'll take full responsibility for this code. I know this man, and I work at St. Luke's. Let's take him to the ER there."

The paramedics agreed to let me take charge, but they seemed a little miffed at the thought. I asked them to watch out for my IV – don't pull it out when we transfer Arne to the ambulance – but sure enough, one of them tripped on it and out it pulled. I was angry. Arne was a difficult stick – I hoped we could get another one placed.

Inside the ambulance, the paramedics – four of them – asked questions and filled out papers, and I wondered why one of them wasn't driving us to St. Luke's. "We have to stabilize the patient first."

That didn't make sense to me. There were three guys and me to work on Arne in addition to the one guy who could be driving, but it seemed as if the paramedics were doing it almost out of spite, taking what little control they did have, and milking it.

I busied myself with the task of putting in another IV. The right arm was shot – no more available veins there. I grabbed a scissors and cut off the clothing on his left arm, then searched for three minutes before finding something that resembled a vein. I tried it, but it was too small. Finally, I went for the antecubital space in the small of his elbow and just stuck blindly; it wasn't the first time I'd had to do that. I was in luck – good blood return through my needle. We hooked him up to a line and gave him some bicarb and more epinephrine.

His monitor showed asystole. I knew it was looking bad for him. "Can we please get GOING?"

We'd been in Arne's driveway while the driver did paperwork for over ten minutes.

When we got to St. Luke's, I met Dr. Bottum in the ER – he was working down there to supplement his income. I was happy to see him – he was an expert at codes – and Arne needed help. We hooked him up and continued the code for 35 minutes more. Arne still didn't respond, even though he was intubated and his color was pinker now. The guy's heart was dead beyond revival.

I wanted to continue with the code, but Dr. Bottum vetoed. It was then that I realized how subjective this all was for me, and how much he was right with anybody else, I'd have called the code off ten or fifteen minutes earlier. With anybody else, I'd have noticed the icy cold of the snow where we'd done CPR, the lack of clothing I had on, and the futility of the situation. With Arne, dear Arne, the only thing I thought about is that he couldn't die – it couldn't really happen to someone I knew that well.

156

I walked out to the waiting room and saw his wife Pat sitting in a chair. It appeared that she was praying. It is said that there are no atheists in foxholes. I had seen this to be true on many occasions during internship, where people suddenly rediscovered their faith in a time of need, or began to believe in God for the very first time when faced with a terminal event. In

Pat's case, I don't think she had ever lost her faith.

"He's gone, Pat." I stated it succinctly without beating around the bush – what was the point? She'd know the outcome with the first intonation I uttered, no matter what the word. I told her that Arne looked peaceful, and that he'd gone suddenly, and that he and I had said a prayer right before he died. She needed to hear that. Then I took her to see him.

He lay there in his ER bed, with his endotracheal tube still in his mouth, because of a hospital rule saying we couldn't remove such items in case there was an autopsy for legal reasons. He looked anything but dignified with the IVs in his arms and the burn marks on his chest where he'd been shocked with the defibrillator. Pat didn't seem to notice those things, even though I did. I thought it was so unfair that he had to look like that. It was just another small example of how malpractice litigation fears had cut into the art, the humanity, of medicine.

All Pat saw was her stubborn old Arne, who'd been complaining of chest pains for the past several days. He'd knocked off early at the auto shop today because of chest pains, and then had decided to get some snow shoveling done with his free time. Pat scolded Arne one last time.

"I told you to see Rich while you had the chance, you old stubborn Polack. See? Look where it got you. I told you we'd never take that trip to Europe together."

She seemed angry, but I guessed that it was a behavior borne of shock, and that the reality of him being gone forever still hadn't set in. Finally, I left the room so that she could be alone with him for a few minutes. Father

Ralph came down to say a few words to her, and then I left to check on my patients in the Unit.

When I arrived, I realized how totally undressed I was – tennis shoes, but no socks, a flannel shirt and jeans, but no underwear. I'd thrown on the bare essentials for winter when the neighbor had summoned me to Arne's house. Nobody in the unit had major problems, the nurses said.

Walter Gould's gases were better on 45% oxygen. I told them I would

157

go home and change, and try to finish my nap, although I knew that my sleeping days were over.

As I left, Walter Gould's nurse Jean asked, "Where's your bowtie, Doctor Mayerchak? We miss it." She smiled. I wasn't aware that anyone had noticed my bowtie style, which was now a whole two days old. I decided that I would keep at it, and persist until I had started a new trend at St. Luke's – the return of the bowtie.

15.45

The Unit called. Tim Kross, a 17-year-old, was admitted with carbon monoxide poisoning. It appeared to be a suicide attempt. I told the nurse I'd be right over.

When I arrived, he was just coming out of the hyperbaric oxygen chamber. St. Luke's has the only such chamber in the city. Consequently, all similar problems come here, ranging from carbon monoxide poisoning to smoke inhalation to scuba diving accidents. Tim had been in the chamber breathing high concentrations of oxygen at high pressure to help rid his body of the damaging carbon monoxide. He'd been discovered sitting at the wheel of his car, in the garage, and his car had run out of gas, so it had probably been running for quite some time. It was unclear whether the hyperbaric chamber would help or not. While I waited for the chamber nurses to finish with him, I talked to Dr. Kindwall, the hyperbaric oxygen director, about the patient's chances of recovery.

"You just can't tell, Rich – sometimes they make remarkable recoveries just when you've given up hope. I had a guy about this kid's age who was apparently brain damaged, had seizures, was unconscious for a few days, then slowly came to, and walked with muscular dystrophy and spoke very slowly for a few months, and then I lost track of him. Five years later, he wrote to me that he was at Harvard, studying medicine and participating on the track team. I was flabbergasted. So, you never know. I'll have to admit, though, it doesn't look good."

16.30

I examined Tim Kross. He reminded me of my brother Marty, who's seven years younger than I am; Tim's face bore a resemblance to Marty. It was haunting to think that my brother could be lying on a bed in an ICU somewhere – how would I react? Would I be as frazzled as these people seemed to be? His parents and sister were worried sick. They waited in the family waiting room at the end of the hall. Finally, I went down to talk with them.

I explained to them that the situation was serious, and that it was entirely possible that Tim could die in the next 24 hours. I did this to start the emotional preparation process that is necessary for accepting death – they would begin to grieve before the fact, so that it would be less traumatic at the time, if it came.

Then I told them that Dr. Kindwall was very optimistic – one had to be and that many such episodes had occurred with others who ended up walking out of here. I gave them as much hope as I possibly could without misleading them, because hope was the glue that kept families from falling apart at times like this. Vic told me to watch out for the family members, and I knew to what he was intimating, for often I'd seen it with my own patients who had loved ones in ICU: they'd get so upset because of their loved one's illness that they ignored their own needs. They would often stay at the hospital 20 hours each day, waiting for improvement, not sleeping, not eating right, running themselves into the ground. I'd had a patient whose husband was in ICU with bad emphysema. She was so worn out after staying with him for a week that I had to admit her to the hospital on the day he was being discharged for home.

With this in mind, I warned the family members to be good to themselves, hard as it might seem, by staying away from the hospital for part of each day, to rest, especially if Tim ended up staying here for more than a few days. I knew I would have to tell them these things again in a few days; right now everything was coming at them all at once, much too fast for them to absorb.

17.30

I went to the caf for a quick supper. John Holtan was eating with Dean, another senior resident, so I sat with them for a moment. Dean was kidding me about my reputation, which had really gotten out of hand by now. The nurses on one floor told me that there was a rumor circulating widely that I had gone to bed with 175 nurses during my internship. A few of the residents were calling me "Doctor 175" now.

Dean ribbed me now about the rumor. "Hey, 175, have you done it in the call rooms yet?"

"Get off it, Dean-o. What do you think – of course not."

"Well, you will, Rich. You've got a year yet. Believe me, you will." He looked at John and they gave each other a confident, knowing look.

I changed the subject. "What's the scoop on Jose?"

"Jose – 100? He's out. Herb canned him today." Dean said.

Jose Ruiz was an intern who had graduated from the medical college here in town, but who had less than full command of the English language. He had made a few bumbles early as an intern, but Dr. Herb Laufenburg, the family practice residency director, had turned a blind eye, until enough protests had forced him to action. Jose's biggest mistake had been on the medicine wards with Jerry Parent. One night, while on call, he'd gone to a patient who was complaining of breathing difficulty. He asked the nurse to give him 100 milligrams of morphine IV. What he <u>meant</u> to say was lasix, 100 mg, which was an unusually high but acceptable dose of a diuretic, a water pill. His mistake of saying "morphine" when he meant "Lasix" was a deadly one. The nurse – a rookie just doing her orientation – began breaking all the 2 milligram vials of morphine that she could find, to put together enough of them to make 100 milligrams, a fatal dose. Fortunately, Dean had been passing by and checked out what was going on, and halted the process before the fatal error was carried through. Hence, the name Jose-100.

The final straw had come at 2 p.m. rounds one day. Jose couldn't pronounce a medication, and he said it six times the wrong way, with Dr. Parent correcting him each time. Finally, Jerry had reached his limit, and a call went out to Dr. Laufenburg, and the next thing we knew, Jose-100 was history.

I shot the bull with those guys for a few more minutes, then returned to finish my progress notes in the Unit.

19.30

Progress notes done, I headed to Dr. Parent's home, hopefully for the whole night. I was happy to note that Susan Graves was doing better, and I had hopes for her eventually making it out of there. Richard Sink,

160

Dr. Wally's patient with leukemia, was continuing to have a good day. I was beginning to think he had better chances than Walter Gould, who was running from the grim reaper at every turn. It struck me so odd that some people could go so suddenly – you'd be talking to them one minute, they'd be gone the next, without warning. And then there were others, like Gould the stubborn Pollack, and Sink, with leukemia, who had every possible strike against them, yet they continued to hang in there, fighting the good fight, as if they had a say in their outcomes.

Poor Arne Celinski – my neighbor – and Pat, his newly widowed wife – I was still in shock remembering what had happened this afternoon as I took the twenty minute drive to the cozy Parent mansion on the Great Lake. (*Editor's note:* Arne's son Dale, the co-owner of the corner automobile service station, was suddenly the sole owner, with his father's passing. I stopped in there one day to get a tire changed. Dale didn't charge me. Over the next four years that I remained in Milwaukee, Dale wouldn't take a penny for anything I asked him to fix on my car. I thought about insisting that he take my money, but eventually I realized that it was something Dale needed to do, out of gratitude for what I had done to try to revive his father, and that I couldn't take that away from him.)

23.30

Call #1: Tim Kross was having a seizure. I started him on valium anddilantin.

00.30

Call #2: Jennifer Lakein's arterial gases are getting worse. She is morbidly obese, at 400+ pounds, and she's definitely tiring now. I asked them to call Dean, who's the house senior resident tonight, and have him intubate her. Then I decided to call him myself. He told me he'd be glad to; he remembered his own rotation in the ICU; I had a feeling that when this month was over, I would be equally be glad to help out whoever else was doing this bloody rotation – it was a pain in the butt.

00.55

Call #3: Dean called to say that he'd intubated Jenny Lakein, and arterial gases were ordered for an hour from now. I thanked him.

Sunday, Day #3

07.00

I received three more calls overnight, evenly spaced to ruin any rhythm of sleep I might had enjoyed.

I started rounds with a big surprise. Sandy Jonathan's husband had arrived and was talking with Dr. Frazin, the neurosurgeon, about her prognosis. Her husband had just flown back from California this morning after hearing of the unfortunate events regarding his wife's brain bleed. I heard him in the family waiting room pleading with Frazin to do something.

"You can't just let her die. Do something, dammit!" He sobbed implacably and repeated his exhortation for aggressive action. He wasn't holding back any emotion. It was quite dramatic, and very sad. I felt bad for Dr. Frazin, who was helpless to change reality, and who happened to be the innocent outlet for this man's frustration with fate.

Frazin left after 25 minutes, with nothing resolved. He was trying to help Sandy's husband see the futility of keeping her on the respirator, but to no avail. For the time being, on she stayed. If nothing else, it would give her husband time to accept her death before she actually "died" – again, the preparatory grieving necessary for the acceptance of the inevitable death.

I looked at Walter Gould – the man was amazing. He was defying death at every turn, and I respected his stamina, but I worried, too – what if Jenny Lakein was coming down with his bug, or Richard Sink? Susan Grimes sure didn't need it either – all three of them had somewhat reasonable chances of making it out of here if we could keep the bugs away.

Tim Kross, the carbon monoxide suicidal teen, was unchanged. His mother sat at his side, talking to him and holding his hand. His girlfriend had recently broken up with him, which apparently explained the suicide attempt.

Richard Sink, Dr. Wally's patient with leukemia, was looking better yet; he had several episodes of consciousness, and his platelet numbers were holding steady for almost 36 hours. His other problems were status quo, which was a good sign. No change was better than deterioration – a cardinal rule that every family member of an ICU patient recited daily.

Susan Grimes, the myasthenia lady, was kicking her pneumonia, slowly but surely. Her strength was improving, and she smiled again for me this morning. Her husband was there to visit with me, and I buoyed them both with hope and positive thinking. She was my age – 26 – I could relate to her predicament. It just wasn't right at our age; she had to make it out.

Jenny Lakein was going bad on me, but why? As I pondered her changes, Vic wandered over to where I sat at the table outside her room. He held her morning chest X-ray.

"What do you think, Rich?"

"Well, here's the culture results, Vic. Staph, and maybe Klebsiella, for starters. She needs broader antibiotic coverage. Then again, the cultures show she's sensitive to the ones we've got her on, so why the fever spikes? Does she need her lines changed already?"

*

"How about an abscess? I smell an abscess, Rich. I wish I could put my finger on where, though. Let's run it by Bottum when he comes in. Okay? He's usually late on Sundays."

"Oh yeah, it's Sunday."

For 18 months I'd gotten used to all days being entirely equal. The weekend had no meaning to me any longer. It was just 2 more days that preceded the 5 other days of the week. I hadn't been to church except sporadically every few months, and that disturbed me. I hoped I would make up for it someday.

Just then, Dr. Wally walked in, so I went over to Mr. Sink to round with him. The nurse was reporting to Dr. Wally that Mr. Sink seemed to be lacking bowel sounds since the last time she checked. He told her not to worry about it, and brushed her off as if she didn't know what she was talking about. How totally typical of Wally, I thought. Nurses were little more than walking uteri, in his opinion.

As we were discussing him, in walked Dr. Jerry Hanson, the GI man on the case. He told Dr. Wally that he'd been by a little while ago and noticed that Mr. Sink's bowel sounds were hypoactive, and he wondered about possible bowel infarction.

Wally brightened. "Bowel sounds quiet, huh? Gee, that's interesting, Jerry. I'll get some films and let you know what I find. Thanks for the tip."

The nurse looked at me, and I at her, as Wally went on to order abdominal films just because Hanson had said something; when the nurse

163

had told him the same thing earlier, he had given her no response. Good old Saul Wally – some things never change.

11.30

The ER called me about a possible admission – a man who was coding silently down there – so I went down to investigate. By the time I arrived, he had been pronounced dead, so I started back upstairs. Out of the corner of my eye, I noticed a man in one of the rooms, talking to the intern, and complaining of abdominal pain. He looked very familiar, but I couldn't place him. I called the intern out of the room for a minute and asked him his name.

"His name is Selwood Bannon – you know him?"

"Bannon, Bannon…yeah – he's the Munchhausen's!" I told him about having Mr. Bannon during my first month, and how he'd walked AMA (against medical advice). The intern called medical records to have my discharge summary sent up. Good old Bannon, up to his old tricks – had diarrhea, needed some morphine to slow down his bowels…

12.30

Dr. Bottum and I did rounds. He also wondered aloud about Jenny Lakein, and thought an abscess was indeed a possibility. He asked me to consult Brian Buggy, the infectious disease man. Why not? He was already seeing Gould and Grimes.

The afternoon and evening was more of the same – a phone call once every hour or two to manage a ventilator setting or address a lab result.

22.15

Call #2: Gould was having some ventricular dysrhythmias – his monitor showed a few beats of ventricular tachycardia, and it looked like he might code tonight if this kept up. Did I want to code him? Tough question. His wife wanted everything possible to be done, which meant yes, we should code him. But, I told the nurse, we both knew the situation here. I instructed her to make it a "slow code", in other words, walk slowly to it, don't get heroic, and call if off early – if indeed, he coded at all. Gould was defiant –

he probably wouldn't code, just to spite us.

23.00

The nurse called again. Gould was coding. I should get in now. I reminded her about what we'd discussed. She acknowledged, and hung up.

23.25

When I got there, an intern from County, who happened to be rotating through Luke's, was writing a note in Gould's chart. It was over. He was dead. I sighed in relief. Finally Walter would rest. I asked him how it had gone, and he told me that CPR had been done. His ribs had been cracked because pulses were weak with compressions, and he had been shocked 3 times for V-fib.

I was angry. What had happened to my orders – the discussion about doing a "slow" code?? These maneuvers were an insult to this man's long fight, and a very undignified way to take his final breaths in this world. Poor Walter – they'd beat on him, shocked him, cracked his ribs – where did they do compressions, with three chest tubes sticking out of his chest? Wow, was I fuming. I asked the nurse about it.

"Well, the supervisor said we had to go all the way with it, and one thing lead to another, and before we knew it, it was done."

I left – ran out of the unit with a mad look on my face – why the hell did I bother to talk to these damn nurses anyway? Just when I thought they had my respect and obedience, they screw up a tacit understanding we had about giving this guy a piece of dignity.

I cried. Walter Gould hadn't had a chance of making it out of this place alive, but he deserved a better end than he got. I went directly home without speaking to anyone.

01.15

Sandy Jonathan's husband finally gave the OK to unplug the respirator. She was the gal with the massive brain bleed. We will leave her on the vent now only until her organs are "harvested" for the donor program.

Monday, Day #4

07.00

I did not look forward to today. I would have to hustle, because I had clinic at 13.00. I noticed that Sandy Jonathan and Walter Gould were missing, it seemed weird not having them around. Two nurses' aides were scrubbing Walter's room with a strong antiseptic detergent. Finally, the culture medium for that deadly Pseudomonas bug – Gould – had been removed.

Tim Kross, the guy with the carbon monoxide poisoning, was no better today. The family was obviously impatient for something to happen, but I emphasized that after the first 24 hours, the progress might be very, very slow, if there was any progress at all. The fact that he hadn't at least come out of his coma was indeed discouraging.

11.30

Rounds were done, and Bottum had staffed everyone with me. I had been very brief with my progress notes – for a change – because I knew I had clinic hanging over me. I'd finished ahead of schedule. I started toward the caf for a quick lunch. On the way I met Pako Acosta, a Filipino internist who was always kidding me about women. Pako had heard the rumors about me, and knew they weren't true, but he prodded me to loosen up a little and take advantage of my position.

"Are you puttin' it to anybody yet, Ricardo? Nothing like a good hump to improve your perspective on life, you know."

I laughed. He was serious, but I wasn't listening as if he was. "Naw, I'm still waiting for the right girl."

"Fine, Richard. But in the meantime, how's about a little fun once in a while, huh? You're too serious all the time. Take me – I'm happily married, I love my wife, she loves me – last week, I had one of the nurses in the CV ICU – she's married too. She loves her husband, I love my wife, but we get steamed up once in a while and it's a good thing for both of us. So why not? And you – you're too moral for your own good, man. It's natural, go have some fun, Ricardo!"

I continued on my way to the caf. Everybody in this hospital seemed to know what I did (even though I didn't) with my sex life, yet they were

166

the ones having all the sex. Pako wasn't the only one giving me little sermonettes.

13.00

I arrived at the clinic for my weekly afternoon session. My first patient was Roxanne Fabinot. She was 22, very immature, and on the welfare rolls like her mother. She was 9 months pregnant, ready to deliver any day now. I would have to juggle my unit patients' needs with her needs in the event she went into labor during this rotation, which seemed pretty likely.

I had first met Roxanne during her second month of pregnancy. She came in asking for birth control pills, and I asked her if there was any way she could be pregnant. She insisted that there was no way, since she wasn't having sex. My exam didn't reveal any abnormalities – it was still too early to feel the baby growing. I started her on the pills, and sent her packing.

She showed up in her 22nd week, complaining of a sore throat. She wore loose clothing to conceal her growing tummy. I smelled a rat when I noticed how full her breasts had suddenly become, and I pulled up her sweater to look at her chest and abdomen. That's when I first knew she was pregnant. I was worried – I'd given her a good three and a half months of birth control pills – what effects would they have on the baby? I was so mad at Roxanne's idiocy that I could scream – she could ruin me just by having a bad baby – despite my careful questioning before I had given her the pills.

Her cervix was beginning to dilate, and the baby's head had dropped – good signs of impending labor – so I told Roxanne to call me the minute she had any contractions. I thought back to the ultrasounds I had ordered to check for any abnormalities of the baby; one of them had showed some possible kidney damage. I was definitely worried about this delivery. I had done close to 200 deliveries already, after four months on the OB service, but this pregnancy outcome had my career riding on the line if that baby was bad.

My next patient was Deb Stine, a 25-year-old mother of one, who'd had 3 miscarriages in a row, and now was pregnant again. I examined her; she was about 10 weeks along; we set up the normal tests, classes, and appointment schedule, and I gave her my home phone in case she had any questions or needed me during the evening. That was the thing I enjoyed about family practice – having patients of my own, whom from time to time would call me in the evenings about problems they were having, and questions. It made it all the more fun to come to this place and see these people time and time again, and get to know everything about them. For the most part, they were poor, on welfare, and satisfied with their lot; most of them were happy just to survive day to day.

Phyllis Minter, my next patient, was a typical example of the chronic repeaters I had. She was 45, had severe hypertension, and was in every other week with one ailment or another. I'd put her in the hospital four times within the past 13 months; she'd had her gallbladder out, a cardiac catheterization for a suspected heart attack that turned out to be a false alarm, a bad uterine infection, and severe contusions suffered when she was robbed while walking down the sidewalk.

Phyllis was an obese, short, jolly lady, and she was always getting robbed. She'd been robbed seven times since I met her. She was a born-again Christian who walked into the clinic each time shouting, "Praise Jesus" and beaming bright as the sun, when ironically she was desperately poor: she was ineligible for welfare because her daughter had violated some provision, and she had no money for her costly blood pressure meds, and between the robbings and beatings and hospitalizations, she was being squeezed for every penny she owned. Often I would end up calling a drug salesman to ask for some free sample meds to give her to get her through until next time.

As usual, Phyllis Minter was happy to see me, and although her pressure was high enough that I feared she might have a stroke one of these times, she pasted a smile on her face and said, "whatever my Lord gives me as a cross to bear, he'll give me the strength to bear it. Praise Jesus!"

Phyllis was in her own little world, a world most of us would have committed suicide rather than survive within. Her optimism rubbed off on everybody.

Karen Ende, my next patient, was 23. Her husband, Pat, had been fighting with her since the day they married four years ago, but now she was in because she'd been knocked out by her husband and had had a seizure. I told her that things had gotten out of hand – it was time to get help. Maybe next time she wouldn't get off with just a seizure.

As usual, Karen refused to press charges or get outside help. This frustrated me, but was typical of many patients of mine who excused their spouse's behavior rather than rock the boat. It really bothered me, but what could I do?

In Karen's case, not only was her husband Pat abusive, but she was abusive to him as well. During their present fight, she'd grabbed the phone, pulled it right off the wall, and threw it at him; it had hit him in the face and gashed him deeply in the forehead. I put four stitches in him in the ER one night a week ago. Another time she had stabbed him with a knife.

17.30

I arrived back at the MRICU for an update on my players. Jennifer Lakein was having problems. She was in atrial fibrillation – why was that? I thought about the many causes for atrial fib, which included thyrotoxicosis, alcoholism, valvular heart disease, none of which seemed probable in her.

Why the sudden change? Could it be a pulmonary embolism? I checked her blood gases. Yes, the pO2 had dropped precipitously. Maybe that was it.

She'd thrown a clot to her lungs, and the atrial fib resulted. The atrial fib was of minor concern – it was easily treated, and played little part in this burgeoning drama; the big question was the <u>cause</u> of this problem, which might evolve to more serious problems.

I ordered a lung scan on her, and I was fairly convinced that it would demonstrate a blood clot in her lungs. It was inconclusive. Reason: it suggested a collapsed lung on the left, and couldn't be interpreted because of that. We looked at her X-ray – yes, there was definitely a mild pneumothorax on the left. I called in Vic Waters: she would need a chest tube.

When Vic arrived, he demurred, then posed the following suggestion: "I don't think this is a PE, Rich. I think she's got a lung abscess."

"Hmmm, maybe that would explain the fevers, the atrial fib, the sudden drop in pO2… maybe you're right, Vic. But a PE is still my guess."

"Well, let's put in a chest tube, and see if we can pull out any lung contents – maybe we'll find some pus to prove me right," Vic replied.

18.30

I made the incision in between her fourth and fifth ribs, and spread the muscle layers with a curved hemostat, and pushed downward with the nose of the instrument until I felt a pop as I reached the lung cavity. I then grabbed the thick-walled plastic tube between the nose of the curved hemostat, and jammed it into her lung cavity. I was amazed to see pus come shooting out through the tube – so much that it shot clear up to the ceiling with tremendous force – and it stunk to high heaven. We quickly hooked her up to the chest tube pump and began the suction. Within half an hour, more than two quarts of pus had been drained from her left lung cavity. It was fetid and foul and turned my stomach into a queasy knot. But because it was successful I overlooked my discomfort. A repeat X-ray showed that the lung was re-expanded, and her atrial fibrillation had suddenly converted back to a normal sinus rhythm.

Vic was cheering like a cowboy riding a wild steer. "Yahoo, I knew it, I knew it!"

Seeing that pus shoot out of her chest was very satisfying for me. Not only was it fun to put the chest tube in, since I had so little experience doing it, but it felt as if I was squeezing one giant zit for all it was worth, and the more pus that came out, the better I felt about it. Jennifer's arterial gases improved tremendously, and within an hour, her fever was beginning to drop.

20.00

I was sitting at home in my apartment feeling good about Jenny Lake's turn for the better, when the phone rang. It was Roxanne Fabian. She was in early labor. Her contractions were 15 minutes apart. I told her to go to the hospital – St. Francis – to be checked out by the nurses. It was too early for her to go, but I figured Roxanne would procrastinate, so I was compensating for that.

23.30

The OB station at St. Francis, where the residents did all their deliveries, called. Roxanne Fabinot had arrived. Her contractions were strong, but 12 minutes apart. She would be waiting awhile. I told them to call me when she began to dilate.

00.30

Deb Stine called. She was having abdominal pains, and spotting. I could have told her to sit them out and wait a few days, but by coincidence Roxanne was in early labor, so I decided to kill two birds with one stone. I told Deb to hurry over to the St. Francis ER and I would meet her there.

01.00

I met Deb and examined her in the ER. She was indeed bleeding – a miscarriage. The fetal tissue – the membranes and tiny fetus – was caught at the opening of the cervix, holding it open so that more bleeding could occur. She could bleed to death if this continued, because it could become massive suddenly. I remembered a case as an intern when I had experienced a patient like that, where a lady bled profusely, went into shock, and was dying right before my eyes. On that previous occasion I had called an obstetrician on the phone, frantic for guidance, and he told me to pull the fetal tissue out of the cervix before she bled to death. I did, she stopped bleeding, and survived. It had been a close call though – she was white as a sheet from the massive blood loss.

Now here lay Deb, faced with the same danger. The blood was coming out at a fast trickle. I grabbed a sterile forceps and teased the fetal tissue free from the cervix. I saw the tiny little outline of a fetus the size of my fingernail; I had just performed a therapeutic abortion. Technically, I had just completed it – it was already separated from the lining of the uterus – still, it left me feeling kind of spooky.

I bedded Deb down for the night, and told her that she would need a D&C in the morning – a good scraping of the inside lining of her uterus – to ensure that all the fetal contents had been expelled to avoid a festering uterine infection or continued bleeding. I would do the D&C, but I would need staffing from an attending doc, and it was impractical to call someone in at this time of night.

It was funny – they didn't allow us to do D&Cs without staffing, but we delivered babies all the time without supervision. Seemed odd to me. (*Editor's note*: nowadays, there is RARELY a time when a resident can perform even a simple procedure without a staff doctor immediately present and available in the same room. Times have certainly changed)

171

02.00

I visited Roxanne, the gal in early labor. Her cervix was dilated to 4 centimeters – she was moving fast for a first-timer. Maybe we'd have the baby by morning – I hoped so. I wondered if there would be any birth defects – I was scared about how I was going to defend myself with this one. After all, I had prescribed her birth control pills when she was 4 weeks pregnant, all because she had told me she wasn't having sex, so I hadn't done a pregnancy test. She had taken the pills all the way until 22 weeks into her pregnancy.

02.20

I drove home to my apartment for some catnaps.

05.15

The labor suite called. Roxanne Fabinot was completely dilated. They were so swamped with work there that they'd forgotten to call me at 8 centimeters. She was being wheeled back to the delivery room – the intern on-call was up and ready to help – I should come right over. BLAST! I was pissed to the max. I knew I should have stayed there and waited, but I was trying to act like a staff doc and stay away until the last minute. Dr. Griesy would never have approved of that. I remembered his admonition as I sped into St Francis Hospital: stay with the mother through the labor – that's when the real doctoring takes place.

I had been sleeping in my scrub clothes, so I threw on a white coat and flew out to my car moments after I hung up the phone. The hospital was 3 miles down the road, with 3 red lights in between. I screeched my tires and laid rubber as I took off, despite the hour, and drove 65 miles an hour down the street in a 30 mph zone, and I ran all 3 red lights. The road was bare of any other cars anyway, and I figured it was the only time I could legally play Mad Max and get away with being a speed demon. Besides, I wanted to be on hand for this delivery – it was especially crucial to me – this baby might be messed up.

05.23

I ran up the stairs to the delivery room on third floor, and found Stev Sirus, the intern, anesthetizing Roxanne's bottom for the episiotomy. The patient sighed in relief as she saw me enter the room. "Oh good, my doctor's here, now I can have my baby," she said. It made me feel surprisingly good even though I considered her a real dirtball of a person – she was affirming to me what family practice thrived on – that doctor-patient rapport that came with knowing and trusting each other.

Steve re-positioned himself so that I could get at her bottom and do the delivery, but I handed him the towel and gave him the nod: this one was his. I just wanted to watch – and pray – that it went well.

Finally, the urge came to push, and Steve guided the baby out slowly. I wanted so much to do it myself, but I fought back the urge to interfere, much as Dr. Griesy must have had to do with me way back when. The baby – a boy – came out looking healthy as can be, and I breathed a huge sigh of relief. Steve then checked the uterus and cervix for tears, a routine procedure, and we proceeded to sew up her episiotomy. I supervised while he sewed, and when it was done twenty minutes later, the placenta delivered. He delivered that as well, and I did an exam of her uterus then to check one last time.

Right then, my heart dropped. Her uterus was still unusually large, given that the baby and placenta were already delivered. Why was the uterus still this big? I could feel a large bulge in her uterus. Then it hit he like a brick- it was another baby. My God, it was dead. The realization broke me into a cold sweat and I felt faint. We had killed the second baby by giving the pitocin, the drug that contracted the uterus down after the delivery was over.

I had left the intern Steve to do the first check, so I wasn't immediately aware of the extra bulge – now it was big and plain as day. (*Editor's note:* back in those days, we didn't yet have ultrasounds readily available for pregnancy care; in fact most of my OB patients never had an ultrasound during pregnancy. Therefore, it was not uncommon to discover twins or other unusual findings immediately at the time of delivery.)

In that moment, I lived a thousand lives, atoned for a thousand sins, and died a thousand deaths. It's the moment of truth that every doctor secretly fears: the moment when all responsibility rests on you and you alone, that moment when you know you must act or lose your patient to catastrophe, yet you don't know what to do. I felt really, really sick inside. This was one mistake that would stigmatize me for life. The error was squarely on my shoulders as the supervising physician. And it was too late to erase...

Just then, Dr. Pagodas, one of the OB men, came by to start his morning rounds. I asked a nurse to grab him and whisk him in here pronto. I explained my concern to him, and he donned a pair of gloves and examined her. He kept his hand in her vagina for a good five minutes, obviously very puzzled by what he was feeling.

Finally, after what seemed an eternity, he removed his hand from her vagina. He looked at me. "It's not a baby – it's a fibroid, I think.

Considering the estrogens you gave her early in pregnancy with that birth control pill, that makes the most sense – it probably grew to large proportions under the influence of the extra estrogen."

I thanked him for his help, and breathed an enormous sigh of relief. It had been only five minutes of psychological trauma, yet in that ephemeral elapse I'd sweated more than I had in the past two months combined. Maybe OB wasn't my thing. I could do without out it when I finished residency, I thought to myself. The thought didn't last long, though, when I thought of all the good times I'd had in this labor room.

I didn't allow Roxanne to see her baby. I was trying to talk her into putting him up for adoption, so I didn't want her to start bonding with him. That had happened so many times before: I'd had the girls ready to give their illegitimate babies up for adoption, then they'd held them in their arms for a few moments, and changed their minds, and presto, we had another load for the welfare rolls.

Roxanne was definitely too immature for kids, and fortunately I had convinced her of that much at least. I still couldn't convince her to use birth control when it was all over; she was thinking of waiting a few months, and then "getting knocked up again so I have something to do with my time."

Just before we finished re-sewing the stitches on Roxanne's bottom – we'd torn our episiotomy repair down to allow Dr. Pagedas to examine her – the phone rang. It was ICU at Luke's – Tim Kross, the 17-year-old who had attempted suicide by carbon monoxide, was seizing again. I asked them to get a blood level of his dilantin, and gave him an extra dose right then.

While I was on the phone with them, and watching Steve finish the

174

episiotomy repair sutures, the nurse handed me the other phone – it was the nurse downstairs – my miscarriage lady Deb Stine's a.m. hematocrit was back – 27. I told them to give her 2 units of packed red blood cells and schedule her for a D&C later in the morning. I would have to try to make it back here in between rounds in the ICU. That would be a trick.

07.15

As I left for St. Luke's, I realized that my car was plowed under. It had just started snowing, and the plow had come through already, and I was blocked. I shoveled for a few minutes with a clipboard I had in the back seat of my station wagon, and dug my way free. It was light out already. Time for another day. Spring was coming, I reminded myself. Spring was coming.

Tuesday, Day #5

07.45

I started rounds with a big surprise. Richard Sink, Dr. Wally's leukemia patient, was conscious again, and seemed alert enough to understand what we were saying to him. His progress, albeit a slow crawl, was very heartening.

Next to him, Tim Kross lay one room over, still unconscious from his carbon monoxide overdose, and giving no indication that he would ever change.

What a dilemma! When did we draw the line and say he'd had enough time to show progress? Sink had been out of it more than a week! Then again, Mr. Sink had an obvious reason for it, a reason that was turning around; his cause of unconsciousness was due to his illness, which was reversible. Tim Kross's cause for unconsciousness was reversible only if attended to early enough. It appeared that we hadn't been in time to save him. Now, how did we convince the family of that?

Susan Grimes, the gal with myasthenia, looked good. She sat up in bed with her respirator tube, complaining that she wanted it out. I was so happy to see her progress. I turned her oxygen down to room air, and figured that was a good start toward weaning her off the machine.

After going over things with Vic, I rushed back to St Francis for Deb

175

Stine's dilatation and curettage – D&C – where the cervix gets dilated by inserting progressively fatter rods into its opening, and once dilated, the uterus gets scraped vigorously to remove any adherent contents remaining from the conception. When all of the lining of the uterus had been removed, the scraping tool makes a grating sound on the muscle of the uterine wall, and that's our signal to stop. We call that scraping sound the "uterine cry".

Dr. Fritz supervised me as I did Deb's D&C, and it went uneventfully. Fritz was a nice guy, and had helped me immensely by allowing me as much hands–on experience as he could; the only drawback to working with him was that he had four daughters with ages close to mine, and he was always trying to set me up with one of them. I'd already dated three of them on a one-time basis; they were all cute, and seemed fun, but I knew right away after the first date with each of them that there was no long-range potential. Yet, every time Fritz and I scrubbed on a case together, we'd be standing there at the sink, talking about his daughters.

As we were finishing up our case, I noticed that in the next room, Dr. Garanamis was scrubbing for his D&C case. The guy really disturbed me. He was epileptic, and took medication for it, but he made a habit of drinking on top of it. He would often show up for a delivery with alcohol on his breath, but the nurses would hush it up by saying it was just his seizure medications. I knew better. I knew the smell of alcohol.

One night, he'd come in to do an emergency D&C, and I was supposed to help him, since I was the intern on call. He wobbled down the hall, and his breath was toxic with spirits. I told the nurses not to light any matches, or we'd all go up in flames, and I went in on the operation with him only out of concern for his patient, who was unaware of his state of inebriation. I was flaming mad at him, but since I was an intern, I didn't know how to express it without losing my job.

The following day I had gone to see the director of the OB department, and we'd discussed this man. The director informed me that the OB department knew full well of his problem, but had decided to turn a blind eye to it. "We take care of our own, he said. Then told me that he'd take it under advisement; meanwhile, I was not to rock the boat.

Once I was back at the MRICU, I buried myself in the patient charts.

The head nurse Sue pinched my shoulder. "Dr. Mayerchak, what do you think?"

As I looked up at her, I noticed she was wearing a bowtie made out of cling, a gauze-like material used to wrap bandages. She was obviously mimicking – or was it mocking – my bowtie.

"We decided to make this 'Rich Mayerchak look-alike day'."

I looked around the Unit. Everybody had a bowtie on – all made of the white gauze. Every patient, every nurse, and even all the doctors that walked through the doors were getting them put on. Dr. Wally was sitting over by Mr. Sink, and even HE had a white gauze bowtie on. Dr. Wally? I was in shock. It was one of the most bizarre, yet gratifying, things that I'd ever seen. It made me realize that even Wally had some modicum of respect for me, even though he would probably not admit it.

I called the hospital public relations director and asked him to send a photographer up right away – I had to get a picture of this. We got a group photo, and then the nurses took me to lunch in the caf wearing their white ties, me in my black bowtie. It was then that I knew I was accepted into their circle; I was a member of the Unit.

13.45

15.15

Another outside page. It was Emily Vance, my lady with breast cancer who had been operated on last year. Earlier this year, about a year after her surgery, we'd found a mass in her lung; the cancer had come back in both breasts, and now in her lung. She was calling to say that she had a fever and was weak, and had shortness of breath. I told her I'd be over to do a house call later in the afternoon. For the past 2 months, Emily had been unable to walk to the clinic, so I'd been stopping in to see her on my way home.

17.45

I went up to the call rooms – I was too tired to drive home – and crashed for however long they would leave me undisturbed. It was such an unsettling feeling not knowing if that would be 2 hours or 2 minutes. I didn't want to fall sound asleep and get woken immediately.

The next thing I knew, I was awake. What time was it? 5:30 a.m.

Wow – I'd slept the better part of 12 hours, almost straight through. How ironic, I thought to myself, to get that much sleep in the hospital call room! Now I was hungry. I decided to get some breakfast at the coffee shop, and get an early start on rounds, so I could get Boy Fabinot's circumcision done. Then I remembered – Emily Vance! I had forgotten to do my house call! It was too early to call. I made a note of it and decided to do it after the circumcision.

Wednesday, Day #6

06.15

I started rounds, and Susan Grimes was wide awake. She wanted her endotracheal tube out. I looked at her gases, and they looked fine. I told her I'd discuss it with Vic, and moved on to Jenny Lake, the obese diabetic with the abscess in her lungs, what we refer to as "empyema". She too was looking better. Her chest tube was continuing to drain pus, but only at a nominal rate. She was one lucky lady, it seemed. I was of the opinion that she'd brought most of this misery upon herself, by being the obese slob that she was, allowing herself to gain that much weight. Walter Gould, too, had been his own undoing, drinking as heavily as he had. They had had many warnings, and many opportunities to change their ways, so their outcomes now were more or less deserved. Tim Kross, the teen suicide attempt, was less accountable, though. He'd done himself in, but it was a sudden mistake, a warped perspective after his girlfriend had dumped him, which led him to his error. It could happen to anybody. I had more sympathy for him than for any of the others – except maybe Susan Grimes, with the myasthenia, who had no control of her plight, and Richard Sink, who woke up one morning with leukemia.

When Vic arrived, I asked him whether he thought we could pull Susan's tube. He agreed to give it a whirl. We extubated her and, for the first time, I heard her gasp out a word of thanks. It was raspy, rough, and obviously painful, because her vocal cords and voice box had been through a beating with her tube in place. We cautioned her not to talk for a while. By golly, another day here, and I might be able to send her to a ward bed, I thought.

On my way out, I stopped in medical records to fill out my paperwork and sign charts. Sue, the records clerk, flirted with me every time I visited the department to sign my charts. Today I noticed that she was wearing a tight sweater and a skirt with dark nylons – whoa, things were starting to get carried away in my mind. On a sudden whim, I asked her to go to a movie later tonight. She smiled and told me she would look forward to it.

11.00

I stopped over to see Emily Vance at her home. She appeared emaciated and wan. She had a fever of 102, and was breathing shallow breaths, with obvious pain. I listened to her lungs, and noted that she had rales midway up both lung fields – water in her lungs, either from the tumor, or from congestive heart failure – probably from the tumor. I gave her a shot of lasix, to help her lose some water, and a shot of penicillin for what sounded like pneumonia in the right lung. She was not able to keep any food down, from the nausea.

Emily looked to be about 75 pounds lighter than when I had first met her a year ago. Most of the weight had come off in the last 3 months. She was nearing her end stages, I knew. It reminded me of that saying: "I complained because I had no shoes, until I met a man who had no feet."

And what a way to go! I looked around her at the mess she lived in – an old house in the Polish section of the south side of Milwaukee. The house was sadly in need of repair, with three broken windows covered over with cardboard, a broken screen door lying on the porch, no lights on in the house, large holes in the sofa in the living room, a broken TV, and six people running around the house. She was the mother of eight, six of whom still lived in her house, even though some of them were grown adults. Two of the guys had their girlfriends living there also, and I saw one of them come out of the bedroom with her hair in curlers. It was quite a scene to behold.

Emily had been married to a man who eventually went to prison; when he was released, she divorced him to raise her kids without his bad influence.

I knew as I left her that she would soon need hospice care; I wasn't allowed to admit her to a hospice unless I could guarantee in writing that she would die within 30 days – that was the new state statute. Maybe now was the time. I asked her about it. She didn't know what to say. I told her to think about it, and we set up a time to discuss it tomorrow night – we'd have a family conference and talk it out with everyone. I left her home feeling like a real country doctor – it was a good feeling knowing that I was doing all that anyone could, and making medicine accessible to someone for whom doors were closed more often than not. Even though I knew the outcome was decided already – against her – I thought of the sign that hangs in the ICU "Caring is more important than curing". How appropriate.

14.00

They admitted a 36 year old guy from the ER with hepatitis – and he was vomiting, so his nurse asked me to place a nasogastric tube down his nose into his stomach. I was in the process of placing the tube down his nostril when I felt a sudden urge to yawn – it was that time of the afternoon. I yawned as I advanced the tube, and suddenly he vomited a mouthful of blood and vomitus, as the tube hit his esophagus. Since I was leaning over him, I swallowed some of the upchuck as I yawned, and then I realized with horror that this man was jaundiced – yellow from head to toe – he had hepatitis. I had just come into intimate contact with his secretions. I was mortified.

In that brief moment, two horror stories flashed through my mind. The first, a recollection of an intern at the University of Minnesota from my med school days, a guy who had stuck himself with a needle that had touched a man with hepatitis. The intern got hepatitis and died from it, and his wife and kids were left out in the cold – no insurance, nothing but sympathy from his residency program.

I also remembered the intern who had been doing a spinal tap, and the fluid had gushed out under such high pressure that a drop had splashed into his eye. The patient he was tapping turned out to have Jacob-Creutzfeldt disease, a rare degenerative neurologic disease which ends with death in less than a year – the intern came down with the same disease and died a year later.

Now I needed help. I called Brian Buggy, the infectious disease man, for advice. Brian told me that I was in good shape – this man probably had alcoholic hepatitis, which was different from serum hepatitis, which was the kind I was worried about. I smiled. I knew that – why hadn't I realized that? I had panicked. Buggy recommended drawing some blood tests and leaving it at that – if anything showed up, there would be time to deal with it. I sighed in relief. This job was fraught with many unpublicized hazards that nobody ever told me about when I was 4 years old and told my daddy that I wanted to be a doctor.

19.30

Time for my date. I picked up the gal from the St Francis medical records department, Sue. I hoped the Unit would stay quiet for 90 minutes. I'd asked them to hold all calls except for emergencies until I called them at 10 p.m. I was learning the tricks of sanity survival.

Sue showed me around her apartment, and we sat on the sofa to talk for a few minutes. All of a sudden, I heard someone fiddling with the lock on her back door.

"What is it, Sue? Do you have a roommate?"

"No… uhh.. listen, just stay here, and promise you won't go, okay? Please, promise you won't go!" She looked worried. That definitely worried me.

"Okay, I promise." I got my feet ready for a quick bolt out the front door if I had to – what in the heck was this all about? Something was weird here. I heard her talking with a man, and then suddenly they were in the living room.

"Rich, this is Jamie. Jamie, this is Rich."

I recognized the man – an anesthesiologist from St. Francis Hospital.

I knew this man was married, so what was he doing here? I told Sue it was time to go, and pulled her toward the front door. We went to a movie, and she explained.

"Jamie and I have been having …"

"Say no more – I figured it out at the house."

"But you see, I was married until a year ago. Jamie's wife doesn't understand him, and I'm good for him. I was lonely all those nights… I decided to go out with you 'cause I want to break it off with him."

I laughed to myself. It was always something. Why was someone as cute as she was throwing it all away on a married man who had the best of both worlds?

After I took her home, I stopped inside for a minute. I noticed that her large color TV and several other large furniture pieces were missing. She explained that Jamie must have borrowed them, but I knew better. Jamie was just taking back his presents now that his sugar baby had dumped him.

181

As I arrived back at my house I stared at the vacant lot full of snow and felt sad to realize that Arne wouldn't be there watering his massive garden this summer. And then I smiled. A wave of realization came across me like an epiphany. I had a sudden gift of knowledge that told me that not only would I survive this grueling rotation, but the residency itself; the day to day uncertainty that I'd lived with was tamed. I was beyond the halfway point of my marathon. From here on in, my crises would broaden, but not break me. I was learning from every failure, and moving on. If I put in my time, I would walk away from here with my Family Practice specialty degree. There was no doubt of it. Where I would find a woman to share it with, I couldn't begin to guess; maybe I wouldn't. Nevertheless, spring was coming. Fire up! Spring was almost here.

Editor's comment:
Richard Sink, Dr. Wally's patient with leukemia, walked out of the MRICU a week later, and lived another 8 months before succumbing to his leukemia. Susan Grimes, with myasthenia, left the hospital two days before that, and she continued to do well for as long as I was a resident. None of the other patients survived, including Tim Kross, the 17-year-old who had attempted suicide.

SENIOR YEAR OF RESIDENCY

St. Luke's Hospital The Final Weeks Summer 1984

Milwaukee, Wisconsin

I spent my final month as senior resident on the medical service where I began- the medicine ward – 6JK with Dr. Parent.

I was in the hallway talking to Konrad when his medical student named Michelle walked over. They were discussing a patient they'd just seen.

Konrad pointed to Michelle: "Rich, do you have any interesting patients on your schedule that my student Michelle might want to see with you?"

I looked at Michelle. She was gorgeous – tall, with dark, curly hair, thin, a pretty face – but she wore a little too much makeup, if that could be considered a fault. Boy, if the year wasn't so close to ending! I thought.

Much too late to start something personal, though. I would be leaving this town forever in a short time. I decided that the best path would be to ignore her. It had taken three years to gain this wisdom, but I had it now.

I replied. "Naw, I really can't think of anyone she would want to see, Con-Man– just a bunch of dull follow-ups."

"Oh, that's okay – maybe another time. C'mon Michelle, let's see my next one." He left with her. I hurried on to finish spying on my interns before rounds with Dr. Parent at 2 p.m.

I scanned the list of clinic patients I would be seeing today. Joe Vance, son of Emily Vance, whom I'd followed from diagnosis until her death from breast cancer 8 months ago, was first. It was painful being reminded of her death and miserable life preceding it, but I realized that it had taught me a lot about the continuity of care that can be offered by a family doctor, who learns to back story to so many of his patients over the years of the relationship.

Another of my regular clinic patients was Roxanne Fabinot, the gal I had delivered last year while covering the ICU. She was now coming in far too often for it to be coincidence. Last night, her mother had called me at the hospital to tell me that Roxanne was in love with me. I realized that today's clinic appointment would be her attempt to express that to me. Fortunately, I was leaving Milwaukee soon – that would solve the problem.

14.00

We waited in the conference room for Jerry Parent to show. Two of the residents were laughing because they'd just played the bingo pager prank on the chief of surgery. I had a good group of guys – it was the end of their internship year, so they were sharper, and more relaxed – we'd had a lot of good times —despite it being medicine wards – together.

14.15

Jerry Parent strode in briskly.

"Sorry I'm late, Rich. How much business do we have?"

"Oh, hi, Jerry. No one to staff – no admits last night. Dan is the luckiest intern I've ever seen. That's three times now, huh Dan?"

Dr. Parent smiled.

183

Just then, Konrad walked in. "Hi, Dr. Parent – do you mind if I drop off this med student with you – she wanted to see you do rounds – her name is Michelle – from the medical college – she's just finished her first year of med school, and is doing a summer externship with us."

Dr. Parent nodded in approval. "No problem, Konrad – glad to have her.

Welcome, Michelle."

There she was again, in her short white lab coat and pink and white striped summer dress. It was hard to keep from noticing her, but I knew it was best to ignore her as much as possible.

"Okay, gang, let's run the list and get out of here," Jerry said.

I started. "Fine with me, Jerry – I've got a meeting with the town of Clarkfield this afternoon. It's a small town in western Minnesota. They really want to hire me."

"Just be sure you know what the town's like – visit it and get a better feel before you get yourself into something bad, Rich." Jerry was acting like my father or older brother.

"Well, it doesn't hurt to listen – they're buying me supper – what do I have to lose?"

Jerry laughed. "Everything. Now let's run the list. Jon Sipes."

Dan cleared his throat. "Jon is the 35-year-old with chest pain admitted yesterday with a diagnosis of rule out MI."

"How did his serial electrocardiograms change?" asked Parent. "Well, I didn't look at them yet, but…"

I butted in to rescue my intern, much as Jill Harman had once rescued me. "No change, Jerry – all three showed sinus rhythm, with no ST-T changes or any signs of ischemia,"

Dan looked at me gratefully. I remembered back to my days as an intern when I could never guess what Jerry was going to ask, or what seemed important to remember. Now it seemed so easy to remember the numbers, the facts about all of the interns' patients, because I knew what was important to focus on.

I noticed Michelle sitting by herself. She wore a ring on her left fourth finger – did that mean she was engaged? Probably. She was too pretty not to be dating someone. It was just as well. The last thing I needed at this point in my life was a romance.

184

Clarkfield Interview 1984

After rounds, I met with the delegation from Clarkfield, Minnesota, for supper at the Hoffmann House at the Midway Motor Lodge. They had flown in on a private chartered plane. The group consisted of the chief of police, the mayor, the president of the local school board, and the sole doctor from town, Dr. Gene, who was in his late sixties. I was surprised to discover that all of the other men were young, in their thirties and forties. We discussed their town's need for a physician, and the benefits of their proposed contract, and I promised that I would visit them later in the summer. They offered me a guaranteed income of $80,000 for my first year, $90,000 for the second, and $100,000 for the third year, in addition to a signing bonus of 10% ownership in the nursing home. The home was worth $2 million, so my stake in the nursing home for signing the contract was worth $200,000. Then, after a mere 90 minutes of chatting, they were ready to leave, and I excused myself to go to the restroom. Dr. Gene followed me in there and looked me squarely in the eye with a stern gaze.

"If you want my advice, Rich, turn down this offer," he said.

"Why?"

"You're fresh out of residency, wide-eyed and bushy-tailed. The kind of medicine you've learned is a long time away from coming to Clarkfield. The most sophisticated lab results we can get in town is a CBC and a urinalysis. We have X-ray facilities, but none of the modern equipment you've been trained to use. We make diagnoses by looking at patients without the aid of CAT scans and blood gases. I don't dispute the value of the technologic lab advances, but the smaller towns will probably always lag behind in getting to use them."

Dr. Gene continued his stern warning. "I'm warning you – you'll regret moving to a small town. Medicine in Clarkfield is different than anything you've trained for. We don't have fetal monitors for delivering babies, and we don't have respirators for people needing ICU care. Most of the people needing that kind of help either get whisked to the big cities by chopper, or they just don't make it.

"The biggest reason for me dissuading you is that you're young, single, and let's face it – you'll never find a suitable woman with an educational background compatible with you – you need to be married before you'll be able to survive in a small town."

I thanked Dr. Gene for his advice, and decided that he was probably right. Still, in the back of my mind, I was sure I wanted to live and practice in a small town. I decided that I would give it a look-over sometime, and thanked them all for flying out to interview me.

During the evening, I went over to St. Luke's to type up some journal notes. I'd been keeping a journal since the first day of med school, and in it were numerous stories of people and events that made medicine so interesting. The only way to keep up with it was by steadily recording it, instead of waiting months and then typing it all at once.

I was typing on the ninth floor – when I suddenly heard: CODE 4CODE 48 JK Room 8108 bed A.

I realized that it was directly below me, one floor down. Should I go to it? I was dressed in cutoff jeans and a torn T-shirt, with tennis shoes that had the sides ripped out of them. Of course I should! I was "Mr. Code"!! I made an instantaneous decision to fly down the stairwell and investigate.

I was the first one in the room, next to the nurse, along with the attending physician, who was shying away from his patient. He obviously wanted nothing to do with this code. I put the paddles of the defibrillator on the woman's chest, who was lying there unconscious. The monitor on the defibrillator showed V-fib, so I charged up the machine and zapped her with 300 joules. Her rhythm converted to sinus, and she immediately came to.

The entire sequence took less than 20 seconds from the time I'd entered the room.

The lady, a 70-year-old cancer patient, looked up at me and frowned. She saw my cutoffs and ragged shirt. "Who are you, young fella? You're not a doctor – get away from my bed!"

I felt like zapping her again – between the ears – but I graciously left the room, wrote a quick note in the chart, and made my apologies to her attending physician for my state of attire. I went back upstairs, and finished my journal, including the episode that had just occurred with the code. Little did I know that it would be my last code at St. Luke's, or that it would go that smoothly, or that it would someday become part of this story.

The following day, Friday, after rounds with Jerry Parent had ended, I sat at the table with my interns Dan, Larry, and Tim.

The med student Michelle sat across from us. Dan was asking Michelle if she was engaged. It piqued my interest.

"How can I be engaged when I'm not even dating anyone? Who has time for dating these days?" she answered demurely.

Dan nodded.

"Yeah, I know what you mean. There's plenty of time, though. You probably won't get married until after internship – that's the worst." Dan was giving her a realistic picture, unfortunately.

I was still keeping to myself, listening to them talk, but staring out the window. There were those pigeons again – dozens of them – sitting along the wall, sunning themselves. They were my ever-present reminder of my imprisonment here, but my sentence was almost over. Soon I would be as free as they were, but changed forever because of what had happened here.

I heard Michelle say something about playing the violin. This was interesting. I turned to look at her. What else did she do that she wasn't telling? I found myself wondering many things about this girl, young as she was, and late though it was for anything to happen between us.

Then Dan and Tim walked out to finish rounds and go home, and Larry got up to leave also. "See you later, Rich."

I looked down at my hands. Why was Michelle still sitting there?

Why hadn't she left at the end of rounds? What should I say? I made small talk.

"So, you play the violin, huh? I once wrote a few violin solos with piano accompaniment. I never did get to hear them played. I also wrote a piano work with a great violin part in the middle – as a matter of fact, there's a piano downstairs – would you like to hear it?"

"Sure," she echoed my enthusiasm.

I started to play. I fumbled and messed up a few notes, and decided to start over. Again, I fumbled through the first couple of bars.

"This is embarrassing, Michelle – I've played this song thousands of times, and I'm never nervous when I play in front of people."

I tried again and I regained enough composure to play the song through. All the while, a whirlwind of thoughts raced through me. Why was I so nervous? What was happening to me? What kind of spell did she place on me? I hadn't felt this uncomfortable playing in front of somebody since the first time I'd played for Toni six years earlier, during my second year of med school.

When I finished, she looked at me.

"That's a beautiful song. I really love the way you play."

"Would you like to play that solo part for me on your violin sometime?"

"Sure! When?"

"Well, how about this weekend? I'm going to Sheboygan tonight, and I'll be back on Sunday morning. How about sometime on Sunday?"

"Yeah, if I can get my new strings by then. The ones I have are shot."

"Well, what's your phone number? I'll call you."

She gave me her number as I walked her to her car out in the parking lot. I told her that I came from a large family, and we made some small talk that would otherwise have seemed meaningless, except that the intonations and inflections in her words told me much more than any words could have – she was feeling exactly the same as I was – something was happening here.

After watching her drive away, I sat outside the drive–around by the lobby of the hospital, where I'd nearly walked away from residency training on my first night on call. I waited for the senior resident who was to watch the house for the evening with the intern on call. As I sat there, Jerry Parent strolled out on his way to his car.

"On your way to Sheboygan again, Rich?"

"Yep, as soon as Konrad gets here for his call night."

Jerry frowned. "Why do you beat yourself into the ground with this moonlighting, Rich? You should be out enjoying the evening!"

"Yeah... Jerry, but it pays the rent... and besides, up until now, I haven't met anyone that I wanted to spend time with, so I'd rather get paid and learn some practical skills in the ER up there. Now, though, who knows... I just might be hanging it all up."

"Really? Mr. Moonlight, hanging it up? Finally had enough?"

"No, Jerry, I still love working the ER – it's very stimulating. But I think there may be a new woman in my life..." I was beaming.

"Yeah? That's great, Rich – let me know if things work out – you can bring her around for supper some night."

"Okay, Jerry... I have a feeling this one's going to work out – don't be a bit surprised if we take you up on your offer!"

Finally Konrad arrived to cover the hospital for the night and I was off on my way to Sheboygan. Darn!

I thought. Now I wished I didn't have to go. I was scheduled to cover the ER at St. Nicholas Hospital in Sheboygan, Wisconsin from 8 p.m.

Friday night until 8 a.m. on Sunday – a 36-hour shift for which they paid $20 an hour. The wages were only half of what the staff docs got, but I didn't complain, because it was a lot more than I made as a resident.

The drive to Sheboygan took me an hour. It reminded me of the drive from Duluth to Two Harbors; the road to Sheboygan paralleled the Lake Michigan shoreline. My mind was preoccupied with one thought – was there a point to getting involved with Michelle? Was she too young – she said she was 24, and I was almost 30. Would I be hurting her – and myself – by starting something that I had no intention of finishing? The thoughts were most unsettling.

Yet, there was a second group of thoughts that were even more engrossing. Who was she? Could she be the one I'd waited to find? She was definitely different than the girls I'd dated before – she had a certain air of innocence and morality to her that was lacking in most. She talked in a manner that displayed her intelligence and discipline. There was no doubt about it – I was intrigued.

When I got to Sheboygan, the ER was already hopping. My friend, Kent Jacobs, gave me the beeper and call room key. I could see that he was elated to be leaving this mess.

My beeper went off as I finished pulling up my scrub pants. "Dr. Mayerchak, come to ER, <u>STAT</u>."

As I jogged down the hallway toward the ER, the overhead PA system boomed the following message: "Dr. Mayerchak, STAT." Damn! Don't they know I'm on my way? I thought. I began to run down the hallway, my stethoscope dangling from my neck and my white coat flapping like a cape; my Nikes squeaked on the freshly waxed floor, and as I passed each patient room they peered out inquisitively to see what the fuss was about. I realized that this weekend was going to be a marathon, and I was grateful that I was in good physical shape. I would take it one mile at a time, one patient at a time. The residency had trained me to stay awake for long durations, and I sensed I would need every bit of that ability this weekend.

Rollie Preder, the p.m. ER supervisor, met me at the door.

"Bad accident coming in by ambulance, Rich. One person is dead, and two of the others are critical. Flight For Life is standing by for our call."

Flight For Life is the helicopter that is part of the Milwaukee County Hospital's trauma center program. The helicopter is equipped much like an ambulance, with a respirator, cardiac monitor and other life support equipment, and scarcely enough additional room for a pilot, a doctor, and a nurse, with a bunkbed type of arrangement for stacking one or two patients for transfer to the large trauma center on the Milwaukee county medical grounds. On three previous occasions, I'd shipped patients via this 'copter, but only one of the three had survived. Even so, the helicopter offered hope where otherwise there was none – all three patients would definitely have perished immediately without the sophisticated life support systems available in Milwaukee.

While we awaited the ambulance's arrival, I did a quick mental review of the ABCs of trauma support. A= airway, B= breathing, C= circulation.

After those three priorities are attended to, check the neurologic status – watch for cervical spine trauma. I psyched myself up for what might be a real ugly scene. One person was dead, one was unconscious, and another one was critical. That's the only news we'd heard on the radio. I began wishing I hadn't agreed to this moonlighting shift.

As we were waiting, Dr. Hermington, the local urologist, passed through the ER with his four-year-old son, who was doing rounds with his daddy.

"Do you think you'll need help, Rich?" he asked.

"Boy, it sure sounds like it – we've got two coming in – both bad.

Would you mind sticking around for a few minutes?"

"Not at all." I was relieved to hear that he would stay to help. I had learned early on to ask for help whenever possible. No longer was I afraid to admit my shortcomings or pretend that I could do it all alone.

The ambulance pulled up into the garage which was an appendage to the emergency room. I noticed that it was drizzling outside, a sort of cold, dreary late-June evening. The back door of the ambulance opened, and I saw five men empty out. Nobody seemed to know who was in charge, or to care they were on auto pilot at this point. All they wanted to do was to wheel their victim-charges into the more sophisticated surroundings of the Emergency Room. I looked at the victims. One was about nine years old, a boy. He was conscious, talking to the driver, and screaming to the emergency medical tech to not cut his brand new pants off.

The tech cut them off anyway, as he was lifted onto a rolling bed and into the ER. As he rolled by, I told them to put him in treatment room one. Dr. Herman went with the boy and began to evaluate him.

The other victim was a female, about fifteen years old, who seemed

190

semi-conscious. She appeared to be pretty badly hurt. Her right shoulder was obviously dislocated, from the way it was hanging, and her right upper arm appeared to be broken as well. She had two large gaping lacerations on her forehead, which I hardly noticed; I was much more concerned with her cardiorespiratory and neurologic status. Broken bones and lacerations always come last in trauma triage – the other stuff is the serious life-threatening stuff.

As I did a quick scan of her body, I noticed an irregularity to the back of her neck – possible cervical spine fracture, I noted to myself. Her spine was immobilized with heavy sandbags just in case. Her chest had a large protrusion underneath the skin just below the collarbone on the left side; possible rib fracture, and possible punctured lung, I thought. Her skin color was pale – she might have a pneumothorax.

Her heart sounded okay, but her belly was tense – probably internal bleeding – maybe a ruptured spleen, I thought. Her blood pressure was 100/65 and her pulse was 130, two very important clues implying internal hemorrhage.

Her lower legs were badly scratched, and the left knee had a deep gash in it. The left upper leg was distorted such that I assumed it was broken also. Her breath smelled of alcohol. The ambulance driver told me that she was 13, and that she had been driving.

My assessment was that she had multiple fractures and lacerations, all of which were the least of her problems. Her biggest problem was that she was disoriented and stuporous – she kept screaming because of the pain, but she would only half answer questions, and her eyes stared dysconjugately off to the upper right side of her head. She knew her name – Lynn – and she told us that she was 13 – but that's all she knew. I noticed that she moved all four extremities, which was a relief – no immediate neurological damage – but her rapid pulse and disorientation was disconcerting.

I asked Rollie to put in two lines. While he was doing that, I put a nasogastric tube in her stomach through her nose. As I passed it down, I heard breath sounds coming out of the tube – I had passed it into her lungs by mistake. I pulled it back as she choked out a dry "take it out", and I reinserted it past her epiglottis into her esophagus and into the stomach.

Immediately, the stomach contents were emptied into the suction bottle attached to the tube – bright red and coffee-ground colored liquid, the result

191

of intestinal bleeding.

Next, I put a catheter into her bladder, and again the contents that were removed were bright red. This girl was obviously bleeding from two sources internally, and most probably from the spleen or another abdominal organ as well. I opened up her IVs to pour in as much fluid as possible.

Next, I obtained a cervical spine X-ray. It showed no obvious fractures, but a chest X-ray showed a rib fracture and a broken collarbone and separated A-C joint. At this point, I went over to the adjacent room to see how her brother, Paul, was faring, and to see if I could get the story behind the accident.

Paul, the nine-year-old victim, was still talking to Dr. Hermington, but had a cervical spine fracture which forced him to lie perfectly still to avoid paralyzing himself for the rest of his life. He had several other broken bones, and several lacerations, but at least he was more alert than his sister.

The ER guy told me that his mother had been a passenger and was killed. Then another guy, a local policeman, informed me that a man, not a woman, had been killed. What was going on? Who knew the real story?

Finally, a farmer who lived near the accident site came forth to relate his version, the veracity of which was later corroborated: the girl, Lynn, was 17 years old, not 13. She had been driving, and her older brother had been the one killed in the accident. Another friend had been riding in the car, along with her brother Paul, who was here. The friend was in less serious condition, and had been taken to Memorial Hospital across town. Two others had been involved in the accident, and were picked up by a third ambulance and taken to Memorial as well. Lynn and Paul's mother was on her way here.

I called the Flight-For-Life helicopter crew and asked them to come for both kids, Paul because of his spinal fracture, and Lynn because of her serious internal bleeding and multiple fractures and dislocations. As we continued to stabilize them, the chopper arrived on the pad just outside the ER; it consisted of a slab of concrete just big enough to park two cars side by side.

The doctor and nurse emerged from the helicopter dressed in bright orange and blue jumpsuits, with dozens of tiny pockets attached to their jumpers, stuffed with scissors, pens, IV needles and every time-saving convenience they needed based on many previous trips. The pilot was similarly arrayed, but without the ostentatious pockets. All three of the crew

192

members were polite, professional, and crisp. They went right to work making their assessments and preparing the stretchers for transport to their copter. I envied them – what an exciting way to make a living, I thought. I likened them to gods, flying in from out of nowhere, promising to take these victims to inevitable cures from ultramodern technology. As they were preparing for transfer to the chopper, the mother of the two kids arrived at the ER. She was unaware of the death of her other son, and had no idea that Paul and Lynn were as critically injured as they were. As we took her to see them, she wasn't too alarmed about Paul, although in my estimation he had a very serious problem on his hands, perhaps a permanent paralysis from a spinal cord injury. Lynn recognized her mother for a second, and then reverted to her nonsensical rambling and moaning about the pain. Her mother told Lynn that she loved her as her daughter was whisked away toward the helicopter.

As I assisted loading them into the 'copter, I was amazed at how cramped they were – worse than a crowded submarine. Paul's wooden stretcher was stacked on top of Lynn, only inches above her chest. There was no room for any of the other members to switch places once they were situated.

As the helicopter started up, its big blades winding up with successively faster whoops, I watched as Dr. Hermington held the hand of his little boy and watched from a distance. It occurred to me that his little boy was totally unaware of the gravity of the situation. His daddy was just doing his job again, just another Friday at the office.

The helicopter always drew a crowd, and this time was no different. The captivated onlookers watched it lift off the ground and suddenly move off far into the distance over the edge of Lake Michigan. Its departure evoked a collective feeling of escape, and a sense of optimism. We were all there in that helicopter beside those patients.

When I found my way back inside the hospital, I noticed that three hours had passed since I'd arrived. I'd survived the trauma of the motor vehicle accident, but in its wake, the ER was full of inmates, people waiting to be seen that had arrived during the ruckus created by the accident.

The evening went briskly due to our steady stream of patients. Each patient was a blur by the time I reached the next room. Time flew by. Then suddenly it was lurched into the slow motion that happens when a real tragedy hits the door. On the gurney rolling through the door lay a 4 year old girl who'd been playing behind her dad's car in the driveway. He'd backed out of the driveway, not knowing she was there, because it was already dark outside. He'd run over her head, and his brother had noticed her there. Dad had immediately begun CPR. Now she lay there, not breathing, no pulse, with her skull crushed in.

I noticed that she was wearing a pretty blue jumpsuit, and her hair was tied in pigtails which half hid the bashed-in skull. Her pediatrician and two other doctors on staff at the hospital were in the room, so I quickly asked, "who will be running this code?" None of them spoke up. Instead, the four of us began doing CPR, tried to put in an IV, and acted busy rather than stating the obvious, which was that this girl was a hopeless case. The back of her head was bleeding and dripping out brain.

I thought to myself, "how stupid is this to be coding her, when she's dead beyond hope!" but I said nothing – here were three doctors who were saying nothing about quitting, so who was I to speak up? Then I realized that this was ridiculous – even if we did save her, there was nothing left to save –her brain was dripping all over the sheet. The surgeon was just getting his line ready to insert.

"STOP!!!", I yelled. "We need to call off this code."

I was stating the obvious fact that she was not going to survive; we all recognized that reality but no one was willing to vocalize it. My proclamation was quickly agreed upon by the others. Then I realized that they were waiting for someone to speak up, and I remembered that most of them were probably not as used to codes as I had been recently.

It was a sad scene facing the parents, especially the dad. I left that to the pediatrician. What a mess. The guy will probably never get in a car again without walking around the back of it twice. Of all the people who heard the story (it was in the local papers), everyone who talked to me had the same comment; the poor father! I thought it was interesting that very few said "poor little girl"– they all seemed to focus on the reality of what was left, instead of what was lost.

As we ushered that family into the library to talk to the priest and the pediatrician, the other became rooms stacked with new patients. The first one was a 104 year old man who was having trouble breathing. I got an X-ray he had a huge tumor in his lung – it was lung cancer without question. He was admitted to the hospital and he died a week later. He was a cute old man, and still pretty alert and functional, all the way until the end.

Then a lady came in having a miscarriage. Then a young man came in with nonstop seizures. Each of these patients would soon become a distant detail that I would later forget.

Mercifully, the ER shift ended on Sunday morning and I drove home to Milwaukee. I hadn't slept a wink. I reflected upon the events of the past several days. Working at the Sheboygan ER had been a good experience, but the last shift there had been the best ever, because it had demonstrated to me just how versatile I'd become after three years in the family practice residency. I was now very prepared to handle most of the acute problems that a family doc would face, even if working in an emergency room. I was no longer scared about what might roll through the door of the ER. I knew enough to keep any situation stabilized until I could call for specialized assistance.

I reflected upon the tragedy of discovering that little girl whose dad had backed over her with his car; there she was lying on the gurney, looking pristine and wearing the pretty blue bib overalls, and then seeing the crushed skull with her brains on the bedsheet… I could barely bring myself to remember it.

When I arrived back in Milwaukee, I called Michelle. I was dead tired but also anxiously hoping she would still go out with me this day.

"Hi, Michelle. This is Rich Mayerchak. How are you?"

"Fine… but, my violin is lousy. The strings won't be ready for a few days"

I was disappointed. Was this her way of telling me that she didn't want to go out? I decided to risk rejection and go for it.

"Gee, that's too bad. Well, how about going to a movie? I want to see that *Indiana Jones and the Temple of Doom*. Interested?"

"Sure!"

"Great!

As I hung up the phone, I realized just how excited I was.

I picked her up for the movie, and we both enjoyed it. When it ended, we drove down to the Bradford Beach on Lake Michigan, and sat with our feet in the sand, and talked.

"Have you ever been in love, Michelle?"

"Yes, but it hasn't ever lasted. Something's always come up after going out for a while. I think the guys get to feel threatened by my education. They're always trying to prove that they can handle it, but none of them has succeeded so far.

"Yeah, I can relate. Every time I go out with someone, they treat me as if I was a god or something. Their mothers have probably told them to marry a doctor, and so they look at me as a doctor instead of a person.

That's one thing that I've noticed that's different about you – you're not threatened by the fact that I'm a doctor. That's great."

We talked for several hours, then took a walk around Jackson Park.

We stayed out dancing until late that night. I realized that I was caught up in a whirlwind romance the likes of which I hadn't known since my days with Toni. I prayed that it would last.

My final week in Milwaukee flew by. Michelle and I saw each other every morning at the 7 a.m. resident lectures, after which I took her to see all of my patients at the clinic until noon. Then we had lunch, then went to rounds with Jerry Parent at 2 p.m. Each evening, we went out on a date and, in that manner, managed to spend 17 hours together each day. By Friday, we were addicted to each other.

At 2 p.m. on Friday, Jerry Parent walked into the 6JK conference room for my last session with him. He was on time, for a change.

"What's this? A little change in attire, guys?" Jerry was taken aback. We were all wearing Hawaiian shirts and sunglasses. One of the interns had a bedpan with him, and I wore it as a hat. It was a fitting way to run the list for the last time.

Before we went to staff the new admissions, Jerry insisted that we change our shirts. We reluctantly complied. Keep a low profile, I reminded myself.

"How's your ex-roomie John Holtan doing out in private practice, Rich?"

"He seems to enjoy it, Jerry."

"That's nice. Are you going to Laurie Kuehn's wedding? Kate and I will be there."

"No, Jerry, I have an interview in Clarkfield. I'm excited about seeing the town."

Jerry gave me one last word of advice. "Just think about it awhile before jumping into anything, Rich."

"Yeah, I will." I was sad to be leaving Dr. Parent's service for the last time. He was a Mensch. Under his tutelage I had learned to treat every patient as a human being first, beginning my history and physical exam with

196

the taking of their social history. I was especially focused on performing a thorough physical exam, because I knew that Jerry Parent just might recheck something I had done. It kept me accountable, and made me a better clinician.

On my way out of the hospital for the last time ever, it felt eerily similar to the day I'd graduated from high school. I strolled down the hallway to the entrance of the ER. I recalled my first night on call, when I'd almost walked away from medicine for good, but walked back in to the ER to repair that bloody head laceration. That was the moment when I became a doctor. But then I remembered Agnes Kinsey, the lady who had died because of my error in reading her chest X-ray. And I remembered my failed attempt to resuscitate my neighbor Arne when he collapsed in the snow in his backyard. Each of my many errors and failures had taught me something. And I knew that there was no way in hell I would ever make the same mistakes again. But the biggest lesson I had learned was that I couldn't be ashamed to ask questions of others even when the questions indicated my ignorance.

That had been the key to my learning medicine – to ask for help.

As I walked out the door, I remembered the expression that Julius Caesar used after defeating Emperor Pharnaces II in battle in 47 BC:" *Veni, vidi, vici* – I came, I saw, I conquered."

Now I was excited to see what lay ahead. I felt omnipotent, and ready for the opportunity to practice medicine in the real world as a private doctor.

*

1984 Clarkfield Interview

I drove to the small town of Clarkfield, Minnesota to interview again, despite the harsh warning I had received from Dr. Gene a few months earlier. He had cautioned me that Clarkfield was too remote for the training that I possessed, and especially as a single young man. Clarkfield is located on the western edge of Minnesota, out in the middle of nowhere, a town of less than 2,000 people. Dr. Gene and his office manager, Dennis Kampstra, met me for breakfast, and proceeded to show me the town. The main street was only three blocks long, and was comprised of a grocery store, a movie theater, and a hardware store, and very little else of note.

They walked me through the tiny hospital, the quaint old rooms and small ward desk, with an older nurse wearing the traditional white cap and white dress, a far cry from the nursing attire at Luke's. The hospital lab was a small room with a microscope and a centrifuge sitting on a table, and several other small machines sitting against the wall. There were two labor rooms and one operating room which served as a delivery room also. Dr. Gene had been right to warn me – it was a far cry from what I was accustomed to. Even Sheboygan, Wisconsin, which I considered a smaller town, had much more in the way of modern facilities and advanced technology that I was familiar with.

Next, they took me on a tour of the nursing home, and then the clinic. The clinic was modern, and when they showed me where I would have my office, I immediately fell in love with the thought – my own office! It hadn't dawned on me that I was this close to actually having a practice of my own. I imagined my diplomas on the wall, my books on the shelves, my desk plaque sitting there for all who entered the room to see: RICHARD E. MAYERCHAK, M.D. It had been a present from the St. Luke's Family Practice Center.

Then they showed me the place where they would allow me to live – a home located one block from the clinic, two blocks from the hospital – I could rent it for a mere $200 a month. The house was a dream, with two stories, plus a basement, and more rooms than I could possibly use, plus a large yard and a garage. Clarkfield was growing on me.

I took a drive with them as they showed me the sights, the river that flowed through the edge of town, the high school, the tennis courts, the pool. I was sold – I wanted to give this town a try.

I signed a contract with Dennis Kampstra, for $80,000 in year one, and a $200,000 signing bonus if I agreed to stay for 5 years. I then drove back to Minneapolis to discuss it with my family. The only reservation I had about the idea was that I was going there as a single man, and I would be very far from Michelle. Still, the other advantages made it very palatable. I called Jerry Parent to announce the good news.

"Rich, are you sure about this? I don't know…" Jerry did not share my optimism.

"Well, I've always wanted to practice in a small town, Jerry. This is like my dream finally coming true."

"But what about Michelle? You'll never be able to work something out over such a long distance. It's either now or never with her, Rich. You know what? Idealists like you fall the hardest when they fall. You have idealistic expectations of how you'll practice in this town, and when the town falls short of them, you'll be setting yourself up for a big fall. Take care of your unfinished romantic business; there's no hurry for you to settle in your small town – that can wait."

I had the sick feeling that Jerry spoke wisely. What a dilemma! I had to choose between the financial and idealistic rewards that this small town had to offer – an easy solution to my long-term debts, and ready acceptance as a vital member of their community – and Michelle, whose time was now or never. If I came back to Milwaukee to be with her, I would have to struggle to make my monthly loan payments, and accept a job doing some type of city practice, which I dreaded.

I deliberated for the weekend, then called Clarkfield and declined their lucrative offer. 80 thousand dollars in my first year and 200 thousand dollar signing bonus!! Was I nuts to refuse them? I took a job at a walk-in clinic in Milwaukee, so that I could continue to date Michelle.

A year passed, and Michelle entered her final year of medical school, and was preparing for residencies. She was getting so busy that she no longer had time for a relationship, so she ended it. I was disappointed, but I remembered back to when I had been dating Toni in med school and I had done the same thing to her. It was a casualty of medical training, an inflexible reality like a law of physics that was impossible to bend.

Now I had no reason to remain in Milwaukee. I decided that I was going home to Minnesota for good, to be closer to my family again. I would find a place where I could be the kind of doctor I'd dreamed of being, despite Dr. Griesy's warnings to the contrary. I was going to be a small-town country doctor like him.

CHAPTER 4
COUNTRY DOCTOR AT LAST

The shrill siren from the squad car screamed through the early dawn as morning broke. It startled me to my core and woke me instantly. It had to be close by! I jerked violently to an upright position and sat on the edge of my bed to process the high-pitched alarm ringing in my ears. Then my half-opened eyes caught the flashing lights circling the walls of my farmhouse bedroom, and I looked out my window. There sat a police car in my backyard, a mere five feet from my bedroom window, with lights and sirens at full blast.

Just then, I heard my kitchen door open, and then Officer Moe walked into my bedroom. He spoke in a serious tone:

"Doctor Mayerchak, I'm placing you under arrest. Please put a shirt on." I was wearing only my boxer shorts. I hurriedly slid my T-shirt over my shoulders and stood up.

"What's the charge? What did I do?"

He pulled out a pair of handcuffs and proceeded to place my hands behind my back and handcuff me. I didn't put up any resistance because I was afraid of the consequences. Then he walked me out my kitchen door into the backyard where his squad car was still shrieking loudly while the lights circled in panic mode. He tucked me into the back seat of the police car, where I sat in my boxer shorts and T-shirt, wearing no shoes or socks. Again I implored him:

"Would you please tell me what's going on?"

I knew I had made some enemies in town. Or was this related to a medical mistake? I caught a glimpse of someone in the front seat next to Officer Moe. It was still too dark outside to see who it was. I heard a woman's voice – was that Tree?

Let's back up several months...

The first week in January of 1986 was bitter cold, and snowier than usual. My brothers and I had just returned from a hot week in Key West, Florida – home of Ernest Hemingway.

My nine year old white Olds Cutlass cruiser wagon contained my every earthly possession. After living in seven different apartments during residency, useless fat such as sofas and dressers had been trimmed off my possessions list. I relied on a futon mattress for sleeping on the floor – better for the back – and as a rolling stone, I had no interest in gathering moss.

I started out for Madison, a tiny town on the western plains of Minnesota, on a cold, windy, snowy January morning. As I left the last Minneapolis suburb behind in my rear view mirror, the wind blew at 35 miles per hour. The single lane empty highway road cut a path through the barren white flatlands covered with drifting snow which blew across and blurred its edges. I could easily imagine that I was driving across the arctic tundra enroute to the North Pole. An hour out of Minneapolis, my wiper fluid froze, and I was forced to scrape my windshield repeatedly while driving, just to see the road ahead of me. In these forbidding conditions, my estimated three hour trip took me almost 5 hours.

On the way, I passed through Dawson, another small farming town that was faring better than most thanks to a soybean factory. The town's doctor was the father of my roommate from senior year at Luther College, Tim Maus. Tim had attended Mayo medical school and was now a practicing radiologist at the Mayo Clinic. Tim was one of the most brilliant guys I had ever met. He had the mentality of a specialist. He had originally intended to practice surgery, but one summer while home from college and working in this town's soybean factory, he injured several fingers severely enough that he changed his plans and became a radiologist. As my dad would have said, "adapt or die". And so he did. Everything Tim did was top notch, so he had lots of options when his first choice failed. It pays to be talented and driven to excellence. On my way through town, I stopped to renew my acquaintance with Tim's parents. Then I was off to Madison, no longer as a tourist passing through. For the first time in my life, I was going to be living in a tiny town, smaller by far than Dr. Griesy's Two Harbors. My stomach rumbled.

As I approached Madison, Minnesota, I came across a population sign: Welcome to Madison, Pop. 2319. Closer to downtown, I passed a large statue of a fish with a large inscription: Lutefisk Capital of the World. It was apparent that the town had personality. That's a good omen, I thought; it's growing on me already.

Madison was buried in snow. It had been hit hard, and the snow

201

removal capacity was inferior to what Minneapolis possessed. As I drove through the residential areas, I had to stop at each corner and inch forward into the intersection, unaware if cars were approaching from my sides; the snow piles were at least four feet deep. It was very much like driving through a corn maze, but made of snow. Now I began to wonder if I had made a huge mistake joining a clinic in this forsaken, desolate farm country.

I drove up and down the town for five minutes looking for the hospital. On the main drag, I noticed two banks, two bars, two food joints, and two drugstores. Little did I realize that my observation about pairs of businesses was applicable to much of the proprietorship of this town.

I wandered the side streets for ten minutes more. There wasn't much to the town; it was nestled around the intersection of county road 40 and highway 75, and extended from there for about a mile in each direction. In that neat little section of real estate was packed a single school comprising all 13 grades, the downtown business area, several churches, a hospital, a nursing home, and lots of closely spaced houses. I thought it odd that with this much land around, the houses should be so tightly arranged.

The blue "H" signs directly me easily to the hospital, nestled on its own sprawling perfectly square tract of land, with its structure attached by a skyway corridor to the adjacent nursing home. It was the only building I'd seen that contained a spacious yard in an otherwise very spacious town. In front of the hospital was a circular drive-through area much like funeral homes and mansions utilize, covering just enough space for two cars. It bordered the front entrance to the hospital and the ambulance entrance to the emergency room. It was unoccupied, so I pulled directly opposite the hospital's front door and parked. I sensed the town's urgency in finding a doctor, and figured that they wouldn't sweat my parking indulgence on this day.

Richard Range met me in his office on second floor. Mr. Range was the hospital's administrator. He began by showing me around the hospital.

I shouldn't have been surprised by its small size, but I was. After all, I had already toured Clarkfield a mere 15 months earlier. The towns were of comparable size. In this similarly tiny hospital stood one small nursing desk at the end of a corridor on the first floor. That was all there was to the wards. Total bed capacity was about 16 people, in eight double occupancy rooms. Just beyond the nursing desk were two smaller wings where the lab, nursery, operating room and emergency room were located. At that moment, the hospital seemed like a space ship, very efficient, but tiny, with one token representation of everything, including a library and a break room where I found the staff having toast and drinking coffee.

Mr. Range introduced me to one of the nurses, Connie Faith, and to Mary Wodrich, R.N., Director of Nurses. Connie seemed to be about my age, slender, with reddish hair, nice looking. I noticed she had a ring. Darn. Mary was of equally pleasant demeanor and appearance, mid-forties, and married as well. Was the staff all this friendly, or were they that desperate for a doctor?

As we passed the hall in front of the nursing station on our way out, I noticed several large, framed photos of doctors who had practiced there in years gone by. Two were distinguished looking gents from the 1930s, with 40 or more years of service to the town. The last three were photos of older looking physicians who were in the process of retiring.

Mr. Range drove me to the clinic, which was only a block away. There I was introduced to Don Mathers. He had recently purchased the clinic from the three retiring physicians I had seen in the hospital photos.

Don was my age. He'd done a residency in Minneapolis, so we had lots in common. He was tall, slightly overweight, balding, and disorganized, from what I could see of his office: charts everywhere, stacks of magazines in piles, apparently no semblance of order. Still, he was upbeat, optimistic about the prospects of growth for his practice, and I got the sense that he intended to stay. That was very encouraging.

On my way out, I met one of the clinic nurses, Theresa "Tree" Bly, just in passing. Her looks made quite an impression. She was lithe and willowy, with long dark hair and a pretty face, and a nice smile to boot; there wasn't anything not to like about her, except that she was married. Still, she gave the clinic an air of ebullience that I carried with me as we left. Don indicated that she would be my nurse, and that left me with a very positive initial impression.

I rented a house three blocks from the hospital, from a farm family living in a neighboring town. Their story was all too familiar for these small towns; their parents had owned the home, but one was now dead, the other in a nursing home. The housing market was so depressed that it didn't pay to sell the house; a later trip to the bank confirmed for me that many homes in my neighborhood could be purchased for $25,000 or less.

My house had two bedrooms, a small bathroom, a modest living room, and a very spacious attic and basement. It was more than I needed; my rolled-up futon mattress was the only space-occupying furniture that I owned. It took me only 20 minutes to unpack my stuff. Then I made my way downtown to get a checking account.

My first conundrum was about how to choose a bank. Across Main Street from each other stood the Klein National Bank and the Madison State Bank. Which was better? Would I offend one by choosing the other? I decided to open accounts in both just to be on the safe side. No sense stepping on toes when I was new in town. I sensed that I would be highly visible as one of only two doctors in town, and I wanted to maintain the right image.

I soon learned that I'd underestimated the status I was assuming as the new doctor in town. As I walked into the Klein Bank, I was greeted by a teller who recognized me before I told her my name. My picture had been in the local paper recently, and everybody was waiting to meet me. The bank's president was quickly informed, and walked out from his office to introduce himself.

The reception was the same everywhere I went. I stopped at the two drugstores to meet the pharmacists. Bill Kenyon represented the establishment. He'd owned Kenyon Drug for 25 years. The town was comfortable with him as a native son. He was in his sixties, graying, and cachectic-appearing. I attributed his physique to the pack of cigarettes I saw sticking out of his shirt pocket. He was very warm in his welcome.

Kenyon's competitor was Oftedahl Drug, two blocks down and across the street. Dick Oftedahl had only been there ten years or so, and as such, was still considered a newcomer, an upstart, not really a Madison establishment. He was in his early forties, pleasant, athletic looking, and invited me out to lunch. I told him I'd take a rain check. I noticed that Oftedahl's place was more contemporary looking, with more of what today's consumers were looking for in a drugstore. But Kenyon's had been just as busy when I was there: maybe there were two camps of people in this town, each choosing one of the stores for personal reasons.

Fortunately, there was only one post office. I did find two supermarkets, both family-owned; Paul's Red Owl was half the size of Jackson's Super Valu. Paul met me as I was paying for my groceries, and asked if there was anything the store didn't have that I might like. I told him I couldn't find any unsalted peanuts. He told me they'd have some there by

204

Friday.

This celebrity treatment was too much! I was having difficulty believing it. I found that Jackson's Super Valu was so large, that it had three times as many customers, and much less personality. I decided that I would stick to Paul's from now on, to help the underdogs who seemed to have more of a personal touch to their business.

Then it was off to lunch. Again, two choices for downtown; the North 40 Café, or the Perkins' family diner. The former choice sounded like a truck stop, the latter like a piece of Americana, so I ventured into Perkins' diner.

I wasn't prepared for the attention I received from the patrons. As I learned later, everyone in this town knew everyone else. When a stranger walked in, everybody wanted to know who it was. In Minneapolis, nobody cared who sat at the next table. These people not only cared, but they rudely stared until I felt so uncomfortable that I walked out before ordering. The recognition of the other townspeople at the banks and grocery stores had been direct and honest; the people in the restaurant hadn't introduced themselves, and their uninvited forays over my shoulder and across to my table with their probing eyes had been unwelcome.

I fixed myself some lunch at home and flipped on the TV to keep me company. I got no reception except the public television station. I called Range, who told me that that was how it was out there; I would have to pay for cable TV if I wanted any TV stations at all. Bummer! I was $70,000 in debt, and not willing to spend money on something as useless as cable TV.

I decided I'd have to be content with public TV. At least they had McNeil – Lehrer news hour. I could handle that.

After lunch, it was time for a nap. It was already late afternoon, and I'd been up since before dawn. The January sun was already going down.

Things would soon be busy enough, I knew; better to be well-rested to start with. One of the most valuable lessons my residency training had taught me was the importance of good sleep hygiene.

The next thing I knew, it was morning. I decided to go for a run.

Running had been my strategy for maintaining my mental health through med school and residency, and I knew I would need it now just as much.

What a joy it was to jog in the crunchy snow! I wasn't going fast like in the days of old, and only for four miles, but it was enough to allow me to think. Today as I ran, I again thought of all the people who I'd buried in residency. I was running for them, to celebrate the life that they were no longer able to live. It was the best way I knew of two regularly renew my perspective of what really matters in life.

Friday finally rolled around and I started my first day at the clinic before a long weekend off. I met the front office staff first. Everyone was close to my age. Pam kept the books. She was obese, very jolly, but shy. Joan Fernholz did the billing and insurance, and went by "Fern", and Tammy , the receptionist, went by "B.T.". Fern explained to me that one night when Tammy had been really drunk she told the girls that guys should call her "Tammy BIG TITS", because the boys all wanted her big tits and she knew it. Hence, she was "B.T."

As I got situated in my personal office, a spacious, paneled room befitting a bank president, I met the girls who worked in back. I remembered Theresa Bly from our earlier meeting. She preferred to go by "Tree". She was to be my nurse. Carol worked as Don's nurse, and I kidded her that with her thick, shoulder-length, beautiful hair I should call her "Clairol" instead. Nowadays, that would be grounds for sexual harassment, at least in Minneapolis, but she took it as a compliment, and we hit it off.

Mary was the lab person. She was curt, to the point, a little bit flat but pleasant, the kind of person you don't usually count on to get your party started.

Don Mathers, my new partner, hadn't arrived yet. I didn't have anything pressing to do, so I hung around the lab and visited with Tree. I noticed a Nerf ball on top of the refrigerator.

"What's that for, Tree?"

"Oh, we sometimes play a little game here when it's slow…"

"Well, how about it – we've got a couple of minutes to kill…"

Tree looked surprised that I wasn't too stuffy for that. I grabbed the Nerf and asked her how the game went. The office was composed of two long corridors with a central open area in between them which comprised the lab and nursing station. Tree stood in front of one hallway, and told me to stand in front of the other. She told me the object was to kick the Nerf, like in soccer, through the lab into the other person's hallway. We tried it a few times, until I kicked her in the foot. Too dangerous, I thought. I suggested a variation. How about throwing it past each other? If I made it past her to her hallway, I got a point.

We played to five. I won easily. We then amended our rules to award a point for catching the other person's throw as well as scoring a goal. The other girls watched, and I could tell they were anxious to try. Tree and I played six games, and I wrote down our scores on a calendar in the lab. We were off to a great start.

Don Mathers arrived, as did Norval Westby. Doc Norval was retiring in July, and his practice was winding down; since Paul's arrival, most of the town had switched to Paul's care, relying on his more up-to-date medical knowledge and training. It appeared to me that that axiom applied to a lot of the town – the newer of the two dentists, the newer bank, the bigger grocery store, the newer drugstore – people switched alliances when a more up-to-date option arose. Interestingly, though, the older people stuck to the old drugstore, the old dentist, and to Doc Norval. Loyalty ran deeper than modernization.

Norval was in his mid-sixties. He was the son of one of the two Westby brothers who had practiced here in the 1930's, whose pictures I'd seen on the wall. Norval's son was a physician also, but to his father's disappointment, had chosen to practice in a large city. It seemed that Norval would be the last Westby to practice in a town where the Westby name had been synonymous with "doctor" for over sixty years.

Don gave me some background on Norval, as we visited in Don's office with the door closed. Norval's health was progressively declining. He had diabetes, and he drank too much, although he didn't admit it. He smoked liked a chimney and his skin bore witness to that fact. He was very wrinkled and looked much older than his stated age. Actually, the town was widely aware of his excessive drinking, but they didn't seem to mind. It was rumored that he was having an affair with one of the nurses who worked at the hospital, Missy, who was in her thirties. For a guy on the way out of life's door, his hormones were still intact. Don told me that a year ago Norval had come to the emergency room with chest pain, had gone into Vfib, and they'd coded him and shocked him back to life. And here he was still practicing. He'd told people that he would work until they buried him. Now, it seemed, it was Don's intention to force Norval Westby's retirement before his antiquated ways of practice dissuaded patients from coming to Paul's new clinic.

I saw my first patient, June Johnson. Her husband was associated with a prominent newspaper, and as such, was a force to be reckoned with. He was in his late seventies already, but still running the business. She, too, was older than retirement age, but she looked younger and had a spry wit about her. I was surprised when Tree handed me her heavy chart.

Inside I noted that June had irritable bowel problems, and she'd been run through the mill with tests, including several barium enemas and other as ambitious exams.

Her symptoms were presently no different, though, and she was here to see if I could offer any new light on her condition. It was as if my youth and urban background alone were enough to make me an expert. I knew that such a perception was far from accurate, and that experience was far more valuable to patient care than raw knowledge, however current it was.

But I wasn't going to intimate to the wife of the town's newspaper mogul that I couldn't help her out.

I ordered a barium enema for her. It had been seven years since the last one, I told her. Maybe something had changed. Also, I scheduled her for a flexible sigmoidoscopy, something I was sure the older guys hadn't done, but that Don Mathers was offering his patients. I would do her procedure at the hospital in the treatment room in one week. June left with a smile and apparent confidence in my approach. I was on the board.

My next patient hadn't arrived yet. People were used to the older guys taking their time in getting to work, so the lobby wait had previously been upwards of an hour, and the patients had figured out how late they could show up and still be on time. I was used to a walk–in clinic where I often saw 50 people in a twelve-hour day. I moved fast.

With another minute to kill, I challenged Tree to another nerf game. I wanted to skunk her at one. She told me that I had to wait until Paul went into his next room – then we'd have some time. When he'd come six months ago, he'd been friendlier, interested in small talk, and more approachable; now he was her boss, and his attitude toward her and the rest of the staff was noticeably different. She had to relegate the fooling around to times when he wasn't watching.

Don Mathers came out of a room, asked Tree to do a white blood count, and walked into the bathroom just before the X-ray room in the center nursing area. Suddenly, he came out and asked: "Tree, were you in the bathroom last?"

"Yeah, I was… why?"

"You left a turd in the toilet."

208

He announced it to all persons present in the lab, loud enough that the front office girls heard it as well. Tree turned three shades of red and left the room. Don went back in the bathroom, flushed the toilet with the door open, then went back to seeing patients as if nothing had happened. That was my first clue that Don lacked a little something in the employee relations department.

I found Tree in the front office, talking with Fern about the incident. I told her it was inappropriate of Don to mention it at all, let alone in front of others. It reminded me of the way Dr. Wally had razed me in front of the entire nursing station on my second day of internship at St. Luke's. I promised Tree that someday we'd figure out a way to get back at him.

Fern and Tree asked me why I was single, and I explained my recent breakup with Michelle, and earlier in Duluth with Toni, and Lisa, my college sweetheart. Fern gestured toward Tammy "BT" and said:

"She's single, you know… and we can tell she likes you…"

I told Fern that BT was not my type. She was wearing a pantsuit that looked like a leopard skin. She seemed much too wild for me. And, she hadn't been to college. After my comment, Fern's impression of me improved greatly.

My next patient was a farmer with a hemorrhoid problem. He'd been plagued for six months, but between planting and bringing in the crop, he hadn't had time to get in. I later learned that the farm seasons had a lot to do with what happened at the clinic. We had 20,000 patient charts on file, many of them from even smaller neighboring towns, and most of them farmers or farm families.

I set up a time to remove his ''rhoids, and moved on. The day flew by fast. For lunch, we went downtown to Perkins café, where I finally had a meal. The staring was again obvious and abundant, but I had a new family now, and I didn't mind it as much. Not surprisingly, Don declined the invitation to join us. I had the daily special: a large plate of roast beef, mashed potatoes, and gravy, with a glass of milk. My bill was $2.50. How did they expect to make any money?

The afternoon was a blur. I was already thinking ahead to my trip home to Minneapolis for the weekend. I did notice that three young women came in to see me that afternoon, all with little or no symptoms to justify their appointments with me. Were they scoping me out? I got that impression.

Tree and Fern confirmed my suspicions when I asked them about it a few months later.

I left for Minneapolis on Friday afternoon. It was a three-hour drive. I'd been in Madison only five days, but the homecoming to the house of my youth, where many of my siblings still lived, was much anticipated. Since arriving in Madison, I'd made a list of some sundries to help appoint my house, such as extra towels, a dish basin, etc. To my dismay, it was hard to find those items in that small town. They had no Target! No Wal-Mart! In fact, the nearest department store of any similarity was the Pamida in Montevideo, 30 miles away.

When I arrived in Minneapolis, I went directly to Target. Never had I appreciated how much we city folk took these big box stores for granted. I knew exactly where to get everything on my list; I picked out a VCR because of the lack of TV stations. I would settle for lots of movies that I planned to pre-tape this weekend while I was home. (*Editor's note:* there was no satellite TV yet, no cell phones or iPads, no laptop computers or easy access to virtual entertainment of any form. Living in a remote town without television or other entertainment was going to be challenging, considering the town shut down at 5 p.m. each day.)

While in med school, I had qualified for a loan program in which I could borrow $6,000 a year for four years. It would be forgiven if I agreed to spend five years in a small town from their list of needy towns. If I didn't last five years, one fourth of my loan would be forgiven for every 18 months I served.

By the time I finished residency, Madison was one of the few towns south of the Canadian border that still made the list. The others were so remote that I doubted I would ever get to travel home. My goal was to try for 18 months, and if it went well, to stick it out for five years. And, after that, to play it by ear. Hopefully the town would grow on me. I would save a lot in loan repayments if that happened.

Don and I had worked out a call rotation that was basically every other night, plus every other weekend. The call thus far had been light, as people weren't sure who I was, and seemed a little reluctant to see me. I'd seen a few major things that couldn't wait until Don was around, but he was definitely getting the lion's share of calls.

Things gradually swung my way as more and more people saw me in the clinic and heard good reports about me from their neighbors over coffee at Perkins' diner and The North 40 Cafe.

In my fourth week in town, that January of 1986, I received my first paycheck from Don. After taking care of morning rounds and clinic, I headed downtown to do some banking. I laughed as I came across the pileons sticking up in the center of Main Street along each block that announced: BINGO TONIGHT. I walked into the Madison State Bank to make my deposit. They were holding a bake sale in the lobby. Not only that, but there was a TV going in a corner of the lobby so that patrons and tellers wouldn't miss their favorite soap operas. Only in a small town could they get away with these kind of personal touches, I observed. Suddenly a news reporter broke into the soap opera playing in the lobby. The space shuttle Challenger had just exploded, with Christa McAuliffe the teacher on board, and all of the crew was suspected to have died in the crash. We were all shocked. A few days later President Reagan delivered a eulogy that was very touching.

One evening two weeks later I was fixing my usual supper in the microwave – a lean cuisine spaghetti – when the hospital called.

"They're bringing in 'Inky' from the VFW. He's not breathing."

'Inky' was a long-established fixture in Madison, a season ticket holder for his favorite chair at the VFW bar. He'd winced, leaned over, and fallen off his perch, and that was it. They were doing CPR and bagging him when the ambulance arrived at the back entrance of the hospital, which was the ER door.

We slapped some pads on him and got a tracing: asystole. His heart had stopped. I ordered some epi and quickly inserted an IV and asked Sandy, the nurse, to give the epi and stand clear while I shocked him. The ambulance crew, all Madison locals who volunteered their time, and Sandy were surprised by my aggressive participation in Inky's resuscitation. None of the older docs had done that. They'd been trained before CPR and advanced resuscitation techniques were developed. They didn't know how to defibrillate or deliver a synchronized cardioversion. But Don and I did, so Madison was getting an overhaul in its capacity for modern medical treatment.

Despite our efforts, Inky died. I thanked the ambulance squad, and Sandy, and asked her where the other nurse had been during the code. She told me it was Leota Wood. That explained it all. Leota was a year from retirement, definitely a dinosaur among nurses, with no clue about codes or what to do in an emergency. When things like this arose, she found something important to do in another patient's room as far away from the action as possible. She was famous for her disappearing act.

The nice thing about living close to the hospital was that I could whip back and forth twenty times if need be without the drive itself wearing me out. I took the liberty of parking in the drive-up circle by the front door. It was a privilege I knew the rest of the staff envied, but since no one challenged me on it, and it was a perk, I took it. It was small retribution for the countless trips and sacrifice of personal time I was already making for the hospital and for the town.

A week later, I was feeling a little weary. Every other night on call was getting to me. I'd joined the music group at church, my only real social activity. Everyone was married, but it was fun to be involved with people that I didn't work with. My nurse Tree and I were getting to be good friends. Her husband Tom, a farmer, was my age as well, and they had the kind of relationship that was rare, where he trusted her so implicitly, that after meeting me several times, Tom was not threatened by Tree's growing friendship with me.

I was returning home from my church music rehearsal one night in early February. I had my electric piano with me. I was thinking to myself that it was time to break down and order cable TV: The Super Bowl was coming up on Sunday, and the Bears were playing. I hated the Bears, but at least it was something to do. There was no health club, no after-hours stores or all-night Perkins or Denny's open, nowhere to go to get out of the house. The most difficult thing about living in Madison was the loneliness, especially for a single guy like me. Without a girlfriend or wife to keep me company, I had nothing to distract me from my job, In some ways that was a blessing, because the job was all-consuming, and I could easily envision how a married man or woman physician could become divorced due to neglecting their spouse in deference to the needs of this town. That same fate had befallen Dr. Griesy, whose devotion to the town of Two Harbors had destroyed his marriage.

Fortunately, I could run, but the four or five miles I was doing went quickly, and then I was stuck inside again. Sadly, I resorted to visiting the tiny little nursing station at the hospital sometimes on my night OFF-call, despite already growing sick of the place, because it was the only place open where I could easily go to talk to someone. I didn't dare go to the VFW or the American Legion, but those were the only other options for

212

night life after 5 p.m.

As I unloaded my electric piano from the back of my station wagon, I noticed that my house lights were off. I thought I'd left one light on before leaving for church. I got in the door and realized that I had no electricity. In the dark, I fumbled for switches, but everyone was impotent; the juice was off.

I had no flashlight, so I grabbed my doctor bag and used my otoscope to find the fuse box in the basement. I restored power and returned upstairs. Gone! It was all gone! The used sofa I'd just bought, the TV, even my bed! I stared at an empty room. I opened my cupboards. The labels had been ripped off all my canned goods. I stood there in a state of shock, assessing the damages. Then, abruptly, Tom and Tree Bly walked in through my front door with two friends of theirs. They were carrying a 12-pack of beer.

They were laughing their heads off. It was then that I knew I'd been had by a prankster.

It was a great housewarming, I told them. They were pleasantly surprised that I had appreciated their joke. They had removed every article from my home, and hidden my furniture. They had taken my suitcoats and sewn the sleeves shut. In short, they had gone to great lengths to get my goat in a very short period of time, and I appreciated all of it. We sat in a circle on the floor of my empty living room and drank the beers. I had two, quite unusual for me. By then, I was looped. I giggled, told them things about me that only my closest friends knew, and we all let our hair down. Tom and Michelle Peterson were along for the prank. I hadn't met them before that night, but after one drinking party, we were good friends. Tom and Tree Bly then helped me to find my furniture, which was tucked away in a corner of the basement.

After they left, I realized why I had let my hair down and imbibed beer (which I don't even like) so readily. I'd been lonely, and I'd needed to share who I really was with people I could trust. Tonight it had happened, and it was a watermark occasion, the moment I would always remember as the first time I'd dared to imagine this town as my permanent home.

The months rolled by slowly at first, because of the deep snow and lack of viable outlets for the stress which was building within me. It was obvious that the only way I would survive would be to marry someone to keep me company, or else I would need to learn to enjoy drinking. With no nearby swimming pool or indoor tennis or any of the extremely diverse options

Minneapolis offered a single person, I knew that my tenure, despite a blossoming friendship with the Blys, was threatened by the limited options for social activity and exercise.

In May, the golf season began officially with the opening of the Madison Country Club. It was the social event of the young spring season.

I was not a golfer, but Don Mathers was quite an avid participant; every Tuesday after that was golf night, when most of the town could be seen putting in their nine or eighteen holes and heading for the party at the 19th hole at the clubhouse.

I had an aversion to the golfers. I was into tennis. When the snow melted, I began hitting with a few of the locals, and that added some welcome diversity to the intense medicine I was practicing. It seemed that the town was divided in this as well: some preferred tennis, others golf.

But there were those who did both, like Don Mathers, who could beat just about anyone at either sport without much effort. He had multiple talents.

I could have admired him more fully except that Don's arrogance was beginning to annoy me. One day I had a visitor, Vickie Nelson, a friend from Luther College who was now in med school. As we conversed at the nursing station, Don walked up, and as I attempted to introduce my friend, Don cut me off.

"Rich, why didn't you see that one-year-old last night? His mom called you to say he had a fever. That was wrong – could have been trouble.

You shouldn't do that with a one-year-old."

His tone was very denigrating. His comment didn't deserve an explanation, but I gave him one:

"Don, his fever was low-grade. He'd only started it that evening.

Otherwise he was fine. I told his mom to call me if the Tylenol didn't work, and she was very comfortable with that approach. She never called back, so I figured he was okay."

Don scoffed and walked away. He'd berated me right in front of an old friend, and again it had been inappropriate. I was beginning to wonder if I could make it in this town for at least 18 months to at least satisfy the first quarter of my school loan forgiveness. It wasn't worth it if Don was going to continue looking over my shoulder as a boss instead of as a colleague. I was the one who was Board Certified in Family Practice – in his disorganized state, he hadn't gotten around to taking the test yet.

214

After clinic that day, I took Vickie Nelson for a visit around town, and then we drove to Watertown, South Dakota, an hour and 15 minutes away.

Socializing in Madison was impossible; everybody had to know what went on and with whom. It was late when we returned, so Vickie asked to stay the night before returning to Minneapolis.

The following morning, after bidding Vickie goodbye, I stopped at the Klein Bank before starting hospital rounds. The teller asked, "did your college friend from Grand Rapids have a good time?" I couldn't believe it. These people had phenomenal nose problems! They were well aware that I had had a guest overnight!! Tree and Fern had been to a recent bridge party where one woman was telling the others just which room in my home I exercised, which was my bedroom, and what hour I turned my lights off at night. The gossip in this town was making me claustrophobic.

Finally, it was June, and I had my first OB delivery, Liz Olson. Her husband was so excited that he passed out Baby Ruth bars to everyone, and to me he presented a huge bar, the $2.00 kind, that was a good ten inches long, with two large logs of chocolate inside. Out of the blue, seeing that giant Baby Ruth bar gave me a major brainstorm. I went to the doctor's lounge at the hospital and shared my idea with Tree by phone. We would put our plan into action the next day.

The following morning, an hour into the clinic day, Tree and I waited patiently for Don to make his customary trip to the bathroom by the X-ray machine. Finally, it happened, and as he exited the bathroom, Tree quietly slipped into the room and stuck one of the large Baby Ruth logs in the toilet bowl. Then she reappeared in the nursing station, and made an obvious walk to the bathroom. From there she called out:

"Hey, Don, you left a turd in the toilet... don't you know you're supposed to flush afterwards?" They were the exact words Don had used on her on my first day in Madison.

Don's face suddenly became a self-conscious shade of red as he darted to the toilet to check. We'd taken a gamble that he hadn't just urinated, and we'd guessed right, because Don, upon seeing the Baby Ruth, 'fessed up'.

"Sorry about that."

He looked embarrassed. We'd gotten him! Fern was on hand to witness our moral victory, an attack on his arrogance. And we vowed never to let him in on it – it was our secret way of getting back at him for the uppity attitude he'd developed since buying the clinic.

215

July arrived.

Fern (Joan Fernholz) was on a diet. She and her husband "Boomer" were going to Hawaii in the winter, and she wanted to be ready. I'd taken the clinic gals over to Willmar to see the male strippers, the Chippendales, and on the way home she'd acted frisky, so I'd put Tree between Fern and me as I drove them home. It had opened up my friendship with Fern, so that she and Tree and I were now pretty close.

The summer was busy from a medical standpoint. Doc Norval Westby had retired quietly, so Don and I were seeing his patients now. The routine was quite predictable: hospital rounds early each morning, then clinic from nine to five-thirty or so. Once clinic was finished, whoever had been on call the previous night was off to bed for the rest of the night. I don't know what Don did, but when I was on-call, I headed home from the clinic and immediately took a nap until I was called. I figured I could always eat or not eat, but to sleep was to survive. Usually, by about 7 p.m. or so, someone would show up in the ER and the nurse would call me over to see the patient. In effect, it was an evening clinic. By about 10 p.m., things usually quieted down enough to retreat home and make supper, and then I caught a catnap until the nurses called again.

People don't realize just how stressful it is being one of only two physicians in a town. There was never a night when I wasn't called in for something. When the VFW and the American Legion closed, I could count on a call from the ER saying someone needed to be seen. After 2 a.m., I could usually count on a few hours of rest unless a woman was in labor or a life-threatening accident or death had occurred. But consider the cumulative stress of doing that routine every other night and every other weekend! My life was not my own. I was already wondering about alternatives.

One day during the first week of July, I remember seeing Gayle Mathers, Don's wife, walking in front of my house past the tennis courts across the street. I ran out to say hello. She showed me her brand-new Reeboks, which she'd bought on her last trip to Minneapolis. I liked them.

I wanted a pair. As she talked, I realized what a wonderful person she was – very approachable, very down-to-earth. It felt awkward that I wasn't getting to be a close friend of her husband Don's, but she didn't let on that she was aware of that.

I thought it unfortunate that I didn't get the opportunity to know Gayle better, because I rarely socialized with Don. Our circles of friends did not intersect. Don and I were fast becoming like Kenyon and Oftedahl drugstores, or Klein and Madison banks, very different people with loyal camps of patients who preferred one or the other of us.

But we knew we needed each other. I respected Don's medical judgment, although his style was different than mine. Neither of us would have lasted long without a night to sleep after the horrendous on-call shifts we took. So we endured each other's personality differences.

One day, I met a girl who was home visiting her parents who lived in Bellingham, just a few miles north. Her name was Nancy Olson, and I enjoyed her from the moment we met. She was two years younger than I, with blonde hair, quite slender and athletic-looking, and demure. She carried herself with a subtle dignity. She worked as a dental hygienist in Willmar, an hour east of Madison. We went on a date while she was home, and decided to keep in touch.

One of the problems with a small town is that the locals consider their doctors as community property, to be accessed whenever the concerned parties feel it necessary. Whether I was at the grocery store, or filling my car with gas, if a person had a medical problem, they stopped to let me in on it, and get my advice. When Don started golfing on Tuesday afternoons, he decided to give me Wednesday afternoons off. The problem was that when people saw my car parked in my driveway, they walked over to ask me questions.

When I was a little boy, imagining being a country doctor, and even when I was studying in Two Harbors with Dr. Griesy, I always imagined that these extra touches, the community interacting with me at the gas pump or in my living room, were what made country practice special. And they were – for the first dozen times or so – and after that, I felt like an animal in a zoo, with 24-hour visiting hours.

After spending a couple of my Wednesday afternoons off by hanging around in Madison but being assaulted with phone calls because people saw my car home, I called Nancy Olson in Willmar and invited myself to visit her on Wednesdays. I discovered that the drive was immensely therapeutic. The whole concept of just "getting out of Dodge" was rejuvenating.

Nancy was usually done by three, so we played tennis, rode bikes, went for walks and out to movies. I became quite attached to her. Unfortunately, she was not really interested in me. She'd had a seven year relationship go

217

bad a while back, and it had changed her outlook on commitment. So we took the days for what they were, and left it at that. Without the seriousness of a love relationship, we managed to have lots of fun. We were both very athletic, and provided the stimulus to keep each other going.

My Wednesday afternoon escapes provided the comic relief and outside friendship that I'd missed in my first six months in Madison. Prior to meeting Nancy, I was very close to quitting and saying to heck with the loan repayment program. That brief Wednesday afternoon and evening respite with her in Willmar each week gave me the patience to return to Madison and endure the madness for another week.

Something else was keeping me there, or I'd have left for certain. It was a sense of God's hand in my life, in what I was doing. For the first time in my life, I actually felt as if this was my calling, what God had intended for me to do, and where. I was seeing suffering, joy, and needs that only I could fill because of what I'd learned and because I was available, not three hours away in Minneapolis. It was filling me with a sense of satisfaction that, in talking with my urban colleagues, was much deeper than theirs.

During the last week of July, all of these thoughts and emotions came into focus to a more profound and enlightening degree, as Don and Gayle left for vacation, leaving me alone for the first time to mind the town for ten continuous days. It is a period of time whose transpired events I will never forget.

Minding the Store

The weekend started out quietly enough. Don wrapped up his patients and signed things out to me. He had three people in the hospital, and two OB patients close to term. Otherwise nothing brewing. After he left clinic for the airport, the gals and I pulled out a six pack of beer and officially proclaimed it "Miller time". I couldn't drink because I was on call but I took a few sips anyway. It wouldn't have stopped the older docs, I knew.

I was tidying up my desk when I saw Tree peeking through the back of my door hinge. She asked me to step out of my office. Why? I smelled a rat.

I walked out, and caught Pam running around the corner with a water balloon. Just then, Tree unleashed her water balloon on me and it was all out war. Some of the balloons they threw at me didn't break, and I made them pay dearly by turning them back on the ones who had thrown them. By the time it was done, we were all soaked. As I drove home for supper, I passed by Don's house. He hadn't left yet! He was mowing his lawn before the vacation. He motioned me to stop, so I did. I was afraid he'd see that I was sopping wet, so I slinked low in my car and talked out the window. He just needed to pass on another tip about a patient from the nursing home.

As I reached home, I knew that Don had seen me up close. I wondered what he was thinking. Ah, screw it, I thought. Life's too short to worry about him. I had the week to worry about. Not since my ICU month during residency had I had to worry about minding a store of this magnitude for so long. On one hand, it meant that Don trusted me to take care of the town appropriately. On the other hand, it was sure to be a long ten days.

Here's how it went, day by day:

Friday Night

I went directly to bed when I got home. My nap only lasted 25 minutes before I got a call from Mrs. Hansen who wondered if she needed a tetanus shot if she'd had one eight years ago. I answered her, and had some supper. I could never fall back to sleep after rude interruptions such as that unless I was dead exhausted. p.m. The hospital called. A little girl was in ER with an earache. Indeed, my exam showed she had an ear infection. I treated her and returned home. p.m. I was home for 20 minutes when a man knocked at my front door. I opened it to find George, sort of a town "character", a guy some suspected of being a little perverted, asking if he could come in. He had a cough, nagged him for three weeks. Could I give him something for it? I wrote him out a prescription after listening to his lungs, anything to get him out of my hair.

11 p.m. I had just drifted off to sleep when Mrs. Peeples called. Sorry about the disturbance, she said, but I was darned hard to get ahold of during the daytime. She was having trouble getting her Blue Cross to pay for a clinic visit awhile back, and… I cut her off. I told her I couldn't help her, that she would have to talk to Fern, our billing person. I wanted to curse at her, but I bit my tongue. Who did these people think they were?

2 a.m. I had to go see another ER patient. Not surprising, since the bars were closed. He'd broken his hand in a fight – what we call a boxer's fracture – but it was too swollen to cast. I told him to put ice on it and see

me tomorrow, and I'd set it then.

Saturday Morning

9:30 a.m. Wonder of wonders, I'd slept almost seven hours! Very unusual for a Friday night. I sat outside in my scrubs on the cement steps in front of my tiny house in the middle of town, and attempted to wake up. A truck pulled up and out stepped Heidi, a blonde, well-endowed college student who kind of liked me, I suspected. She was dating someone from town, but they fought a lot. She told me she had a surprise for me: she wanted me to meet one of her girlfriends. She said she was cute, and real nice. I said I'd think about it.

The next thing I knew, I was riding in Heidi's vehicle to a house four blocks down the street. She knocked on the door but nobody answered. I told her we should come back another time. No, she insisted on going in to wake the girls up. She roused up my blind date to be, and ten minutes later, the mystery woman was staring me in the face through the eyes of a hangover, trying to look cute. She had hickeys on her neck. I told Heidi I'd seen enough.

Heidi told me I was too picky. It wasn't her friend's fault that she had hickeys: it was her boyfriend's idea. Oh yeah? I asked. Since when did it take only one person to tango? I told Heidi that I would pass on any of her future dating arrangements.

10:15 a.m. I went to the hospital to do rounds. The first order of business was to sit at the nursing station and decide a plan of attack. I opened a bag of Doritos and sipped on my can of Mountain Dew, my usual breakfast routine that the hospital had grown accustomed to. Nurse Sandy Hoium was in charge this weekend, so we reviewed the patients I needed to see:

First was Roy Fudge, a pleasant gentleman in his seventies dying of prostate cancer. He was in with a bladder infection, and he had an overall decline in function.

Next was Ann, one of the girls in my church music group, which I never seemed to get to anymore because I rarely got a chance to make it to church without getting paged. She had severe gastritis – just short of a stomach ulcer – and her symptoms were improving with treatment.

Next was Luke, recovering from an appendectomy done two days ago.

He could go home today if he was eating ok.

Harold Shepard was a farmer in his late fifties who I'd done a sigmoidoscopy on a few days ago. I'd found a large colon cancer. Dr. Briones, a surgeon from Montevideo, had explored him and found extensive spread to other organs. He was recovering from the surgery and hoping to go home in a few days, to spend his last viable days getting his things in order before his time to die.

Esther Olson was a woman in her fifties who had pneumonia, and renal insufficiency – her kidneys were working only borderline well – so I had to be careful what I treated her pneumonia with, to avoid making her kidneys any worse.

11:45 a.m. I finished rounds, and attended to the guy with the broken hand. The swelling hadn't gone down a lot, so I postponed casting and put a plaster "ulnar gutter" splint on instead. He'll have to come into clinic on Monday to have the cast done.

12:30 p.m. I finished my hospital business and decided to go for a run. I felt adventuresome, buoyed by an unexpected, good night's rest. I planned to do eight miles today. I had a locker in the doctors' lounge which held my running gear. Kind of funny that it should be named doctors' lounge when there were only two of us, I thought. How about "Don and Rich's room" I mused. It underscored how small was this town and this hospital. I changed and took off for the highway, after informing Nurse Sandy of my route. Since I didn't have my pager with me, they had to know where I was headed.

There is something absolutely glorious about running in the country, especially when one is contemplating going further and exploring uncharted territory. My stress level from practicing here was forcing me to run further, and the marathon bug was biting at my brain.

I got almost three miles north of town on highway 75 when a police car pulled up to me. I recognized officer Doug Moe. The hospital had sent him for me: I had business in the ER that couldn't wait. That was all he knew.

Doug was in his mid-twenties, lighthearted, a fun guy to be with. I'd gotten to know him fairly well from ambulance runs and various emergencies. He lived in a trailer on the outskirts of town, like James Garner in the Rockford Files. He loved pigs, and had pictures and stuffed animal facsimiles of pigs around his place.

Doug swung me around to the back door of the hospital and I ran in to see what was up. I was topless, with running shorts and shoes on and nothing else. I was sweating like a pig.

The moment of truth for a doctor like me was always walking in to see what I was up against. It could be literally anything under the sun. No accidents or illnesses were pre-screened and sent to the appropriate specialist to examine. I was pediatrician, surgeon, orthopedist, or neurologist, depending on what was waiting for me. And worst of all, there was no other doctor to help me if it was REALLY bad.

And when I had been in residency, it scared me to death to think that someday I might face these challenges, freak accidents and medical conundrums, that came out of the blue when I was least prepared for them. But somewhere along the way I'd learned a few basic rules about how to order my thinking to cover the most essential priorities, step by step, to keep the patient alive so that I could work on the rest of the problems. The time I'd spent moonlighting in that ER in Sheboygan had been invaluable for giving me the skills I needed to practice on my own out in this remote wasteland.

As I stood in front of the room, I could see it was an elderly man.

They couldn't quite get him out of his wheelchair. He'd fallen from his bed at the nursing home, and they'd wheeled him down here. He was apparently bleeding from the face.

Closer inspection revealed that he was bleeding out of his nose, and from his right ear, and from his mouth. He appeared to have suffered a stroke as well, and his body was limp on the right. So what to do first?

It was a struggle just to get him on the table. Blood coming from the ear might be from a ruptured eardrum secondary to the fall, but I suspected that it represented a far more ominous problem, a bleed around the brain. He was coughing and spitting up blood, and I was afraid he'd inhale it, so I put in a central IV line and then attempted to place a tube through the non-bloody side of his nose and into his stomach. That didn't pass well, despite several attempts. I still remember how odd it must have looked for me to be working on this guy, sweating like a pig, without a shirt on, on that hot July afternoon. It happened so fast that there really wasn't time to change. My white running shorts were soaked red from this patient vomiting blood on me.

It was soon apparent that this guy was going out on us. His breathing changed abruptly so I had to decide whether to intubate. I told Sandy to call his relatives to help me with the decision. I reached a daughter who explained that they'd talked about it previously, and their dad would not want that. I was glad she'd said that, because I agreed wholeheartedly in this case. The patient was 76, frail, bedridden: it would not have made sense to aggressively treat his problems.

His respiratory effort was less each minute, and within twenty minutes he was gone. It was divine mercy that he went so quickly, I told myself. It was much better than trying to live with whatever cerebral insult he'd suffered.

After talking with his family who had just arrived after his death, I showered and changed clothes and took off for home.

3:15 p.m. I called Tree and Tom to invite myself over for supper. Tree and I worked together as doctor and nurse five days a week, and she and Tom and I ate together at least once a week, so we were becoming close friends; theirs was my home away from home, my escape to the country. They lived on a farm just on the outskirts of town. The phone rang 8 times before I remembered that they were going shopping in Watertown, South Dakota this afternoon. They wouldn't be home all evening. I got a sudden brainstorm.

I called Steve Townley, the city administrator. Steve was a couple of years younger than I, but single, which gave us a lot of mutual ground to relate. He was a transplant from Cleveland, Ohio. This was his first big undertaking since college, although he'd had several smaller jobs prior to coming here. I often pondered the fact that a lot of the professional, service-oriented people in this town were imported from larger cities. We were a social group unto ourselves which had banded together to survive the loneliness of the long winter indoors.

I asked Steve if he was up for a little excitement. I explained my plan and he dropped by. We headed out to the Bly farm, and passed Doug Moe, the local police deputy in the black and white along the way. I flagged him down and he turned on his flashers, to flaunt his authority.

"Hey Doug, what gives? Have you got a few minutes?" I asked.

"What've you got in mind?" he asked.

"Breaking into Tom and Tree Bly's Place... that's what!"

Doug shook his head at first, then flashed a devilish grin, and turned the squad car around to escort Townley and me to the Bly farm.

We had to figure out how to enter the premises first. I found a way in

223

that I'd experimented with during my last dinner with them. I let Doug and Steve in the back way once I'd crawled through. The plan was to do unto them what they'd done unto me last fall when they had snuck into my home and removed all my furniture and taken all the labels off my canned goods. And I was going to videotape it! I set up my camera and interviewed Doug, in his police uniform, and Steve, the city administrator, as we three sat in the Bly kitchen, helping ourselves to their jar full of cookies, and drinking pop from their fridge. I then pulled out a dozen rolls of toilet paper and some tape, and set Doug to work covering the living room. Townley and I tried to mix things around in the kitchen before completely covering it with TP also. Then we retreated to the bedroom, where I removed every available piece of clothing from their closet. Tree would have fun finding something to wear to work, I laughed.

We dawdled making the video, then realized we'd better bug out of there before the Blys got back. Doug made me promise not to tell any townsfolk about his role in this while he was on duty. It was okay if the Blys knew, because they were pretty cool heads.

5:45 p.m. I ran up to ER to see a little three-year-old who'd been pulled across the street while holding onto her mom's hand. Her arm hurt now, and she wouldn't use it. Mom wondered about a broken arm. From the way she was holding it, and her age and history of the mechanism of injury, I suspected a subluxed radial head. I knew I would only get one chance to snap it back. I had to take the child by surprise. I gingerly touched her arm while sneaking my other hand behind her elbow. With sudden deliberateness, I grabbed her elbow and jerked her hand upward and we all heard a CLICK as the subluxed head snapped back into place. She cried for a minute and still refused to use the arm. Her mom was not happy, but I told her to give it a minute. I was sure of what I'd felt and heard when the bone clicked back into joint. Sure enough, a couple of minutes later, the child was using her arm as if nothing had happened. Her mother was smiling, and thanked me several times. I smiled to realize that it was simple things like that that made medicine fun, and was good PR as well, as contrasted with the old man I'd watched die just a few hours earlier in the afternoon.

8:00 p.m. I had some supper and took a nap.

10:30 p.m. The evening shift nurse, Missy, the one rumored to be having the affair with old Doc Norval Westby, called to tell me that my patient with the pneumonia had low urine output. I ordered a metabolic panel, because this lady had tipped over the edge before, and might need dialysis.

The problem with ordering any lab or X-ray was that the person had to come from home to do it. Today, it was Lisa's turn to be on call, and she lived 20 minutes away, so there was no point in my hurrying in to see the results. It would be a while by the time she got things going. I always felt a twinge of guilt when ordering lab or X-rays after hours, because it meant I had to pull somebody out of bed or at least away from home and family.

And sometimes, they held it against me, too, if they couldn't see a clear-cut reason for the test I was ordering. It was tricky to stay on everybody's good side.

11:00 p.m. I was in my bed trying to get a little nap. I knew I'd have to check on the lady with the low urine output eventually, but it was a warm Saturday in July, so I knew the ER would eventually bring me back to the hospital. And they were having a street dance downtown. I always left my front door open on these summer nights. My neighbors were too nosy for me to worry about my stuff getting stolen. From my bedroom, I heard my front screen door creak open, and into my bedroom walked Heidi, the girl who'd tried to set me up with her friend earlier that morning. I was somewhat surprised, but not really; this town didn't seem to be able to draw lines about what access to me was appropriate, and what wasn't.

Her breath reeked of alcohol. She'd gotten into an argument with her boyfriend at the street dance, and she wanted some advice. She sat down on my bed as I tried to wake up and listen to her. The audacity! And to top it off she was pretty and well-endowed. She walked right into my bedroom and plopped down on my BED to talk! I half-wondered about her motives. She flirted, but I was intractable. I was sorely tempted, but I remembered the stern scolding that Chief of Staff Dr. Palese had given me at St. Luke's regarding propriety. "A doctor is highly visible. Keep your nose clean", he had admonished.

I listened to her sob, inveigle and flirt for 15 or 20 minutes, and then I told her she was a good person, and told her to let herself out. I laughed – they wouldn't believe this in Minneapolis. This is what small towns are all about. I rolled over and fell back asleep.

1:15 a.m. Hospital called. Maynard Porter brought his wife in, in active labor. Maynard worked for the local radio station; he was somewhat of a celebrity for the whole region. His wife Deb was one of Don's patients.

They belonged to the social elite that were included in Don's circle of friends. I hoped that she would feel comfortable with me, since we hadn't met before.

As I was examining her, the ambulance arrived with two victims from a car accident. They had minor injuries, but they'd both been drinking. It reminded me of an accident I'd seen while moonlighting in the Sheboygan ER, where the driver had been crushed to the wheel and died instantly, with a beer can in his hand, which was trapped between the steering wheel and his chest. This guy had been found with beer in his hand also, but suffered only a minor head laceration which I quickly repaired. He had legal problems to deal with that were worse than the cut on his head, but at least he hadn't killed someone, like an accident I'd managed recently.

I walked back to Deb Porter and finished my exam. She was 7 centimeters, and would deliver in an hour or two, I estimated. I decided to hang around the hospital; more action was likely.

2:30 a.m. A five-year-old who had fallen off a swing was in with her parents. They were concerned because the swing had hit her in the back of the head, and now she had a bump and was whining. She'd vomited once right after the fall. She'd slept all evening and that concerned them. After debating for a few hours, they couldn't get any sleep, so here they were.

My exam revealed a small hematoma – bleeding under the skin – and was otherwise normal. I reassured the parents. It was sometimes difficult practicing without better facilities. Here was a case in point: the child seemed fine, but if she got worse, they were an hour and a half away from the nearest hospital that had a CT scan. I explained my findings as sensibly as I could and told them that it was unlikely she would need further X-rays. She was probably drowsy from the long day in the sun and excitement from getting hit. They took her home after promising to watch her closely and call me if anything changed.3:30 a.m. Deb was almost completely dilated. Sandy Mattson, one of my own OB patients, came in in early labor, and waved to Deb as she was wheeled past Deb's room.

4:00 a.m. Deb's labor was arresting. If it didn't progress, I was going to have to help her along. Sandy's was going rapidly.

5:15 a.m. Deb was done pushing, and the baby was crowning. Again it was my moment of truth. Never is this experienced more intensely than when a family practitioner is working in a small town without backup. And this week I didn't even have Don to call if I needed help. He and I had both assisted with C sections so that we could be prepared to do an emergency case if necessary. I'd assisted with almost fifty cases in residency, but hadn't ever done one completely by myself. The surgeon from Montevideo had supervised me through a case earlier in the year, helping me step by step.

Then, three months ago, I'd done my first unassisted C-section with the surgeon Dr. Briones looking on. Still, I didn't want to ever be forced to do one without another physician around. The anatomy scared me- even when I had the surgeon there beside me. The blood vessels on pregnant ladies are HUGE. It was a nightmare that both Paul and I dreaded.

The delivery went smoothly, and I soon presented Maynard and Deb with a little boy. Just then, the nurses told me that Sandy was completely dilated and pushing, and I ran next door just in time to do her delivery. The two babies were born on the same morning. It was almost as if they'd been racing each other. I had the nurses take a picture of me holding both babies. I wondered whether they would grow up in the same town. A hundred years ago, one could count on that. Today, the odds of that happening were very slight indeed.

6:30 a.m. I ran home to catch some winks. I pleaded with the nurses to call me only if a dire emergency arose.

7:00 a.m. The church secretary called. Father wanted to know if anyone could get AIDS from the communion wine. I told her that I knew the answer, but that I wouldn't give it to her until I woke up, and that I would call her back – at a decent hour. I think she got the message. I didn't plan on calling her back. That was too rude.

Sunday Morning

11:15 a.m. The hospital called. I had a coroner's case. Don Mathers was the coroner for the county, but in his absence, it was my responsibility to take care of this problem. They gave me directions to the farmhouse where a lady had died. I had to investigate the circumstances and pronounce her dead before they could remove the body.

It was a beautiful summer Sunday morning, but I was too tired to notice. I was absorbed in trying to find the back roads to the farmhouse where the dead body lay. I sipped on my Mountain Dew as I studied the little map I'd drawn.

After 20 minutes of driving back and forth, I stopped to ask directions. After the farmer got me pointed toward the right house, I had time to become apprehensive about what I might find. Well, at least it couldn't be as bad as the case Don had had in the spring, where they'd called him to examine a body that they'd found in the river that had been there since the previous fall. It was bloated and stunk to high heaven, Paul had said.

As I pulled in to park, I found six cars in the driveway, and an ambulance to boot. Inside the small, antiquated farmhouse sat half a dozen family members, talking in low voices, obviously waiting for me so that they could get on with the show. I introduced myself, and then the oldest son showed me the body of his mother lying on the floor in the hallway between the bathroom and the bedroom. A small flashlight was lying on the floor by her side. Her body, clad in a white flannel nightgown, was stretched out as if she was reaching for something, and I noticed a small cane a few feet from her grasp. Her nose was full of clotted dried blood and she had a bump on her forehead. Her skin was cold and white. She'd been dead a few hours.

I told the ambulance crew that they could move her. This was obviously an accident, and I felt bad for the family that they'd had to endure the wait for me to arrive while their mother lay there in such an undignified way.

What is it with our society that everything has to be done by the numbers? Would I have left my mother or father there just so some coroner could come along and tell me to move him? I think not. No one in the family suspected foul play; it was just that they wanted to do things according to convention. After calling the hospital, they'd been told to leave everything alone until I arrived.

I conveyed my condolences, explained to the family that she probably fell in the dark on the way back from the bathroom (there was no urine or feces on the floor), and hit her head and bled internally and died. I reassured them that she likely lost consciousness upon falling, so I doubted that she'd suffered any. They seemed to accept that explanation, and I'm sure that in their hearts, they wanted to believe that it happened that way.

As I drove home, I realized that these were the moments that most defined being a country doctor. I filled a need for these people. And I had enough sensitivity to do a halfway decent job for those who really needed my sympathy. But for those who abused the privilege, like the guy who walked in the front door of my house complaining of the cough, or the church secretary who inconsiderately woke me up at 7 am, I'd give just as little as I could get by with without getting into trouble.

2:15 p.m. I was just finishing rounds when Tree called the hospital looking for me:

"Hi Richie Poo! Ha ha ha! Now WHERE ARE THEY?" She was looking for her clothes. She was also alluding to the toilet paper strewn across her kitchen walls that officer Moe and city administrator Townley and I had done the day before. We had also hidden all of her clothes.

I played dumb. "Where are what? By the way, how was your visit to Watertown yesterday?"

"If I don't get my clothes back today, you'll pay big time for this… Tom and I loved the video – that Douggie and Townley… boy are they gonna hear about this…" We had videotaped the whole toilet papering affair and it was set up in their VCR to watch when they'd arrived home.

Tree's new nickname for me was "Richie Poo". I called her "Tree Tree" and "Treesie True", because she was true to her husband Tom, and Tom was certain of that, which is what allowed our friendship to grow. Meeting Nancy Olson and escaping to see her in Willmar on Wednesday afternoons had been extremely therapeutic, but without my friendship with Tom and Treesie, I knew the days I spent in town would not have been tolerable.

4:30 p.m. The Madison Lutheran Home – the nursing home attached to the hospital – called to inform me that Jacob Bly wasn't doing too well. He had a fever and a cough. I ordered an X-ray and a white count, and told them I'd be up to read the film in an hour.

Jacob Bly was Tom's grandfather. He'd been a farmer all his life. One of Jacob's sons Robert was a writer who'd made a name for himself. He'd written a best-seller called *"Iron John."* I knew my dad had read it. Tom Bly's father, another of Jacob's sons, had been killed in a head-on collision while driving over a hill in the course of doing his daily work as a farmer. Now Tom's mother lived in town, away from the farm, and Tom was running the farm.

Jacob now lived in the nursing home with his wife. He was frail, thin, a shadow of the strong farmer he'd once been, with leathery arms that shook with a tremor when he spoke. His mind was confused, and most of the time he didn't recognize anyone. Tom related to me a story about Jacob that describes the kind of man he once had been:

Jacob had a hired hand who worked seasonally and lived in Mexico during the winters. One summer evening, the man got drunk and, in the process of defending himself, killed a man who had picked a fight. He'd been arrested and it appeared that he would spend the rest of his life in prison. The man had no money for legal fees. Jacob took it upon himself to hire a high-powered attorney and went to work fighting for his release. The court eventually ruled that the hired hand had acted in self-defense, and let him go free.

A few years later, Jacob took a trip to Mexico to visit his friend. Upon his arrival, he was surprised at the warm reception he received. The whole town seemed to know about him, and they treated him as a hero.

They wouldn't let him pay for any of his meals or trip expenses.

5:30 p.m. I had to see a 10-year-old boy in ER who'd caught a fishing hook in his finger. I injected his hand to numb it up, made an incision, and pulled out the hook. I threw in a couple of stitches and told his parents to bring him back a week from Monday.

6:00 p.m. I trekked to the nursing home to visit Jacob, whose X-ray showed that he had pneumonia, so I admitted him to the hospital. As I passed the rooms of residents on my way back to the hospital, I was moved by the sight of one of my patients in the last room, a blind man in his seventies. He was sitting in his rocking chair, listening to the Minnesota Twins' baseball game. The nurses told me it was his only love, all he looked forward to out of each day. Thank heavens for radio! I thought. I wondered if the broadcasters had any idea just what a vital part they played in this man's lust for life. He had nothing else to live for. He was smiling, so I assumed that the Twins were ahead.

7:30 p.m. After tucking Jacob Bly in to a hospital bed with labs and orders, I headed home for supper. I got halfway home when they called me on my two-way radio. Ray Severeid had had a stroke. The ambulance was on its way.

The ambulance and I arrived together. Ray was co-owner of the appliance store downtown. He was a young man, in his fifties. I was concerned that his stroke was evolving, as if it might be caused from bleeding inside the brain, so I called the helicopter people – North Air Care– which was based out of North Memorial Hospital in Minneapolis. I explained my findings, and they agreed that he should be flown in for an emergency CT scan. They assured me that they were on their way.

I got a central line in him and other essential supportive tubes/attachments, and had the nurses assemble his records for transfer. We had to intubate him because his breathing was changing. We didn't have a ventilator, but we could breathe for him easier with a tube in place.

The helicopter arrived and landed in the open grass in the front yard of the hospital. The nurse and pilot pulled out a stretcher and portable IV tubing poles, and prepared the patient for transfer to the chopper.

By this time, a crowd had gathered. We flew people out regularly, since we were three hours away from any tertiary hospitals, but the news of a helicopter evacuation always drew a crowd. The town was sorely lacking in entertainment options. As we wheeled Ray out the door and across the lawn, I noticed that the edges of grass in all directions were lined with spectators.

As the helicopter ascended, the crowd of onlookers clapped and cheered, and then slowly dispersed. I walked back inside the hospital, and had a Mountain Dew from my stash in the fridge. Sandy Hoium, the day shift nurse, was just signing out to Missy, taking the night shift. We hashed out what had happened, and concluded that we'd done a decent job with Mr. Ray Severeid.

I liked Sandy – she was young, motivated, and cool in emergencies – good to work with. I liked Missy too – but I was somewhat negatively biased about her because of the rumors about her alleged affair with retired Doc Norval Westby. As I sat there chewing the fat with both of them, I decided that I should give Missy more of a chance, the benefit of the doubt, and forget about this fling rumor. After all, think about all of the rumors that had circulated about ME when I had been a resident at St. Luke's. She deserved a better opinion from me. And besides… Norval was too old – who would be sleeping with him? And especially Missy – she was cute, full of vivacity and verve – naw… it couldn't be.

10:15 p.m. I finished my supper and tried to sleep. I had known it would be a long week. By tomorrow morning, I would just be finishing a normal weekend on call, and I had a whole week of Don's vacation to cover yet. I prayed for a quiet night.

3:00 a.m. The hospital called. A man who'd stepped off a curb had sprained his ankle – drunk, of course. I told them I didn't need to see something like that – he could wait until tomorrow. But no, they told me…

the patient was insisting… and he wasn't leaving until I came to see him. I cursed over the phone, and dragged myself out of bed and over to the ER.

A big part of the problem with the hospital was their attitude that if they had nurses working, they might as well see anybody or anything that presented to their one-room ER. And to cover their butts legally, that meant that the doctor had to see the patient and sign the ER record. Don didn't want the community to have a negative impression of the new doctors in town, so he forbade me from chewing anyone out who abused their access to care, such as now, when I was pissed off at this guy for demanding me to see him with a swollen ankle at 3 a.m. I thought I deserved to chew him out when I'd been up day and night delivering babies and saving lives all weekend. A sprained ankle could certainly wait until morning.

I told Missy as I walked in the hospital entrance that this whole ER abuse was going to have to change or I was history. It wasn't an idle threat – I was serious. I saw the guy – nothing like an abusive drunk at 3 a.m. to spoil your ideals about God's calling and medical benevolence – and I bit my tongue instead of lecturing him about why his selfishness might someday cause the disappearance of doctors from small towns.

Monday Morning

8:30 a.m. Almost as if on cue, Mary Wodrich, the director of nurses, told me that Clarkfield was closing their hospital. I wasn't surprised. They'd been struggling with only Dr. Gene for three years now. I remembered back to 1984, a month before I finished residency in Milwaukee. Clarkfield had hired a private plane, and had flown the mayor, the hospital administrator, Dr. Gene, and the chief of police to Milwaukee just to have breakfast with me and to tell me about their town. I smiled as I wondered how things might have ended up differently had I not met Michelle. Maybe Madison would be the town closing its hospital today.

Fate's quirks are interesting to ponder.

They'd thrown big money at me to join them, but I'd chased a dream with Michelle instead. Now, Dr. Gene had had enough, and without a doctor, the hospital could not stay afloat.

I used the demise of Clarkfield Community Hospital to underscore my beef about the ER policy as I talked with Mary Wodrich, head of nursing. I would be leaving too, I told her, if I was taken for granted and continually abused by these drunks each night. There had to be a way for nurses to figure out when a patient could wait until morning, and when it was necessary for me to respond immediately. Triage was the key. Just as the family who left their dead mother on the floor was unable to take some responsibility for their actions by using common sense to move their mother without a doctor's okay, the nurses were reluctant to send anyone out of the ER without a doctor having seen them. Mary was worried about the legal ramifications. I told her she'd have no legal worries if there were no doctors and no hospital. I wished Richard Range, the hospital administrator, was around to hear this, but he was on vacation too. He was a good listener, and often a source of comfort when I was frustrated by the town's lack of appreciation for the absolute round-the-clock accessibility of Don and me.

After rounds, I made it to clinic where I was hassled for being late.

They had no clue of what kind of weekend I'd had, so they didn't – and couldn't – understand. I was grouchy. I went through the morning with a bad attitude, then took everybody out to lunch as an apology.

In the afternoon, Missy, the night nurse from the weekend, brought her son in to clinic. He'd been shot point blank with a BB gun. He'd put his hand over the end of the gun barrel. He had a hole in between the webbing of two fingers, but no sign of an exit wound.

An x-ray revealed that the BB was still lodged in the hand, in between two hand bones. I saw the opening in the skin where it had entered, so I enlarged it and began digging. After two hours of painstaking effort, and after threatening to send him to a surgeon in Willmar, I was finally able to remove the BB without damaging the nerves and tendons in his hand. He was the last patient of the day, fortunately, as my back was sore from leaning over his hand for that long. Missy told me she was grateful, and complimented me on the job I was doing in town. It made me feel good again and my attitude perked up as I left for home. That was often how it went out here – a good vibe and then a bad vibe. Just when you thought you were down for the last time, something picked you up and you decided to give it one more round.

7:00 p.m. I crashed before making supper; the old survival routine was in full swing now, on red alert, with a long week ahead.

8:45 p.m. Mary Wodrich called from the ER. They were bringing in a little girl who'd had a seizure. I jumped in the car and flew up to the hospital. Marv Doeden, the chief of police, saw me speeding down the

233

street, and followed me, not aware that it was my car he saw. I pulled into the hospital drive-through, and I saw him drive on by. I knew then that he'd planned to ticket me until he'd realized who it was. One of the perks of being the town doctor was that the police wouldn't dream of ticketing me.

Marv was my patient.

I arrived before the ambulance. Mary told me that the little girl was three years old. She'd had a seizure and was drowsy. That was all she knew at this point.

I told Mary that it was probably nothing more than a febrile seizure and she would likely be awake by the time the ambulance brought her to us, butto be on the safe side, to have some IV valium on hand in case she seized again. As I'd predicted, she arrived in her parents' arms, sleepy but able to speak coherently. My exam of this toddler was pretty unremarkable.

I was in the process of explaining to her parents what a febrile seizure was, when Mary grabbed my arm and spun me around. The little girl, Angie, was seizing again. I told Mary Wodrich to give her 3 milligrams of valium through the IV. Her parents stood by, helplessly watching her jerk, as her eyes rolled into the back of her head. A minute after the valium was administered, she relaxed. They sighed in relief.

She was drowsy, almost stuporous now; it was due to the valium, I explained. But I was concerned. This was a typical for a febrile seizure, which usually happened once and recurred only if the fever remained.

Angela had no fever. I told her parents we would have to keep her in the hospital to watch her closely and do some tests. They agreed that that was wise.

Suddenly, she began seizing again. I told Mary to grab some IV dilantin and phenobarb, and to give her 2 milligrams more of valium right away. I asked her parents to leave the room for a moment. Sandy Hoium led them into the doctors' lounge to wait.

I was afraid that she would stop breathing if I gave her any more valium. It was time to use other drugs, like dilantin, but that had to be administered slowly. This little girl could ill afford to continue seizing like this and still hope to come away from it without suffering brain damage. During every moment of her seizure, her brain was burning up sugar like crazy.

I increased the IV rate since it was giving her glucose to replace what she was losing. I had one of the ambulance drivers begin bagging her since she was breathing ineffectively. I was getting ready to intubate her when I realized that we had to make our move and transport her to Willmar.

Nothing else would be fast enough – not even the helicopter.

I told nurse Sandy to get her parents, and then I explained to them that she needed more help, and that shipping her to Willmar was her only chance. I reassured them that I would ride along in the ambulance, and I asked them to drive along behind us.

Riding in the ambulance, as we pulled away from the hospital, I realized that I was abandoning the town, and that they were temporarily without any physicians. I felt guilty, as if I should have arranged for some coverage in my absence.

That thought was short-lived as I turned my attention to sick little Angie who was still seizing, now with small subtle jerks. She was still breathing, but I held the laryngoscope in one hand and a tube in the other to intubate here at any moment if she stopped breathing. Mary rode along with me, and I complimented her on her sense of calm which I was sure had helped the parents. Mary was the best nurse we had – the most experienced – and Sandy was just as competent. I was glad that both of them were working tonight. What a difference good nursing made in these crises.

As our ambulance made tracks down County Road 40, going 65 miles an hour, I reflected once more about God's calling. I was his instrument at this moment. I had no idea yet of the outcome, but regardless of her fate, I could be of great help to her parents in assisting their ability to cope and to understand what was happening. During my reflection, I said a prayer for Angela. I believe in the power of prayer as much as in any other medicine we have at our disposal.

By the time we arrived in Willmar, an hour and 15 minutes had passed. She'd been seizing off and on for over 2 hours already, and was still at it. We got her in the ER and they immediately intubated her and put her on a ventilator. After passing on the history to the ER doctor, I went to talk with her parents in the waiting room. My job as Angela's physician was temporarily over, but my job as her family's physician was just beginning.

I decided that it was time to start bracing them for reality. They needed to know the truth, that she might die in the next hour; by hearing it now, they would begin the long road to accepting it, and better they heard it from me than from total strangers.

At the same time, I offered them hope. It was important to keep their hope alive, so I told them that little kids sometimes endure these seizures remarkably well – they have a resiliency unlike adults in this situation – and the next hours would give us a better indication of her chances. I continued to inject some reality into our discussion, though... I had a sense that she wasn't going to make it, and I felt they needed to know the true gravity of the moment.

I went back to check on Angela. An X-ray revealed a possible reason for her seizures – she had a pneumonia in the left lung. Either she had meningitis due to the pneumonia, and was seizing from that, or the infection in her lungs had caused a fever which triggered the initial seizure, and the other seizures were triggered by the first one.

I waited with her parents for three hours. Finally, her seizures stopped, and her condition seemed more stable, although critical. Her parents decided to stay with her, and as I bid them goodbye to ride the ambulance back home, they gave me a heartfelt handshake that said it all; they were grateful beyond words.

When we arrived back in Madison, Sandy Hoium told me that North Memorial had called; Ray Severeid, the appliance store owner who we'd flown out by helicopter, had died. He'd had a brain bleed, as I'd suspected. Sadness overcame me again. A real tragedy – a relatively young man... made me ponder again that thin line between life and death.

When I reached home, it was after midnight. I was really beat. I didn't bother to turn on any lights; I walked straight into the house and into my bedroom – I was going to sleep in my clothes. I lifted the blanket and crawled in... AAAYYYYYY! I jumped up and turned on a light. Someone was in my bed. I turned back the blanket and gasped... it was FULL skeleton, dressed in a nightgown with a hole cut out of the crotch for easy intimate access. The bed was covered with rice – probably symbolic of our wedding night – and I knew who to blame. Those Blys!! I'd been truly HAD– it had scared me. Never again would I enter the house without thinking twice, and definitely I would be turning on my lights from now on. It was too late to call them, so I cleaned off the rice, removed my bony bride in her negligee', and plopped on the bed and collapsed.

Tuesday Morning

Maybe it was my previous ragging on the nurses, I'm not sure, but the hospital left me alone all night, and I slept like a baby. At the Willmar hospital, they told me that the little girl Angela was doing better today, and that they'd actually taken her off the respirator. She hadn't woken up yet though so they weren't sure of her mental status.

After taking care of morning rounds and clinic, I headed downtown. It was hot, and someone was selling ice cream cones outside. I bought one and started back for my car, which was parked by the courthouse.

Two blocks up the street from me, as I walked licking my ice cream cone, Joey Miller suddenly dropped to the concrete. As he fell to the ground, he hit his head on the curb of Main street. I ran up and took a look at him. He was one of my most familiar patients. He had a problem with complex seizures and, despite being on three different seizure meds, he continued to have an occasional seizure. The funny thing was that he was always pestering me to sign his medical release so that he could get his driver's license back. Episodes like this one convinced me that I was right to refuse him.

The ambulance arrived while I was finishing my cone. The passersby must have thought it an odd sight, me eating a cone, sitting on the concrete sidewalk cradling this guy's head in my other hand, his bloody nose dripping on the street. Perhaps I was getting a bit cavalier about my job, but I realized that this was my life – I didn't turn it on and off like another job – it was anytime, anywhere, 24/7. So I figured I deserved the right to be casual and eat my cone while I served my public.

The afternoon at the clinic went better, and I came close to skunking Tree at our favorite Nerf game. Fern even tried me for a couple of games, but she was no match for me. At least Tree gave me a run for my money – sometimes.

The week wore on and I endured. Friday came, and as I walked out to my car at the end of the day, I found a pair of my underwear stretched tightly over the steering wheel of my car. Where in the… how did someone get my underwear… I was perplexed. Tree again? I walked back inside and stared her down, but she wouldn't budge. I walked past Fern, and she laughed.

Fern?? Yep, Fern had an underwear fetish. In fact, it was Fern's garment with the hole in the crotch that Tree had put on the skeleton in my bed the other night. It was a fitting end to the week, and I retreated to home to crash again while I awaited the weekend onslaught.

Diamonds and Rust

The months passed. In October, the thought of enduring another winter in town with my neighbors watching my every move was sickening me. If my car was home, I was home. If I took my phone off the hook, they walked over to my house to find me in person. Tom and Tree suggested that I move out to the country. Jacob Bly's farmhouse was available; I could rent it from Tom and Tree. In November, I made my move.

The place was a mile down the street from the Blys. Tom still farmed the acreage, but nobody was living in the house. The homestead consisted of a large barn, a two-car garage with a basketball hoop, and an old two-story house with a view of wonderful acres of brown dirt.

I found the winter much more bearable without the townsfolk knowing my every move. No more bridge parties where they discussed which room I did my exercises in, what time I went to bed, what I had for supper. Out at the farm, the following April came around before I knew it.

One weekend, my family drove out to visit. My brother Mike and sister Ceil came out before the rest. I showed them my outdoor speakers, which I'd attached to the large barn, so that I could shoot baskets and listen to my stereo as loudly as I wanted without complaints. Shooting baskets had always been my solution to stress. It had been the means by which I'd decided to come to Madison in the first place.

We shot some hoops and listened to Joan Baez songs on the outdoor stereo system. *"Diamonds and Rust"*, the tune she wrote for Bob Dylan, was our favorite, so we cranked it. I decided that someday I'd like to own a place like this where I could be as loud as I wanted and still have privacy.

The following morning, the rest of the family arrived. Mike got the tractor working and gave the other sibs lessons on how to drive it. Ceil and I went for a nice three-mile run.

When we returned, Mike asked me where he could get some gas. The tractor was low on fuel. I gave him directions to the station downtown, and he took off.

He was driving along highway 75 into town when a police car pulled him over. Out stepped Marv Doeden, chief of police. He walked over to Mike.

"Sometimes it's faster to go slow, sir..." Marv told him. "Let's see your driver's license."

Mike pulled out his license and handed it to Marv. When he saw the name, he asked:

"Are you related to the doc?"

"Yeah, he's my brother. I'm visiting for the weekend."

"Oh... (pause)... The doc likes to speed, too. Well, take it easy from now on, okay?"

Mike came back and told us the story. We all laughed.

Mike was impressed. "You've got a good racket going in this town, Rich."

"Believe me, it's a small perk considering what I have to do for this town," I answered him.

Everybody enjoyed the weekend, and it made me homesick. I began to wonder how long I would last in Madison. I needed companionship of the female persuasion, and single eligible females were scarce in these parts. In fact, of all that was missing in this town – no evening entertainment or cable TV, no Target or Wal -Mart, no indoor health club- the deficiency that stood out far and above the rest was the lack of eligible female companions.

Without the chance for romance, I was not going to last.

A few weeks after my siblings came to visit at my new digs at Jacob Bly's farmhouse, I was in the clinic one day finishing up with patients when I was greeted by a surprise visitor; it was little Angela, the girl I had taken to Willmar by ambulance, with the seizures. She was four years old now, and doing well. She'd recovered without any obvious mental damage. She brought me a little gift and a thank you card. It made my whole week. I went to bed that night thinking that I had a future here in Madison. Maybe I would make it after all. But things were about to change.

The shrill siren from the squad car screamed through the early dawn as morning broke. It startled me to my core and woke me instantly. It had to be close by! I jerked violently to an upright position and sat on the edge of my bed to process the high-pitched alarm ringing in my ears. Then my half-opened eyes caught the flashing lights circling the walls of my farmhouse bedroom, and I looked out my window. There sat a police car in my back yard, a mere five feet from my bedroom window, with lights and sirens at full blast.

Just then, I heard my kitchen door open, and then Officer Moe walked into my bedroom. He spoke with an ominous tone:

"Doctor Mayerchak, I'm placing you under arrest. Please put a shirt on."

I was wearing only my boxer shorts. I hurriedly slid my t shirt over my shoulders and stood up.

"What's the charge, Doug? What did I do?" I had thought Doug and I were friends.

He pulled out a pair of handcuffs and proceeded to place my hands behind my back and handcuff me. I didn't put up any resistance because I was afraid of the consequences. Then he walked me out my kitchen door into the backyard where his squad car was still shrieking loudly while the lights circled in panic mode. He tucked me into the back seat of the police car, where I sat in my boxer shorts and tee shirt, wearing no shoes or socks. Again I implored him: "Would you please tell me what's going on?"

I knew I had made some enemies in town. Or was this related to a medical mistake? I caught a glimpse of someone in the front seat next to Officer Moe. It was still too dark outside to see who it was. I heard a woman's voice- was that Tree?

I shifted my weight until I could make out the person in the passenger seat of the squad car. Yes, it WAS Tree!! What was she doing there? Had I offended her in some way?

The squad car pulled up in front of Perkins' family diner. Doug Moe ushered me out of the back seat of the black and white squad car and into the restaurant. 'HAPPY BIRTHDAY'!! a small group of my clinic friends cheered as I entered the eatery. I'd forgotten all about it being my birthday today!! Tree gave me some clothes to put on while Doug took off my handcuffs. Only in a small town! I chuckled to myself. They had scared the living crap out of me.

June 1987 came, and with it, my second summer in Madison. I was restless for change. Don and I weren't getting along. His arrogance hadn't changed, and he continued to look over my shoulder as if to check my work, using the excuse that he was just checking that the clinic charged appropriately for what I did. We weren't fighting, just not really relating with a level of mutual admiration that I had hoped to earn from him.

One afternoon, I was over at the hospital finishing a breast biopsy, when the ambulance brought a boy into the ER. He'd been working in a grain elevator where his clothing had been caught in an auger, and had pulled his body in, and in the process of tearing off his clothes to escape the machine, he'd gotten cut in 11 different places. Some of the lacerations were long and deep. They covered his arms, back, chest, and face; the largest and most significant was a cut that extended from the right corner of his mouth all the way back to his ear.

His mother eventually ran into our one-room ER and I told her that he was okay, but that he'd need a lot of work. She waited outside as I worked on each cut separately. It took me three hours to get the pieces back together. The mouth wound alone took over an hour to repair, and required multiple layers of stitches to approximate tissues.

When I finished, his mother was amazed. I took pictures before and after, just in case she later complained that my cosmetic repair wasn't satisfactory. I heard a few days later that she immediately went downtown to Perkins diner and began bragging about what a good doctor I was.

Despite episodes like that, when I felt very useful, I yearned for more.

Those moments of joy realizing what God was doing through me were like diamonds, but the rest of the time I felt as if I were wasting away, like rust. I shared my frustrations about being lonely and overused by the town with Richard Range, and he understood. Finally, one day, a day both Don Mathers and he had seen coming, I told them I was through. The 18-month period necessary to forgive one-quarter of my med school loans would be over on July 1st. This would be my last month.

I wrote a letter to the townspeople. Babe Henningsgaard, the newspaper editor, agreed to print it without changes. It explained that I needed a social life, and that I was leaving for personal reasons which had nothing to do with Don, or any dislike of the town. The explanation was generally well received.

Because I was going, many patients scrambled to see me one last time. Among them were several of the office staff who wanted to get their pap smears done before they were stuck with only Don as an option. Fern's was a classic:

I walked into my exam room and found her draped and lying in the lithotomy position-in the stirrups – legs spread apart, ready for her pap and pelvic exam. I sat down to do it, and discovered that she had on that slinky pair of panties with the hole cut out of the crotch that she'd given Tree to put on my skeleton that night in July. When I saw the pre-cut panties, I laughed, and got up to leave the room. It was too much for me. I opened the door and found three office staff leaning against the other side, listening in for my reaction to Fern's practical joke. It was classic Fern; only she would have the guts for a joke like that.

And people were lining up for cardiac stress tests as well. As of last fall, I'd convinced the hospital to let me begin doing them, to screen the townspeople for heart disease. The hospital had provided a room, and I had trained Sandy Hoium as my assistant, and we'd picked up a number of people with underlying coronary artery disease, who later had successful coronary artery bypasses.

Tree's dad Norbert was one of the guys who came to see me during my last week at the clinic. He had diabetes and had not been following his diet too well. He was a hard-working farmer who paid attention to his health only after the crops were in for each year. Even then, his cattle kept him busy… he always had an excuse. But since I was leaving, he had decided it was now or never.

He'd been having chest pain, he told me. Norbert seemed like the stoic type, so I wondered if he was holding back on me. I suggested a stress test before I left town, since Don didn't do them. Norbert consented, and we set it up for Friday, two days later.

Early on in Norbert's stress test, the reason for his chest pain became apparent. It was a strongly positive test suggesting underlying coronary artery disease related to his diabetes. I stopped the test after only several minutes. I told him to seriously consider traveling to Minneapolis to see a cardiologist about an angiogram as soon as possible, and he promised me that he would make arrangements after checking with his insurance agent.

That evening, Norbert and his wife stayed with Tom and Tree at their farm outside of Madison to discuss his options and make arrangements for watching the farm. On Monday, he'd get an appointment for a cardiologist.

Don was on vacation again and wouldn't be back until Monday. I had one weekend left to cover, and I would be done. The call shift started suddenly on Saturday morning. It was an urgent phone call from Tree.

Norbert wasn't feeling well… she was bringing him right over to the hospital.

I met them at the front door, and ushered him right into a patient room where I sat him down and slapped EKG leads on. He was feeling nauseated and had a little bit of chest pain. The EKG confirmed my suspicions; he was having an MI, a heart attack.

242

We got him on a monitor and put in an IV. I put him on oxygen and began giving him meds for his pain and to open up his arteries. Quite abruptly, he developed lots of PVCs, extra beats, and I knew that implied that trouble was on its way. I asked Sandy to get me some lidocaine. By the time we had him bolused, he'd gone into V-tach so we started a lidocaine drip, and I thumped him on the chest to get him out of it. Over the next several minutes, his rhythms changed several times, and he had two more episodes of sustained V-tach. I pulled Tree aside and told her that this was serious, that the rhythms didn't seem to be responding to lidocaine. I told Sandy to start a second drug, pronestyl, and got on the phone to North Air

Care, the helicopter. They agreed to send someone, and to bring him to Minneapolis. I placed an internal jugular central line like I had been taught in the ICU at St. Luke's.

I knew that Norbert was a religious man, so I told Tree to call for the local priest, who was a good family friend. His EKG showed evidence of a large heart attack, and with his rhythm changes, I realized that he might not be with us long.

The wait for the helicopter was longer than usual. It was a rainy, blustery day, and they told us they might have some trouble finding us because of the thick cloud cover. Finally they arrived, and explained that initially they couldn't find us, and had decided to turn back. Then, at the last moment, a hole had opened in the clouds and Madison was directly below them, as if God had invited them down.

We loaded him on the chopper as the usual hoard of spectators lined the periphery of the hospital lawn and watched from a distance. I told Tree that it was out of our hands, and that all we could do was pray. I'd made several phone calls to line up my personal choice for a cardiologist to see him when he arrived in Minneapolis.

Tree told me she was going to Minneapolis. Something very weird possessed me at the moment and I realized that I was going to drive there with her. Norbert was more than a patient; he was like family to me. I told the hospital that they would simply have to go without doctor coverage for a while, maybe the whole day. If Don didn't like it, he could lump it. I would deal with the consequences when I returned. Right now, I was worried about Norbert and I didn't want Tree driving down there by herself, as worried as she was.

We drove together. We talked about many of the episodes we had shared in Madison over the past 18 months. I remembered my birthday, when officer Doug Moe had pulled his squad car right up to the back window of my bedroom and had arrested me, in my boxers and T-shirt, and handcuffed me. Only in a small town would that happen!! We shared a lot of heartfelt closeness during that drive to Minneapolis to see Norbert, and I realized that this, as much as any other gesture, was a gift of God working through me. I prayed that Norbert would still be alive when we reached the hospital.

He was. He went on to complete the heart attack, despite an angioplasty. But he recovered uneventfully and returned to Madison after a week. The events of that week in the Twin Cities forever cemented my relationship with Tree's family. Tree Bly credits me with saving her father's life; I realize that God had more to do with that than anyone, but I do acknowledge my part in the outcome. Had Tree not lived so close to town, and had her dad not stayed with her that night, he would probably have died en route to seeing a doctor.

In a funny twist of fate, Norbert was my last patient in Madison. The intensity of pain I felt with Tree as I saw her experience her dad's mortality was emotionally crippling; I discovered that it was hard caring for someone personally and then being responsible for saving his life as he knocked on death's door. It was perhaps fitting, after utilizing the helicopter so many times over the 18 months, that I should call upon it one last time for Norbert as my last patient. After that experience, I knew I couldn't come back and finish my weekend on call. I called the hospital, told them to call in Paul when he returned from vacation, and that was it. I was done.

Several weeks later, in mid-July 1987, I packed up my office things and cleaned out my furniture from Jacob Bly's farm house with the help of my brother Mike. I swung by the hospital on my way out of town to pay my respects to Richard Range, who'd always been on my side. He wished me well and I him. On my way out the door, I passed by the large photo of me on the wall, next to the retired doctors who'd devoted their entire lives to that town. These 18 months had seemed like a lifetime to me. I knew I would never work in a town like this again. In that moment I felt as if I had failed. I couldn't hack it. I smiled to think about how my perceptions of small-town practice had changed since I'd first seen their pictures and idolized them. There was more to life than the sacrifices they'd made, although I admired how fully they'd given of their lives. I would have to find a different formula that would incorporate sanity time as a trade-off for the time I gave of myself to others. But finally I knew what small town practice was like; I could say I'd been there. As I drove away from the turnaround driveway in front of the hospital, I held back a tear. Medical practice would never be the same for me, or mean as much to me after this. I'd turned the page on a milestone. As I took highway 75 south of town, I saw Chief of Police Marv Doeden in the squad car out of my rearview mirror. I put on the brakes and reminded myself that I couldn't get away with speeding anymore.

1992 Phone Call Flashback

I was playing "Laura", one of my favorite songs, on "Antoinette", my glossy black satin Yahama concert grand piano. The phone rang. It was Tree. It was the summer of '92, almost five years to the day since I'd left Madison. She'd called to tell me that Doc Norval Westby had died.

I flashed back to those golden days as a country doc, and all the changes that had occurred since then. I thought about a sunny summer's day six years ago when Gayle Mathers had proudly showed off her new Reeboks to me. How vibrant she'd seemed. But she was dead now. She'd succumbed to a cerebral aneurysm three years back. She had had a thunderclap of a headache one day, while talking on the telephone, and she was gone.

As a result, Don had left town, and eventually he'd remarried. I had been dating a girl, who, by freak coincidence, was his old high school girlfriend. When he'd found out I was dating her, he cut in on my dance. It was just like old times; one final slap in the face from Don. He now practiced with Methodist Hospital in Minneapolis. I completely understood why he left Madison, and how hard that must have been for him. He had invested much more in that town than I had. Although he and I never really got along well, I respected his medical knowledge and expertise. He was a very good physician. He had been a Godsend for that town, and no doubt they missed him terribly.

Richard Range had been deposed by the hospital board, which was demanding more success in recruiting physicians for the clinic. It wasn't Range's fault that the town was so hard on doctors. He was lucky to have gotten out before the walls tumbled down though. And Mary Wodrich had moved on from her job as director of nurses.

245

Officer Doug Moe had taken a job as chief of police in a neighboring town, and had married "Jugs", who was aptly nicknamed.

Steve Townley had moved on to greener city administrator pastures. Bill Kenyon, the pharmacist, had died of complications from smoking.

Tree's dad Norbert was still alive and feeling better than ever. Tom's grandfather Jacob Bly had died. Tom and Tree now had two children.

Of all the changes, Gayle Mathers' passing had been the least anticipated and the most traumatic, even for me who hadn't known her well.

She meant a lot to that town. We all grieved tremendously when she died. She's buried in a cemetery in Madison now. In a way, part of me is buried in that town as well. It is unlikely that I will ever again find an endeavor as emotionally and physically demanding, as time-consuming, as underpaid, oras spiritually fulfilling as the job I had as the doctor for the little town of Madison, Minnesota, the Lutefisk Capital of the World.

CHAPTER 5
CITY DOC

Dr. Pendleton, the head physician, stomped his way up to the clinic manager's office.

"Where's Dr. Mayerchak?? You tell him that he can't get away with THAT while he is practicing here!! We'll fire his ass!"

The entire front office staff watched him as he left the building and climbed in his car and hastily drove away, ostensibly still fuming about what I had done…

In the summer of 1987, immediately after leaving Madison, Minnesota, I moved to Minneapolis. Having failed at small town medicine, I decided to try my hand at city medicine, which was much more familiar to me, since I had been trained in the big city of Milwaukee at St. Luke's. At this point I was less than three years out of the family practice residency. I found a job working for one of the major clinics in the northern suburbs of Minneapolis. with all of the other partners of the Coon Rapids Medical Clinic.

The first thing that amazed me about city practice was that the pay was substantially better. The Madison Clinic was paying me $60,000 per year, and the Coon Rapids Clinic started me at $110,000. That allowed me to accelerate my medical school loan repayments. I was still deeply in debt.

Working and living in an urban environment was a refreshing change, and it allowed me to join a large heath club and have a social life again. The major difference between working in Madison and now was that I was only required to be on call once every 12 nights. I actually felt guilty having so much free time. My sister Ceil and I joined the health club together, and we began meeting at the club for running and exercising. We had already run a marathon together, and we planned to do another one.

After having spent endless nights on call at St. Luke's, followed by 18 months of every other night and every other weekend on call in Madison, I was like a coiled spring. Imagine a car that drives over a big hill at high speed, and lands hard on the road on the other side of the hill. At the moment it lands, the springs are compressed and the car scrapes on the ground. Then, a moment later, that car frame shoots off the ground as the springs release all of their compression. I was that car spring, wound so tightly that I was ready to finally unleash all the potential energy I had stored up, and explode into having fun. Now that I was on call only once every 12 nights, I was able to sleep a lot more, and I caught up on lost sleep from working 18 months in Madison. I had more free time to date, and there were more opportunities for that in the large city. My seven sisters and other friends set me up on dozens and dozens and DOZENS of blind dates, all without a successful outcome.

*

Several years passed.

On a Saturday in the spring of 1993, I drove up to Duluth from my apartment in Minneapolis. On this beautiful Saturday in May I had decided to go for a long run along Lake Superior to train for Grandma's marathon. I had recently run my second Boston marathon, and I was looking to achieve a PR (personal record) at Grandma's marathon later that summer in Duluth. I ran 17 miles along the marathon route, beginning from Two Harbors. I finished just before entering the city limits of Duluth. I felt so good that I decided to stop at Holy Rosary church for Saturday evening Mass on my way home to my apartment in Minneapolis.

When church finished, I noticed an old friend sitting up near the front. It was Mike Cohen, a local attorney. Years earlier, when I had attended med school in Duluth, I had directed the youth choir at this church. Mike's daughter had been in the choir and I had given her guitar lessons. Mike asked if I was still single. I confirmed that I was. He suggested that I call a girl he knew in St Paul, from a large Catholic family that had lived in Duluth a few years back. Her name was Mary Terese Weiland. He told me that she was very Catholic, and had a beautiful voice, and that she was single and a very lovely girl. He asked if he could call her and ask for her number and then forward it to me. I told him I would be agreeable to that, but as usual, I was skeptical. Nevertheless, I had to remember that this was Mike Cohen. He knew the importance I placed upon a Catholic spiritual foundation in a relationship.

The night before we were to meet, I was on call for my clinic. I was up most of the night admitting patients to Mercy Hospital, and I was exhausted.

I finally made it to bed at around 4 a.m. We were supposed to meet at Lake Como at 9 a.m. At 7.30 my alarm rang and I slammed it off and turned over. I decided that I was going to blow her off, not show for the date. I was too exhausted. I knew I was taking a risk that she wouldn't go for another try, but I didn't care. Blind dates had never worked out for me anyway, and this was going to be a long drive, on no sleep. After 15 minutes of lying there feeling guilty, but very tired,

I dragged myself out of bed, but I was NOT looking forward to the long drive to St. Paul.

I arrived at Lake Como and began looking for Mary. She had described herself to some degree, so I had a vague idea of what to look for, but just vague. On previous blind dates, many a time I had approached a rather attractive-looking person and had hoped that that was my blind date. Each time I had been told that no, she was not the one I was looking for. And every time, I had been disappointed when I finally found my date. The day was warm, sunny, and there was vernal optimism in the air. I saw a girl standing alone in the parking lot, and she was drop dead gorgeous. I noticed her curly hair and beautiful face and smile. As I approached her, I kept reminding myself that the beautiful girl always ends up not being your blind date, so don't get your hopes up here, bud… and then I was right in front of her. I asked her if her name was Mary, and I held my breath.

Yes! It was Mary!! I was so relieved! Our phone conversations had piqued my interest in her, because of her intelligent responses and depth. But seeing her for the first time, how beautiful she was, I was instantly smitten. I completely forgot how exhausted I was from being on call and we walked twice around the entire trail circling the lake. Then I asked her if we could continue the date over lunch at TGI Fridays. We headed to Fridays and afterwards spent more time talking. The date lasted most of the day.

I remembered back to when I had started my third year of medical school, and I was standing in front of a sink, scrubbing my hands before entering the operating room. My senior resident was about to perform a Cesarean section. He was quite attractive (for a man), and had plenty of female suitors. I asked him why he wasn't married yet. His answer to me was "I have known many women I could probably live with, but I haven't ever met one I couldn't live without."

Now, on this marathon first date, I knew that this was the one I couldn't live without. I have always struggled to make even the most trivial of decisions. I will pore over a cafeteria menu for twenty minutes before deciding, and then regret what I ordered. I can truly say that proposing to Mary was the easiest decision I have ever made in my life. It was totally spontaneous, no ring, no prior plan. On New Year's Eve, I just realized that the time was right, and without even blinking she said yes. I can say without hesitation I have not had an unhappy moment since that day. Not long after we began dating, I whisked her off to Milwaukee to visit my great friend and mentor Dr. Jerry Parent and his wife Katie, to receive their approval.

Jerry gave a toast at the wedding reception. He said that his observation was that my dating of females was more like a job interview. He observed that my quest in search of a life's partner had been severely challenged by my utilization of a rigorous checklist that was almost certainly impossible to fulfill… until he had met Mary. At that point he realized that I had found the perfect woman, impossible as that had once seemed.

Most of my prior dates had been with women whose parents had encouraged them to marry a doctor. Mary's parents did the opposite: they initially encouraged Mary NOT to marry me because I was a doctor. The demands of a medical career often place a great strain on a marriage.

Indeed, Dr. Griesy's first marriage, to the lady he referred to as the "Funny Frau", had failed. In her wisdom, Mary made sure to court me for 18 months before the marriage commenced. During those months she was able to understand the type of life she was committing to.

Now I was happily married, but I was miserable working in the big city of Minneapolis. I paid a steep price for practicing family medicine in a large city, so very different from the way I had worked in Madison. In a large group, being on call once every two weeks allows for wonderful free time, but diminishes one's hospital skills dramatically. The internal medicine docs who worked exclusively in the hospital didn't want me managing the ICU patients any more. Also, the OB/GYNs in my own group wanted to deliver my pregnant patients. They told me that a family doc had no business delivering babies. The pediatricians in my group wanted to take care of my younger patients. The orthopedists wanted to manage my patient who needed a case for his leg fracture. That left me taking care of elderly patients with chronic medical problems. While I didn't object to seeing older folks, it was quite depressing to lose the option to manage my pregnant patients, and their kids, and the variety that is supposed to be family practice.

Then one day an event occurred which drove me over the edge. The chief medical officer of our clinic, Dr. Pendleton, came to visit my branch clinic one afternoon while I was out. I had decided to take one of my three patient exam rooms and convert it into a personal office for myself, similar to what I had enjoyed while practicing out in Madison. This branch clinic hadn't provided any space for the doctors to have offices.

When Dr. Pendleton discovered what I had done, he went ballistic. "Where's Dr. Mayerchak?? You tell him that he can't get away with THAT while he is practicing here!! We'll fire his ass!"

When the clinic staff told me that I was in trouble for having my own office, I knew that I'd had enough.

I had to think outside of the box and find a way out of this misery. I had a wife and family to support. Something seismic was needed. I was definitely unhappy. As had happened so often in my medical training and career, once again I had to adapt, or die.

THINKING OUTSIDE OF THE BOX

The cathedral in Florence Italy was begun in 1296, but the dome of the cathedral was not finished until over 150 years later, because the science behind the architecture of dome construction was complicated and lacking. The span over which the dome was to extend was sufficiently large that none of the known building techniques could accomplish the feat without the dome collapsing inward under its own weight. After several unsuccessful attempts at completing the dome, a competition was announced in 1418 to find an architect who could design a successful structure to span the opening in the cathedral with a dome which would support its own weight.

The contest was won by Filippo Brunelleschi. One of the contest problems proposed by the architect search committee was to challenge each contestant to balance an egg by standing it on its end. Whomever could successfully stand the egg could secure the contract to design the dome.

None of the architects succeeded, until Brunellesci stood before the committee and took his egg and firmly planted it onto the table, crushing one end of the egg so that it was flat. At that point the egg sat squarely on the table, perfectly balanced on its end. The others immediately cried foul-he had cheated. Brunellesci argued to the committee that he had used this example to make them realize that they needed an architect who could "think outside of the box" in coming up with a revolutionary design to span the cathedral with a dome. The committee selected him as the architect, and he subsequently developed a revolutionary design of concentric bricks which formed a dome supported by its own sound design.

The tyranny of my clinic withdrawing my option to deliver babies, and not allowing me to take care of kids, and now forbidding me to have my own personal doctor office was too much to bear. I couldn't make a lateral move to another urban practice. The same problems existed all over the Twin Cities. Thinking outside the box prompted me to make a profound decision. That night, I decided I would go back to residency training. What did I love about medicine? I knew that I especially loved cardiology, and also emergency medicine, as well as OB/GYN. I typed up a letter addressed to ER residencies all across the country, and another to cardiology fellowships, and a third letter addressed to OB/GYN residencies. I ran off 50 copies of each, and researched every address I could find for each of those areas offering teaching programs, and mailed off the letters. I decided that I would let fate decide which way I should turn.

A week later I received a call from the University of Kansas OB/GYN department, asking me to come to Kansas City for an interview for a second-year resident spot that had been vacated. The residency was four years in duration, but they were willing to credit me with a year, because of my previous internship at St. Luke's in Milwaukee.

One of the second-year residents had dropped out, and of 20 + candidates who had applied, they had narrowed it down to 4 for interviews. They invited us all on the same afternoon, in early April, 1996. It was the Monday after Palm Sunday. Mary and I drove to Kansas City and my hopes were sky high. As I sat in the large conference room with the 3 other candidates, my optimism swooned. I noted that each of the 3 females was about 26 years old, and I was 41. I got the impression that I was completely outmatched and way too old for the interview.

The interviews were hard to interpret, polite and cordial but not very reassuring. As we drove home I was fairly sure that I had lost my chance. As we approached Iowa, my car phone rang (*Ed note:* we didn't have cell phones yet) and it was the KU residency director- I had won the spot!! I was ecstatic. I called my partner Tom Blankenship, but no answer... so I sang a message on his answering machine which said: "I'm going to Kansas City, Kansas City here I come… they got some crazy little pregnant ladies there, and I'm gonna C SECTION me one…"

I looked over at Mary, who was driving. It was dark outside by now, yet she was still wearing sunglasses. I removed them and noticed that she had been crying crocodile tears. I asked her to pull over at the next exit. It was Lamoni, Iowa. I looked her squarely in the eyes and told her that I promised that when we finished those 3 years in Kansas City, wherever she wanted to be for the rest of our lives, I would go with her. She dried her tears and I took over driving. I could hardly contain my glee for the rest of the ride home.

CHAPTER 6
RESIDENT AGAIN

We started the hysterectomy. We made the long vertical incision in her lower abdomen, and dissected the underlying layers until we reached the uterus. At that point, our staff physician Dr. Weed had just entered the room. As he took his place alongside us at the operating table, the uterus came into full view. He took one look at the bloated uterus, gasped, and uttered:

"What the hell? SHE'S PREGNANT!!"

Then just as abruptly, he backed away from the table, ripped off his gown and snapped his gloves loudly as he ripped them off his hands. He threw them on the floor to telegraph his disgust, and strode briskly out of the room. We looked at each other in horror. Then we sewed her back together as quickly as we could. All hell was about to break loose, not to mention the lawsuit...

A few months earlier, as I drove into Kansas City one week before starting the OB/GYN residency as a second-year resident, I was scared silly. I was 41 years old. I harkened back to my previous residency and the toll it had taken on my body as a 26-year-old. Did I have the stamina for this?? I was petrified. But I remembered how frustrated I was with my clinic telling me that I couldn't see kids, and that I couldn't deliver babies, and I was basically left seeing elderly patients with chronic problems that I couldn't fix. That was sufficient motivation for me to summon up all my courage and decide that I had to succeed so that someday, somewhere, I would be able to deliver babies again AND take care of their kids. And I WOULD HAVE MY OWN OFFICE SOMEDAY, I vowed.

I drove down to Kansas by myself. Mary and our son Isaiah would remain behind, living with the grandparents, just in case I flopped.

However, we had sold our house in Minneapolis, so in my mind there was no looking back. One of the most difficult questions they had asked me during my interview for the second-year position in the residency was, "How are you going to manage taking orders from a 29-year-old senior resident, when you are 41 years old and have been out in practice for a decade and a half?" I convinced them that I looked at it as a tradeoff… I was highly motivated to learn surgical skills, and perhaps I could share some of my knowledge of the real world that could benefit them as well.

Each time I became overwhelmed with fear, and doubt that I might not make it through this residency, I told myself: "DON'T DIE WONDERING!!"

On the radio was playing that Whitney Houston song, *"One moment in time"* which was written for the 1988 Olympics.

"I want one moment in time.

When I'm more than I thought I could be… When all of my dreams are a heartbeat away… And the answers are all up to me…"

I had a lot riding on this success. I had sounded off on my partners over this issue: how dare the OB docs tell me I could no longer deliver babies as a family practice doc? Or let me take care of my patients' kids?? My resignation was not well-received, and I was now "persona non grata"; they told me not to come crawling back if I changed my mind. If I failed at this residency attempt, I would have egg on my face. It would be difficult to live this down. This was my "one moment in time". As I was fretting over what failure might look like, I summoned all of my marathon experience. I remembered what I had done before Part 1 of the National Boards, during those tough first two years of medical school. I had taken each step as a mile in the marathon. Ok, I thought, I will just try to finish the first year of this residency – that will be the first segment of the race. I will take it day by grueling day. After a year, I can quit with my head held high. I should be able to come back to Minneapolis with some pride, and demonstrate that I have obtained more training. Maybe some clinic will let me deliver babies again once they know I have finished a year of an OB/GYN residency. It was enough to calm my trepidation about failing. Take it one mile at a time, one month at a time. I heard my dad's voice over and over in my head: "when the climate changed, some species didn't make it, Rich… they couldn't adapt… stop whining… ADAPT OR DIE." I also reminded myself of what I had learned from my St. Luke's family practice residency training: sleep hygiene is critical. I told myself I would choose sleep as often as I could over any other option. And I remembered all of the mistakes I had made in residency, those skeletons that I still carried in the closet inside my soul. I thought of Agnes Kinsey, the gal who had died because I missed a critical finding on her chest X-ray. Those mistakes still haunted me, but I resolved to learn from the mistakes to come, and try to ask as many questions as possible to avoid causing patient harm as I trained anew. And I reminded myself that I needed to keep running, which always maintained my mental health, and also helped to maintain my stamina for the long nights on call.

But did I still have that kind of stamina?? The doubts plagued me. I was paralyzed with fear. As I was showering on my first evening in my rented house in Kansas City, I stared at the shower tiles in horror as I realized that I wouldn't make it through this long residency. I was too old. 41 years was just too old.

Yet, for every moment of fear, I had a moment of awe. Wow, they accepted me, at age 41!! I would be allowed to train to do surgery!!

Hysterectomy! C section! Emergency surgery!! Cancer surgery!! The thought of learning new procedures was tantalizing. My imagination ran wild. I only prayed that I would have the stamina to succeed. That was the disadvantage of being 41. I might have more experience and maturity, but whether I could survive the physical demands of call nights without sleep, that remained to be seen. (*Editor's note:* If I had had any idea of how difficult this residency would actually turn out to be, I would never have signed up for it. At age 41, it took a toll on me that I grossly underestimated.)

On July 1st, the traditional day when all residency training programs begin anew, I drove onto the campus of the University of Kansas Medical Center. I was instantly struck by its enormity. It dwarfed St. Luke's Hospital in Milwaukee, which had been my reference point. I had considered St. Luke's to be a fairly large institution. KUMC (Kansas University Medical Center), as it was commonly referred to, was at least twice that size, with 910 beds. There were 23 residency programs attached to it, including most of the specialties, such as General Surgery, Orthopedic Surgery, Radiology, etc. The medical schools in the area rotated many of their students through KUMC. The institution was bustling with activity. In the center of the hospital stood a large atrium with 6 banks of elevators from which to choose, whisking doctors, nurses, and patients up and down through many floors of specialty clinics and hospital wards.

I had interviewed for a second-year residency position, to replace the resident that they had lost. She had quit due to exhaustion. The residency

256

program gave me credit for the internship year since I had already completed a residency in family practice at St. Luke's. They knew that I would likely be lacking in some basic OB/GYN skills that their interns had acquired, but since I was a seasoned doc out in practice, they thought I could catch up to the others in my class by the end of this year. I was assigned to obstetrics for my first two-month rotation. I was happy to discover this, because it would give me the opportunity to hone my Cesarean section skills for the times I was on OB call during subsequent rotations. No matter what service we were assigned to during the day- oncology, gynecologic surgery, obstetrics, etc. – we all rotated through OB/GYN call each evening, where we were expected to cover all deliveries and manage any consults from the ER, which usually required a surgical procedure. We had a staff physician assigned to take call with us each evening, but they typically camped out in their offices, removed from the hospital, unless there was a situation that the senior resident was uncomfortable managing.

On my first official day as an OB/GYN resident I was introduced to my senior resident, Stephanie Carpino. She reminded a lot of my former experience with Jill Harman, my senior resident when I began my internship at St. Luke's 15 years earlier. Both of these senior residents exuded a confidence that comes with having experienced lots of challenges over the previous three years of residency. Whereas I was quite intimidated about beginning the OB rotation, Stephanie walked through the ward with a noticeable swagger.

The first- and second-year OB/GYN residents were considered junior residents, and the third and fourth year residents were considered seniors. When we took call shifts, there would be a junior and senior resident paired together for the night. Since I was starting already as a second year resident, I would have only one year to completely get my act together before I would be the senior resident in charge of supervising a junior resident while on call.

I was one of only 3 male residents. The balance of the OB residents from all four years were female. This reflected a growing trend in the OB/GYN specialty, which was evolving to almost complete dominance by female candidates.

Just as had been the case at St. Luke's, the residents had a conference room in which we met each morning. This room was located close to the obstetrical nursing station where the labor nurses congregated. It was hard not to notice the kinetic swirl of activity at the station. This was a busy labor unit.

At 7 a.m., Stephanie Carpino introduced me to the other residents on our service, and to our medical students. The addition of students was definitely different for me. At St. Luke's we had only occasional medical students. Luke's was private, and less inclined to host anyone other than interns and residents. By contrast, the University of Kansas hospital was teeming with students.

We sat in steel chairs padded with thin cushions – not comfortable at all – but emblematic of the bare bones accoutrements of a university teaching hospital. In the front of our small resident conference room, nicknamed "the war room", stood a tall whiteboard on which all of the OB ward patients were listed. It indicated how far each patient was progressing in their labor, along with other details about them, such as how many pregnancies they had had, and whether they were high risk for some reason. As I soon learned, most of our patients were high risk for one reason or another.

The University of Kansas Medical Center took on all-comers as patients.

A large portion of our customers possessed either no medical coverage, or Medicare/ Medicaid, which was equally as bad. Because they had no insurance, we would often get phony names and addresses from these patients as they walked through the door to have their babies. Many presented with no prenatal care, ready to deliver. It was quite a distinction from St. Luke's in Milwaukee, which the nurses had referred to as St. Lucratives. When it came time to pay their bills, or make arrangements for after-care in the clinic, these people at KUMC would leave a slippery trail. They would be what we referred to as "lost to follow up". But by that point they would have had their babies, or their emergency surgery, or whatever urgency they'd presented with.

I had observed over the years that those same people who lacked medical insurance coverage were the most likely to suffer significant medical consequences and be considered high risk from a medical standpoint. And so here we were, sitting in this "war room" and discussing our "players", much as we had done at St. Luke's over a decade earlier. And the majority of these players were of the high-risk, uninsured variety.

I was nervous as hell. I surveyed the residents and students packed in this small conference room. There were 11 of us on the service. My senior resident Stephanie looked to be about 25, but by doing the math I knew she had to be as least 30 years old. The students looked so young. I felt awkward and out of place. Steph began our sign-out rounds in the usual fashion. The senior and junior resident who had been on OB call the night before walked up to the board and began discussing each labor patient so that we were all brought up to date on their progress.

After we finished the sign-out rounds, Stephanie wasted no time getting started on actual rounds with the patients. I marveled at her sense of purpose and the ease with which she flowed into the work of the day. She was obviously comfortable with her skills at this point. I remembered back to my insecurities as an intern at Luke's. Back then, by the time my senior year arrived, I was walking around with that same swagger and confidence. I was the man. Almost too cocky, I recalled. And now I was reduced to the same insecure feelings that all interns experience at the start of a residency.

Unfortunately, this time I was older than these folks by a decade and a half, and my self-doubt was twice as palpable.

Stephanie Carpino walked into the first labor room, followed by me, and then a trail of three other medical students.

We were introduced to a young gal in her early twenties, and she had two small children with her. Her boyfriend was sitting in the corner playing a small portable video game. The children were not her boyfriend's kids, but were each fathered by different men. This couple was living on welfare, and they had no intention of marrying lest they lose that welfare income. As she labored, she instructed the kids, ages 2 and 3, to sit in the corner and watch TV. She told her boyfriend to find something appropriate for them to watch.

He scanned through the channels, and settled on Jerry Springer. The episode depicted two people fighting over an affair the man was having. Perfect, I thought. What a way to raise kids.

That thought would have ended the conversation in my mind, but something had changed between this residency and the last, when I was 26-year-old. I was now 41, Marriage had succeeded in giving me a more mature perspective on situations such as this. So instead of completely writing off the chances of these kids, I reminded myself that I too grew up in poverty. I had lived in a trailer in a single room with 7 kids. I was the oldest.

Eventually the family grew to 13 kids. My mother was an alcoholic. My parents eventually divorced. Yet, I had persevered, and hung onto the ideal I had had at age 4, to be a doctor. So in this present situation, with the kids from two different fathers, and a new boyfriend with their mother, watching Jerry Springer on TV, I reminded myself that anyone can succeed; don't write them off yet. Admittedly, they were starting at a disadvantage.

As we left the room, I surveyed the nursing station again. There were several nurses writing in charts. (We had no computers yet, no electronic medical records.) There was a large bank of monitors which displayed the fetal heart rate patterns of all the ladies who were laboring. The monitors beeped in their own particular low tones. The sliding glass doors that led into each labor room were closed, but I could make out the muffled moaning of the patients laboring in each room. The cheers of a labor coach yelling "PUSH!!" could be heard through one of the doors. The nursing station was full of other peculiar noises that are indigenous to each specialty area, much like the noises I heard when I was working in the MRICU at St. Luke's many years earlier. And I surmised that these noises never ceased, just as had been the case at the MRICU. As we passed by the station, an alarm sounded loudly as the fetal heart rate pattern on labor room # 12 took a dive. Stephanie immediately walked over to the monitor, and after absorbing what she saw, she dashed into room 12 to get a closer look. Inside was Monica, a 21-year-old unmarried gal who was laboring for the first time. There were no other people present. I heard the fetal monitor alarm chiming a high-pitched continual alert noise. It was distracting to me, but Stephanie didn't seem to even notice it. The nurse told us that she was 6 centimeters dilated, and contracting frequently, without using any other medication to stimulate her labor. All of a sudden the baby's heart rate had dropped. Instead of the usual 130 beats per minute, it was now down to 50 beats a minute.

Stephanie asked the patient to shift to her left side, and instructed the nurse to give her some oxygen. Then she had the nurse administer a shot of terbutaline, which slowed down the uterine contractions to allow the baby's heart rate to recover.

As I watched Stephanie work, I was reminded of the times I had been running a Code 4 in my senior year at St. Luke's. Eventually they called me "Mr. Code" because I was quite proficient at them, and exuded a certain calm that I saw in Stephanie now. I realized that this was basically a Code

4 for a laboring patient. The baby was in serious trouble, and might die, if not for Stephanie's competent medical experience. She quietly instructed the nurse to call out to the nursing desk for more help, and then she calmly spoke to the patient about what she was about to do, and she reached her hand in the patient's vagina and pushed on the baby's head. By lifting the head up out of the woman's pelvis, the baby's heart rate improved.

At that point Stephanie looked at the three nurses now in the room, and nodded. "We need to do a stat section NOW", she stated matter-of-factly.

The nurses offered no resistance. They seemed to respect her word as the final judgment on the matter, and they scrambled off to make preparations. Stephanie explained to this frightened single mother, who had no support person to help her through this labor, that this baby needed to come out now. We would have to do a Cesarean section. The patient seemed to comprehend the gravity of the situation, and agreed.

The moment that Stephanie called for a STAT Cesarean section, the well-oiled machine that was the labor unit whirred and roared into action. There was an even bigger hustle and bustle at the nurses station, as preparations were quickly made for the C section.. The anesthesiology senior resident came running up the stairs, along with his junior resident, and their students right behind them. The nursing station ward clerk, who handled the phone calls, was instantly converted into the scrub nurse for the operating room.

She retreated to one of the two operating rooms we had right down the hall. I hadn't noticed those rooms until this moment. How nice that we have our own ORs so close!, I thought to myself. Very convenient.

Stephanie assisted the nurse in pulling the patient Monica's bed down the hallway to the OR. Then she asked me to help her to transfer Monica to the operating table. Wow, this is happening fast, I thought. I realized to my horror – and delight – that I was about to be involved in my first Cesarean section. I had done several C sections in Madison, with the general surgeon from the neighboring town guiding me through them. But in truth, I had never understood the anatomy. In fact, those extremely large blood vessels in the pregnant uterus scared the hell out of me. His "see one, do one" approach with me had failed. Without his coaching, I wouldn't have known where I was or what came next. I was a neophyte surgeon in every regard.

This would be quite a novel experience.

The patient was quickly prepared for the procedure. The

anesthesiology team sat her up and placed a spinal block, numbing her nerves from the lower chest down to her legs. That way she could be awake for the surgery but would be numb where we operated. She was quickly scrubbed by another labor nurse while the ward clerk who doubled as a scrub nurse counted the surgical instruments. I marveled at how efficient this process was, utilizing the personnel they had immediately available on the nursing floor to double as the assistants in the operating room. It was obvious that they had done this a million times before.

Stephanie called the attending physician for the day, Dr. Tom Snyder. He was over in another building in this huge complex that was the Kansas University Hospital system. He told Stephanie to get started with the surgery, and he would scrub in as soon as he could get there.

We started the surgery without Dr. Snyder. Stephanie took the knife from the scrub tech and assertively made the first incision in Monica's lower abdomen. In that instant, I entered into a world that had hitherto been denied to me, the world of surgery. In recent years, the obstetricians in Minneapolis saw no reason for a "mere" family practitioner such as me to be delivering babies or entering the operating room, not even to ASSIST with a cesarean delivery. The idea that I was now afforded this opportunity to learn these surgical skills and to one day be a surgeon was a thrill beyond description. I watched with fascination as she moved quickly through the layers of tissue and advanced deeper and deeper into the pelvis. With each layer she cut, there was more bleeding, but that did not distract Stephanie's advance with deliberate, decisive technique. Despite my best efforts to assist her, I couldn't discern the anatomy. I realized that I wasn't helping the way she had hoped I would. She had to repeatedly instruct me about what to hold and where, so that she could see what she was doing. Despite having done this surgery several times in Madison, I was hopelessly lost about what layer of tissue I was seeing and what to expect next.

Then suddenly to my surprise she was at the uterus, and she made a small cut through the lower part. Almost immediately there was a large gush of amniotic fluid splashing upwards at us, and soaking the floor around both sides of the operating table. Stephanie pulled the baby's head through the cut she had made, and then the rest of the baby popped through. Then we saw the reason for the drop in the baby's heart rate: the umbilical cord was wrapped around the baby's neck three times! Steph uncoiled the tightly wound cord and then blurted out:

"It's a boy, Monica!! Woo hoo! Congratulations!!" The baby screamed loudly as he was carried to the baby warmer to be examined by the pediatrics resident.

I heard Monica sigh, and then she began to whimper, and then she cried. Tears of joy.

I looked at Stephanie as she returned to her calm, steady work on repairing the wound she had made in the uterus. Her hands moved quickly and assuredly, and by that time Dr. Snyder had arrived to assist and supervise. I stepped out of the way to allow him to help her close up the wound. I noticed that I was getting very excited. The thought that I could someday do this same surgery was exhilarating. But could I ever be this competent, or confident, or cool under pressure as Stephanie had been today? I seriously doubted it. Yet, the prospects for growth in this new frontier before me were endless. My previous residency had taught me how to resuscitate people who were dying from heart attacks, how to manage people on ventilators, how to do spinal taps and to place cardiac catheters and chest tubes. But never had I learned any significant surgical skills. I was both frightened and eager to see what lay ahead.

After we finished writing post-op orders on Monica, it was time for lunch. We were way behind in our morning rounds, but Steph said we should always eat when we could, because we never knew what crisis might be just around the bend. And she reminded me that surgeons need to eat, or they might pass out from low blood sugar. She brought me to the gigantic cafeteria on the main level of the hospital. There in front of us lay a long salad bar replete with every kind of fruit and vegetable and dressing choices. Also a grill where we could order a specialty burger or choose from a large assortment of precooked items. I was not expecting this stroke of good fortune. I surmised that my nights on call would be better fueled with this beast of a cafeteria at my disposal.

My first day of residency was also my first night on call, just as it had been with my last residency. We finished lunch, and then proceeded to finish our rounds. It took the rest of the afternoon. In the course of rounding, we were interrupted twice to deliver babies. Then, at 5 pm, we met back in the resident sign-out room in front of the big white board which was constantly being updated all day long by the nursing staff. I glanced over at Monica's name, and it showed that we had done a C section on her and she had a new baby boy.

Since Stephanie and I were on call together, and this was our service, we didn't have to sign out to anyone. We were "it" for the night. We briefly instructed our students to meet us at 07.00 tomorrow and we dismissed the rest of the team. We had one student to spend the call night with us.

The day's activities had been exhausting. Already we had done a C section, as well as two vaginal deliveries. For the first delivery, the nurse had paged me "stat" to the room, and Stephanie saw me running down the hallway for the delivery She had met me halfway and grabbed my arm to slow me.

"Why are you hurrying?" She asked.

"The lady is about to deliver. They are waiting for me. I have to hurry."

"And why do you have to hurry? "she asked again.

"Well, so that I don't miss it?" I was becoming confused. But I had to stop and listen to her, because she was my senior resident.

She finally explained what she was getting at:

"Rich, think about it. If you miss the delivery, they didn't need you, did they?… remember that even a cab driver can deliver a baby. They only need you if the baby is stuck. God forbid that happens."

She had a good point. I had never thought about it in that light. I stopped running to the delivery from that day on.

I was worried about how I would manage an entire night at this pace, followed by a long day here until tomorrow evening at 5 pm.

Stephanie walked me to the call rooms, so I could see where I would sleep, if I was lucky enough. I remembered back to St. Luke's, where the intern rarely slept, if at all. I recalled the painful experience of walking out of the ER after my first night on call, vowing to quit for good. I prayed that this current experience would be kinder to me.

Steph told me that I was now on my own unless I felt I couldn't handle something. She rightly assessed that I had a certain maturity about me. I felt it. I had medical judgment and experience. The biggest tool I possessed was my ability to realize when I was in over my head, and to ask for help. I wasn't going this alone. I had already resolved to ask for help early and often, until I had my feet firmly under me. Steph knew I had a lot of experience delivering babies the usual vaginal way, so she told me to go ahead and do this if I felt comfortable. Call her if I had trouble. I assured her that I would.

As soon as Stephanie retreated to her call room, I called Mary to update her on my first day. I didn't own a cell phone. They were a brand new phenomenon, and way too expensive. Aside from the $1,000 for the phone, the phone service charged $2 per minute for the phone calls. And they were too large to carry around as a resident. I asked the ward nurse for the long-distance code to allow my call to go through, and called Mary at her parents' house just south of Minneapolis.

I told her about the wonder and awe I had experienced with that first Cesarean section. The day had flown by. I confided that I was very unsure if I had what it took to finish this call night, let alone the residency. I was tired already, and the night was just beginning. She reminded me that my strategy was to take it one mile at a time, just like the marathon. Just get through tonight, she said. Let tomorrow take care of tomorrow. I bid her goodnight and prayed for a quiet night.

Having survived St. Luke's, I knew that sleep was the number one survival key. I forced myself right then to take a nap even though I was hungry enough to head down to the caf for supper. Sleep first – always – that was my mantra. I was able to fall asleep at 6 p.m. and awoke an hour later – surprised that I had been able to sleep. Now I was somewhat armed for what faced me this evening. After quickly refueling at the caf, I headed back to the OB ward to catch up on our four laboring moms.

Just as was the case at Luke's, the hospital wards take on a different complexion at night. After visiting hours expire at 8 pm, the lights are dimmed to allow patients to transition to overnight slumber. It is a more relaxed atmosphere, quiet, with much less hustle and bustle than is present each morning and afternoon. If not for the fact that I need to sleep at night, I would choose to always work in this calmer, more relaxed environment.

By 9 p.m. I had delivered my first baby of the evening, and as I was instructed to do, I called Stephanie to notify her that the lady was ready to deliver, and she instructed me to call the attending physician for the night, Dr. Weed. He was a prominent gynecologist oncologist, who specialized in treating women's cancers, such as ovarian and uterine cancer. Because he was part of the OB/GYN department, he was required to supervise our OB service on call twice a month, as was the rest of the faculty. But he wasn't wild about the prospect.

According to Stephanie, Dr. Weed was an interesting man. His dad had been a prominent OB/GYN, and had taught his son well. Dr. Weed was tall in height, about six foot three, and he stood tall in the OR. He was a surgeon's surgeon. When any of the other faculty experienced unexpected bleeding during an OR case, they would put a call out to Dr. Weed to put out the fire.

He was one cool customer, the story went.

Dr. Weed stood over my shoulder as I delivered the baby, and walked out of the room without saying a word. That was my first clue about his indifference toward obstetrics.

As I was finishing my delivery note in the chart outside of her room, the ER paged me. I walked over to the phones at the nursing desk and called the ER. The senior resident informed me that we had a patient down there who needed a D and C – she was miscarrying. I smiled. Finally, something I was more familiar with! I had done them in my previous residency, and when I was practicing at Madison. I called Stephanie, and we headed down to the ER to evaluate her.

Sure enough, we confirmed that the pregnancy on this 17-year-old wasn't viable. I thought the girl would be relieved, but she was shaken to the core. Her boyfriend wanted this kid, she told me. She was sobbing. We gave her the options for surgery and medical management, and she chose to have us do the procedure to remove the dead embryo inside her uterus. Had the embryo been alive, this would be considered an abortion. But since it was confirmed to no longer have a heartbeat, it was acceptable to offer her the D and C without any question of impropriety.

Stephanie assisted me and commented that my technique was quite good and that I would no longer need her to be present when I did my next one. I was happy to get such positive feedback, especially when I had felt so out of place during our C section earlier in the day. I could see that she had realized during the C section how inexperienced I was in the surgical realm as compared with my vaginal delivery skills. After the D and C, I think she was relieved that I wasn't completely green.

As we rode the elevator up to our call room, I heard an overhead speaker call out CODE BLUE, 4TH FLOOR. CODE BLUE, 4TH FLOOR.

I looked at Stephanie, then punched the button for the 4th floor. She put her hand on mine as if to cancel my thought.

"We don't respond to code blues. The internal med residents will take care of it."

'But Steph, we are right here! Let's go take a look" I hurried out of the opening elevator door and Stephanie followed me with a quizzical look on her face. We were the first residents to reach the room where the code had been called. There were three nurses in the room. One was giving CPR to a man in his 50s who was lying lifeless on the bed. I noticed that his nurse had brought a crash cart into the room. He had EKG pads on his chest and was connected to a telemetry – a cardiac monitor – which showed his heart rhythm on the screen above his bed.

I quietly asked the nurse his code status and for a little information about him. He was in the hospital recovering from foot surgery, she said. He was diabetic and had some known heart disease. I told her that I could see his rhythm was ventricular tachycardia. Did he have a pulse? I instructed the nurse giving CPR to halt for a moment, and to Stephanie's surprise, the nurse stopped and obeyed my instructions. I checked for a pulse. No pulse. At that point I called out some instructions in a low but authoritative voice, like a police officer talking to his dispatch agent en route to an emergency:

"His rhythm is V tach. He is pulseless. We need to shock him. Everybody stand back."

At that, everyone moved away from his bed. I grabbed the paddles on the defibrillator and touched them to the gel pads we had placed on his chest. I then yelled "CLEAR!" and discharged the defibrillator. His body immediately bounced about 2 inches off the bed as he reacted to the jolt of electric current delivered through it.

I then watched the monitor. The rhythm returned to a normal sinus rhythm. I asked his nurse to check for a pulse, and as she did so, he came to, and began complaining of a pain in his chest. Most likely from the shock I had given him, I thought. I told the nurse that it might be a sign of a myocardial infection, and that she should get lab tests to check it out. Just as I was saying this, the internal medicine resident arrived. He had been stuck in an elevator that wouldn't open. I told him what had transpired, and then we left the room.

Back in the elevator, Stephanie was grinning.

"Wow, Rich, that was amazing! You just saved that guy's life!!"

Stephanie then proceeded to advise me never to do that again. She explained that there were politics in a university teaching hospital. I had probably stepped on the toes of some internal medicine team, and it didn't matter how altruistic my intentions were. Nevertheless, for one brief shining moment I was thrust back in my element, running a code, and it made me remember what had got me to that point. Nick Bollettieri, Andre Agassi's tennis coach, famously said: it isn't the better player that wins the match, it's the one who wants it more. I was going to "want it more" when it came to learning these surgeries. As I had once been referred to as "Mr. Code" at St. Luke's, I was now going to earn my way to achieve the same echelon of prowess as a surgeon.

The night dragged on as I labored patients into the morning, and delivered one more vaginally. Again Dr. Weed showed his face just long enough to see the baby pop out, then disappeared to his office where he slept on his couch when taking call.

We had morning sign-out rounds at 07.00, then headed over to the auditorium which was a giant lecture hall, with movie theater style seating and a front podium with a lectern and a microphone. The entire faculty of the KU OB/GYN department was gathered to participate in the weekly "Friday Meat Market" activities. It was the nickname the residents had given to the proceedings. The morning's agenda began with a lecture from one of the senior residents, on the latest surgical technique for removing an ovarian cancer. Then we were handed a stack of papers which contained the names of every patient the residents had operated on the previous week. The reasons that the surgeries had been performed were listed, as well as the outcomes. There was a place to read the pathology reports of the specimen they had removed.

First up was Maureen Smith King. She was a senior on the general gynecology service. She stood at the podium while the faculty read her list of surgeries. Then a call rang out from one of the faculty docs:

"tell me about case 14… why did you remove her uterus? She was only 28 years old!"

Maureen cleared her throat. I could see she was squirming and fidgeting. "Well, she had severe pelvic pain, and she didn't tolerate birth control pills, so we decided to take out her uterus. She was done having kids…"

The faculty continued their badgering.

"What about trying Lupron? Did you consider a laparoscopy first, to confirm your diagnosis before taking out her uterus??

I could hear a dull murmur travel throughout the faculty as they whispered in disapproval of what she was saying. After all, this was a young girl, losing her uterus at 28.

Another faculty member joined the feeding frenzy:

"What did the pathology report say about the uterus? Was there endometriosis in the path specimen??"

Maureen was sheepish and obviously uncomfortable.

"Well, no… it just showed normal tissue…."

By the time the faculty had finished deriding Maureen, I understood why they referred to it as the "Friday Meat Market". It was if she had been cast overboard into a sea full of sharks.

The meeting with all of these highly renowned faculty members left me with a lasting respect for the OB/GYN department. It wasn't going to be sufficient for me to merely operate successfully on my patients. I was going to have to justify to this angry crowd why I had decided that surgery was necessary in the first place.

After the meat market concluded, we headed to the caf for lunch, and finally finished our day on the OB ward with sign-outs at 5 p.m. The only sleep I'd gotten all night was that one-hour nap I had forced myself to take at 6 p.m. last evening. Without it, I wouldn't have survived. Even with the nap, I was truly exhausted. I called Mary using our long distance hospital code so that I could avoid paying for the call personally. Then I drove home to the house we were renting which was five minutes away. I was happy that I had survived my first night on call. However I was truly scared at the toll it had taken on me. I could tell that I wasn't going to handle these long nights as easy as I had done at St. Luke's 15 years ago. I admonished myself to remember the marathon, to pace myself, and to sleep at all costs. I wolfed down a microwave dinner in ten minutes. Then , at 6 p.m., I dropped my severely exhausted body onto the bed and slept all night.

During my third week on the obstetrical service, I was called to admit a 21-year-old Caucasian female who was 33 weeks pregnant. She had been lying at home for three days with a bad headache. She had presented to her local doctor in a small Kansas town, and was noted to have severely high blood pressure. The local doc didn't feel comfortable managing her, and immediately transferred her by ambulance to KUMC.

When she arrived, she was alert and oriented but still complaining of a headache. Her blood pressure was alarmingly high. She told me that her name was Amanda, but her friends called her "Mandy". She was single, and lived by herself in an apartment in her rural Kansas town. By her symptoms, physical signs and the laboratory evaluation we performed, it was obvious that this was pre-eclampsia, which is potentially quite serious. It represents a syndrome which, if left untreated, can progress to eclampsia, where the patient has seizures. It can be fatal. Her blood pressure was still quite high, 190/110, despite the medications she had been given at her local hospital.

We added more medication, and began inducing her labor. The best way to manage preeclampsia is to deliver the baby, provided the baby is mature enough to survive outside the uterus. At 33 weeks, our NICU would be able to handle that gestational age without difficulty. Delivery usually reverses the mechanisms that lead to preeclampsia.

My senior resident Stephanie advised me to watch her very carefully, so I remained on the ward and checked on her frequently. Two hours after she arrived, her blood pressure was under control, and we had her on magnesium sulfate, which is given to help prevent seizures. However, as I examined her, she seemed to be confused, and I detected that her mental status was changing. I discussed it with Steph, who was in the main operating room on second floor at the time. Stephanie decided that we couldn't wait for her to deliver vaginally, and we had to deliver her by Cesarean section to begin the process of reversing the preeclampsia symptoms. We had our own OR on the labor unit, for C sections, but the main OR was located a few floors down, and was used for every other type of surgery, including hysterectomies. She called me to the main OR:

"Rich, would you come down here before we do that section? I have an EKG for you to look at."

I met Stephanie just inside the preop holding area where a patient was about to have her tubes tied. She needed an EKG before surgery, and Stephanie was looking for an internal medicine resident to read the EKG for her. I was surprised… she didn't know how to read an EKG??? I read it.

"It's normal, Steph…"

In the months to come, one of the biggest revelations to me was just how limited a scope these OB/GYNs had practiced within. My senior residents commonly called me to ask me to read an EKG or a chest X-ray for them.

Amazingly, they didn't care to learn how to read them. On numerous occasions, a staff doc at the KU OB/GYN clinic would call me in their office to ask how to treat a new diabetic, or someone with heart disease, etc.

Stephanie did the Cesarean section on the gal with preeclampsia, and I

270

assisted. I was not yet ready to be the chief surgeon on this procedure, but she told me my time would come eventually. I was eager to see that day arrive, but not too soon.. Since it was early afternoon, our staff physician Dr. Weed was in the hospital, and joined us for the surgery. We delivered the 33-week little girl without incident, and the NICU (neonatal intensive care unit) residents were standing by to receive the baby.

I was assigned to do her post-op orders, so I sat at the nursing desk completing the orders. Just as I finished, the anesthesia resident who had put her asleep informed me that she was not waking up as usual. He could not arouse her. We went back to the post-op area to examine her, and realized that she was exhibiting signs of a progressive decline in her mental status. I ordered a CAT scan of her head, which showed that she had incurred a stroke during the surgery. A blood vessel had burst, and she was bleeding into her brain.

We transferred her to the ICU and obtained a neurosurgical consultation.

It was determined that the bleeding was massive, and not something that could be accessed by surgery. Her only option would be to use medications to decrease the swelling in the brain. Her prognosis was bleak. We attempted to call her family members to notify her next of kin.

Her admission and symptom progression had been so rapid that we hadn't yet reached any family before her C section had been performed. Now we were scrambling to find someone who knew her. We discovered that the father of the baby was serving a ten-year prison sentence. She had no other immediate family in the area. She had been spending the past three days alone in her apartment, with no one to help her, despite her severe headache and probably severe high blood pressure. Even her boyfriend was already in prison at that point.

Mandy's vital signs worsened overnight, and by the following day, we reached her grandmother, who drove to Kansas City to talk with us. The neurosurgeons informed us that the brain bleed was massive and incompatible with normal brain function in the future, and after several other services consulted on her case, a decision was made to turn off her ventilator about 10 minutes before midnight on the day after her little baby girl was delivered.

The grandmother then told me that her husband had died in this same ICU, 10 years earlier, on this same date. It was such an eerie story that we

271

all shuddered. The newborn baby girl remained at KUMC for several weeks, and was eventually discharged home with the grandmother.

In my second month on the service, we were rounding one morning and Stephanie mentioned that we had a C section to do at 10 a.m. It was a planned repeat section on a lady who had delivered two other babies that way. She was now in her 39th week and ready for her final baby to be delivered. Stephanie called Dr. Snyder, our faculty for the day, and the three of us scrubbed for the surgery. As we scrubbed our hands at the sink, Stephanie asked me about how the residency was treating me.

I told her that the major difference between this one and the time I had spent at St. Luke's was that OB/GYN residents at KU never slept on call nights. We were busy 24/7. As a 41-year-old, it was taking its toll on me. And I noticed that there was much less talk among the residents regarding extramarital sex; it just wasn't happening as it had at St. Luke's. My theory was that ever since Rock Hudson had died of AIDS, and now Magic Johnson was HIV +, we were all scared of contracting it. I know the surgeons were deathly afraid of getting it by poking themselves during an operation. I suspected the hospital staff were now much more wary of the risks attached to extracurricular activities. But the biggest positive change was that I was married. I now had the support of a spouse to come home to, so I was no longer alone and searching for love in the off hours in between my call shifts. I could instead spend that time sleeping in order to survive. Mary was still living in Minneapolis with our son Isaiah – staying with her parents. We were still very uncertain about how I would fare in this nascent residency experiment.

Stephanie nodded. She too was married, and acknowledged the value in a supportive spouse. We walked into the OR with our hands wet from the scrub sink, and we were handed sterile towels to dry off. Dr. Snyder got the first towel, since he was the faculty. Then Steph was handed a towel, and finally it was my turn. Then we donned out gowns and gloves, and I took my usual place alongside Stephanie who would be doing the surgery.

The scrub nurse handed the scalpel to Stephanie, and then she looked at Dr. Snyder, and he nodded, and she handed the scalpel to me. She looked at me quietly and gave me a glance with her eyes that said, "it's your turn – take over".

I was dumbfounded. I wasn't expected to be the chief surgeon, and I certainly wasn't prepared. We had done about 10 C sections together, but I had felt secure in the idea that Stephanie would continue doing them as long as I wanted to assist. Now she was insisting that I do the cutting. The skin incision was easy – that much I knew without question. As soon as I got inside the skin though, I fumbled. I was so unsure of where I was that my hands began to shake noticeably, as if I had a tremor. At that point, Dr. Snyder let out a big sigh and grabbed the scalpel out of my hand. He handed it back to Stephanie and I could almost see him frown at me underneath his surgical mask. He was disappointed in my lack of progress at this point over a month into the residency. In less than a year I would be a senior resident (the third and fourth years were considered seniors). How was I going to be able to guide the interns unless I improved substantially?

After the C section was finished, Dr. Snyder met with me and shared his disappointment.

"You have a lot to learn, Rich… you'd better be prepared if you ever want to be handed the scalpel again."

And then he walked away in obvious disgust. I was very ashamed of my incompetency. I vowed right then and there to never be unprepared for surgery again. I would learn that procedure inside and out. I would find a way…

The next morning, I met with Stephanie and asked her what I could do to catch up on the skills I lacked. Shen suggested that I offer to assist some of the docs at other hospitals when they were on call at night. She told me that many of the private docs did the C sections by themselves at night, and would welcome an assistant. I called around to several of the OB/GYNs in the area and let it be known that I would be willing to assist them for C sections.

Within a week, I received my first call at 2 a.m. one night, from a doc in the area who needed an assist with his C section. Afterwards, he told me he would tell his partners. The following week, I did 4 more assists.

Stephanie began to see steady improvement in my skills, and on the last week before my two-month OB rotation ended, she handed me the scalpel again. This time, I was ready. I confidently took the knife from her and made the incision. I made my way through the layers underneath and got to the uterus, made my incision, and removed the baby. Stephanie was impressed.

"You've come a long way in just a few weeks, Rich," she told me.

I could see that she was proud of my improved skills, because she deserved a lot of credit for her contribution to my education. But in large part it was due to my willingness to scrub in on every available C section in Kansas City, whenever I was called. The sheer volume of surgeries was my educator.

I was reminded of that saying that musicians and performers espouse: "Amateurs practice until they get it right. Professionals practice until it won't go wrong."

Now I had demonstrated to myself that I "wanted it more", to the extent that I would become a professional.

"Mr. Code" was history. Now I aspired to be "Captain C section".

Just before my two-month OB rotation finished, Mary decided it was time to move down to Kansas City and bring our son Isaiah, who was 15 months old. I had asked her to stay in Minneapolis with her parents, because I was so unsure I would make it this far. Now the time had finally arrived for her to join me. On the evening she was to arrive, I stood in the street in front of the house, pacing impatiently. Finally I saw her car three blocks up the road and slowly advancing in my direction. I bolted down the street toward her. As I approached, the car slowed to a stop in the middle of the block, and Mary let little Isaiah out of the car to run toward his daddy. He hadn't seen me for over a month. I wasn't sure he would even remember me. I scooped him up in my arms and began to cry tears of joy. That emotional rush empowered me. Now I knew I had to finish what I had started with this residency quest.

After finishing my two-month OB rotation with Stephanie Carpino, my second rotation was on the gynecology service. I was introduced to Kermit Krantz, MD, who was a world-renowned figure in the OB/GYN arena. He had served for over 30 years as the Chairman of the KUMC OB/GYN department, only the third chairman in almost 100 years that the department had existed. The very first chairman of that department had delivered Ernest Hemingway's baby by Cesarean section. Hemingway had no money at the time, so in lieu of currency he presented the chairman with a hand-written rough draft/first edition of his novel *A Farewell To Arms* – which was eventually worth a hundred times more than a surgical fee. Dr. Krantz was at one time the personal physician for Senator Bob Dole. His claim to fame had come years earlier when he had pioneered the bladder suspension surgery known as the Marshall-Marchett-Krantz procedure.

On the day I was introduced to him, he shook my hand and announced:

274

"I'm Dr. Krantz. I can do the MMK in 12 minutes skin-to-skin." (skin to skin is the time it takes to make the first incision until the incision is closed up again).

He then informed me that he had done the procedure over 5,000 times in his career.

At this point, Dr. Krantz was an emeritus professor and he had a clinic each Tuesday morning for only 2 hours a week, and he was allowed to operate with the residents one morning a week. He was already in his early eighties. When we operated together, he regaled us with stories of the good old days, before rubber gloves were available for surgery. He told us that he would have his entire surgical team take a betadine shower in the morning, and then scrub at the sink outside the OR with a steel wire brush for 10 minutes, and then they would pour alcohol on their hands and start surgery – without gloves. One day he told me that he is no longer worried about sticking himself with a needle during surgery. The hepatitis C or HIV he might get from the needle stick would take enough years to do him in that he had nothing to fear. Of course he was right. I envied him that luxury.

Kermit Krantz began his career by earning a PhD in anatomy, and then following it up with a medical (MD) degree. He became the chief medical consultant for Pan American Airways in the 1950s, and at that time the first oral contraceptive pills were introduced. He was tasked with providing birth control pills to all of Pan Am's flight attendants. He amassed a wealth of experience with the side effects and assisted the pharmaceutical industry with the early studies regarding safety. He then developed a world class preeminence in his field. One Tuesday morning as I sat in his office during his clinic hours, he told me a most interesting story. He said that he was once invited to visit India by Prime Minister Nehru himself, and that he was taken on a private tour of the Taj Mahal with the prime minister in late evening. From a tower in that magnificent structure he watched the full moon rise over the Taj Majal at midnight, alone with Prime Minister Nehru. That story underscored to me that this was a man with serious connections. When Bob Dole ran for president, Kermit Krantz went into hiding for two months, as the press was hunting him down for information about an alleged abortion that Dole had arranged for one of his staff members years earlier.

One day I was assisting in a Krantz case, a sacrocolpopexy, which is a more complicated surgery where a prolapsed or fallen vagina is suspended back up into the abdomen. We had a third-year medical student assisting on our surgical team. She was holding a retractor while Dr. Krantz was operating, and my senior resident was doing most of the work. At this point in his mid-eighties,

Dr. Krantz had such a hand tremor that he couldn't hold any instrument steady. He relied on his senior resident to get the surgery done. However, he seemed particularly irritated on this morning. He kept yelling at the medical student to hold the retractor steady. It was so ironic, because he was shaking so noticeably that everyone in the room silently agreed that she was the least shaky person there. Finally, he lashed out at her. GOD DAMMIT, YOUNG LADY!!! CAN'T YOU KEEP THAT RETRACTOR STILL??? WHEN I WAS YOUR AGE, YOUNG LADY, I ALREADY HAD A PhD BEFORE I EVEN FINISHED MEDICAL SCHOOL!!!!

The tension in the OR was so thick that you could cut it with a knife. The weirdest part of the situation was that, unbeknownst to Dr Krantz, this particular med student DID already possess a PhD! Not a single person dared breathe a word of it to Dr. Krantz, though. We just let it pass.

Several weeks later, while still on the gynecology service, I was invited to scrub in on a hysterectomy. One of my fellow interns had done her evaluation leading to the decision for surgery. She was 30 years old, and had two children at home, both from different fathers. Now her latest boyfriend didn't want her getting pregnant anymore, and she had chronic pelvic pain, so she asked for a hysterectomy.

The morning arrived for the surgery, and the intern who had done her workup was ill. My senior resident now asked me to fill in and join the surgery.

We started the hysterectomy. We made the long vertical incision in her lower abdomen, and dissected the underlying layers until we reached the uterus. At that point, our staff physician Dr. Weed had just entered the room. As he took his place alongside us at the operating table, the uterus came into full view. He took one look at the bloated uterus, gasped, and uttered:

"What the hell? SHE'S PREGNANT!!"

Then just as abruptly, he backed away from the table, ripped off his gown and snapped his gloves loudly as he ripped them off his hands. He threw them on the floor to telegraph his disgust, and strode briskly out of the room. We looked at each other in horror. All hell was about to break loose, not to mention the lawsuit…

276

At that instant, I knew I was not culpable for this very unfortunate disaster. I had just joined the surgery at the last moment, and had not been involved in the evaluation. When the patient had complained of pain and requested a hysterectomy, her intern had neglected to check a pregnancy test before setting up the surgery. She had assumed that the swollen uterus was due to fibroid tumors. On the day of surgery, the senior resident blindly assumed that the intern had done her job in checking for pregnancy before operating. Although the patient didn't even want a pregnancy, when she miscarried a month later, she became a victim, and landed on a jackpot. It became her opportunity to reap a large settlement from a lawsuit. We never heard the final outcome, but the rumor went out that the hospital settled out of court for a seven-figure sum.

I learned a valuable lesson that day. This time it was a skeleton in someone else's closet, but it taught all of us how important it was to CHECK A PREGNANCY TEST BEFORE OPERATING- ALWAYS!!!

SENIOR RESIDENT

My first year in Kansas City concluded and I was now a third-year resident, having been given credit for the internship year. That meant that I was a senior resident, and had a junior resident paired with me each evening when on call.

My original goal had been to survive only one year of this residency, in order to save face with my former partners in Minneapolis, who had predicted that I would never make it this far. Now that I was through with my year of being a junior resident, the idea of finishing out the whole residency was more appealing. Only two years to go!! I felt strangely confident. When taking call as a senior resident, my responsibilities were different. My intern did most of the routine deliveries. I might actually get some sleep. This strategy of taking the marathon one mile at a time was working. I had made it through a year, and now I was well into the race. I decided to go for broke and see if I could finish the whole thing.

When taking call as a senior resident, my intern did most of the routine deliveries. I was called to a labor room only rarely, to help with a difficult delivery. Often the first year residents would labor these people and I would get called only for the C sections.

One night in my second year of residency, there was a particular lady who was out of control and her nurse asked me to come into in the room to help her get through the last part of the delivery. The junior resident was two rooms down doing another delivery.

I walked in and noticed a very large 340-pound female writhing on the bed and screaming in pain and seeming inconsolable. Her girlfriend was on the chair alongside the bed and holding her hand and trying to calm her down. The girlfriend was just as heavy. The girlfriend told me that they were both hairdressers. They worked at a salon in the neighborhood. This laboring gal was a single mother-to-be and the girlfriend was her chief support.

I've often found that if the laboring mom doesn't have a good support system the labor goes poorly. I've been in rooms where there are two guys fighting in the corner over which guy is the father. I remember seeing that situation with two guys, fighting over a woman and each claiming that this kid was theirs. That poor woman couldn't control herself in labor because she never got a handle on her pain, and we had to deliver the baby by C section. It underscores the point that a woman needs calmness in the room in order to get a successful vaginal delivery. All too often we end up doing C sections because the woman screams that she's had enough of this stress and she is done laboring.

So this morbidly obese gal was screaming bloody murder about the pain of her labor, trying hard to push this big baby out, but not making much progress. I was trying hard not to even imagine how difficult the C section will be on this morbidly obese lady if we don't get this baby out of her vagina.

Her girlfriend was trying her hardest to console her by rubbing her hand. It wasn't working. This gal was screaming at the top of her lungs and none of the effort was going into her vaginal area. I was sitting in a chair at the end of the bed watching to see if the baby was moving at all but the head wasn't dropping because of all the wailing. It was 2 a.m. The rest of the ward was quiet.

Then, out of the blue, she stopped her wailing and the room went deathly silent. It was completely unexpected and a very welcome relief. She paused, looked me over carefully, and asked: "Who does your hair, doc?" (I had my hair cut real short like a military haircut) I told her "my wife cuts my hair with a shaver we bought at Target – she usually gives me a number 2 haircut."

278

She then looked over at her girlfriend with a knowing glance, and nodded and said: "he gettin it for free"

Then without missing a beat, as if the eye of the storm had passed, she went back to screaming bloody murder.

We ended up doing a C section to deliver the baby.

Every so often Mary will remind me of that night, as she cuts my hair. "He gettin it for free."

Midway through my second year, I received a subpoena in the mail to appear in court. I was being sued by a patient I had managed while practicing in Minneapolis a few years earlier. I flashed back to my first encounter with lawyers, on a rotation in my third year of medical school, on the psychiatry ward at the St Paul county hospital:

On that particular day, I was writing notes in all of the psych patients' charts as I did my morning rounds. One of the new patients was admitted for alcoholism, and was being held for 72 hours against her will before she would be committed to long term alcoholic treatment. She had been drinking for so long that she had dementia, and couldn't manage her bills, etc. As I got to recording my chart notes regarding her day's progress, I remembered that today was my birthday. I wrote in her progress notes "HAPPY BIRTHDAY TO ME! It's my birthday today!!" And then I proceeded to write my usual medical comments.

Two days later, that person with the alcoholism was presented before the circuit court judge who was conducting court in the courtroom that we had located on our locked psych ward. The alcoholic patient was brought before the judge to officially commit her to long term alcohol treatment, against her will, as ordered by the head psychiatrist. However, her attorney asked the judge if he could call a witness before she was officially committed to treatment. The judge agreed, and her defense attorney said:

"Your honor, I'd like to call student doctor Mayerchak to the stand, please."

I was surprised and baffled as to why he would be calling me to testify. I was brand new to psychiatry, and my testimony would not matter. Once the judge had sworn me in, the attorney asked me to read my chart entry from March 7th. I gulped, and read my note aloud to the courtroom: "HAPPY BIRTHDAY TO ME! It's my birthday today!!"

I was so embarrassed. The defense attorney looked at me, with a very knowing smile.

I am sure he knew that his client was demented, and needed to be committed, but he used that moment to teach me a lesson that I have never forgotten, that the chart is a legal document, and should be revered as such. Since that day, my notes have always been written as if they may one day be read aloud in a courtroom. It's one of the nicest things an attorney has ever done for me.

Now, 18 years after that embarrassing moment in med school, I was being sued, during my second year of KUMC residency. It was bad timing on steroids.

I had treated an 11-year-old boy three years earlier, in 1994. He had originally presented to my clinic with a sore throat and vomiting. His strep test was positive and I had treated him for strep. I had assumed his vomiting was due to the strep, since that was a commonly associated symptom. A few days later he came back to my clinic and still complained of vomiting, but his abdominal exam was reassuring. The tummy was soft. He had bowel sounds. Nothing to direct me to another diagnosis. However, a day or two later he presented back to clinic and he looked sicker. At that point I ordered a CT scan of his abdomen, and it revealed that he had a ruptured appendix. He had surgery, spent a few days in the hospital, and recovered without any long-term complications.

Two years passed, and the boy and his parents were sitting at a party.

The parents were relating the story of the boy's appendicitis, and an attorney attending the party overheard the story and convinced them that a lawsuit was needed to rectify the gross negligence of my having missed the appendicitis. As I later explained in court, it is common to have vomiting with strep, and his abdominal exam did not initially point to appendicitis.

As I endured the depositions and long intervals of time waiting for the court trial, it couldn't have arrived at a worse time, during my residency. I was exhausted. To make matters worse I had to burn up my only two weeks of residency vacation time for a two-week courtroom trial in Minneapolis. It was very inconvenient.

Finally the trial occurred. It was hardly a jury of my peers. Our defense lawyers did their best to throw out any potential jurors with tattoos, while the prosecuting attorneys tried to eliminate any jurors who had finished college. The best thing I had going for me was that I had taken good clinic notes. They were very detailed. Because of the unfortunate experience I had endured in medical school years before, where I was ordered by the judge to read my notes in the courtroom ("Happy Birthday to me!!"), I had learned to write my notes as if they would later be read by outsiders. My attorney Mr. Hagen had my notes blown up into large posters almost as tall as I was, so the jury could clearly see the detail I had put into them.

At one point I asked my attorney how this prosecuting attorney could live with himself; this was clearly a "nuisance" lawsuit. After all, this child was doing well, and hindsight is 20/20, and it was clear in my mind that I had done my best as a physician with the information I had had at the time.

My attorney responded by regaling me of the following story:

The scorpion wants a ride across the lake. He asks the frog to take him across. The frog tells him, "no, because you will sting me if I let you ride on my back across the lake."

The scorpion replies, "no, I won't sting you, because then you will die and I will drown in the middle of the lake."

Then the frog agrees to take the scorpion on his back, and swims across the lake. Halfway across, the scorpion stings the frog.

Just before they both drown, the frog asks the scorpion," why did you do it?" The scorpion replies: "because I'm a scorpion."

Some attorneys are just slime buckets who crawled out of a swamp and who will sue anyone for no good reason at all, just because they are snakes. This prosecuting attorney was that type. He was short, fat, and bald, and worked in a law office with his dad, who looked exactly the same as the son did, except that the dad was older, balder, shorter, and fatter.

I had Mary and my small two-year-old son Isaiah with me in the courtroom for the trial. I wanted the jury to know what pain they were inflicting upon my whole family. After two weeks of anguish and grueling courtroom testimony, the defense rested its case. Our expert witness stated that he was the head physician of an emergency room in St Paul, and even he had missed appendicitis on his own son.

Before the verdict was announced, we drove back down to Kansas because I was expected to start another grueling call shift at KUMC in the morning. Halfway into Iowa we got a call that the jury had decided the verdict – I was found innocent of all charges. I was so relieved.

When I returned to KU the following morning I begin my call shift as a free man again, now that the lawsuit was finished. My intern Beverly Tong called me because she had just admitted a lady in labor who had previously had a Cesarean section, and now the lady was in full blown labor. We had to do a Cesarean section as soon as possible. I instructed her to make all the preparations and told her that I was on my way. I stood in front of the giant atrium which held the bank of 6 elevators whisking doctors and nurses through many floors of this giant complex. I stepped in the elevator on the second floor and punched the number 7 where the OB unit was located. The door closed, and I was in the elevator alone. I heard *"Closing Time"* by Semisonic playing on the overhead speaker. As the elevator ascended I shuddered as I thought of what might have happened if I had lost the lawsuit. There would be all of the extra paperwork to fill out every time I applied for a job somewhere, and more paperwork and explanations for each hospital I requested privileges to work. Not to mention the stigma of having lost a suit, which implies guilt. My thoughts were interrupted as the elevator violently jerked to a halt. The button indicated I was on the fifth floor but the door wouldn't open. I hit the "open door" switch, and as the doors swung open I realized that I was stuck halfway between floors. I could see the fifth floor; it was actually at the level of my chest nipples. I waited a minute, and nothing changed. I reached for the emergency phone in the elevator. As I grabbed it, I discovered that the cable attached to it was cut, and it was a detached phone which had been stuffed back in the holder with no cable attached. I was in trouble and no one was the wiser. I had no personal phone or way of calling for assistance. I yelled out into the hallway as my eyes stared at the objects even with the 5th floor. It was likely how a small animal would view that floor. I began to panic a little. Should I jump through the opening? What if the elevator continued to ascend at the moment I jumped through? I would be crushed or cut in two. I remembered reading about a surgeon in Houston whose tie had become caught in the elevator doors and as it rose it had strangled him.

I waited for 10 minutes and vacillated between my options. I steadied myself for a leap like Superman would make, through the midway opening, and to slide onto the 5th floor. As I readied myself to jump, the doors suddenly closed, and the elevator continued its rise to 7th floor. As the doors opened, I bounded out of the elevator and wiped my brow. It had been a nerve-wracking experience. I vowed to take the stairs from that moment forward.

I arrived on the OB floor and assessed the situation with the lady in labor. Sure enough, her contractions were strong. Her brow was sweating and she was panting through every one of them, and the pain on her face told the story. I called our attending physician on call, Dr. Weed. He told me to start the ball rolling and he would be along soon. Beverly Tong was our brightest intern, short in stature but obviously ahead of her peers in what she had learned in medical school. She carried herself with a certain dignity and humility that indicated that she wasn't really aware of how far above the other interns she stood. I was paired with her on the OB service, and I had watched her progress steadily in her surgical skills. However, she was only an intern, which meant she still had a lot to learn.

Beverly and I began the C section with Dr. Weed scrubbed in alongside of us. The scrub nurse handed me the scalpel, and I looked at Beverly and winked.

"Your turn..." I said in a low voice.

Beverly was eager to accept the scalpel, but her hand shook. I could see that she was nervous – her first crack at being the chief surgeon. She was a quick learner, but surgical skills take time, and they require repetition that only happens once you have been handed the reins to actually perform the surgery. She didn't hesitate to incise the skin, but she struggled to free up the adhesions in the underlying tissues that resulted from the patient's prior Cesarean sections. As she struggled, I placed my hand on hers, and showed her how to free up the tissue. At this point I had well over a hundred cesareans under my belt, having decided to earn the title of "captain C section". I had driven all over Kansas City to multiple hospitals at night when an obstetrician had needed an assist with a C section. It was now second nature to me.

After Beverly removed the baby, she began to repair the uterus. The bladder was stuck, and needed to be released from its attachment to the uterus before she could continue. As I picked up the Kelly forceps and Metzenbaum scissors to demonstrate how to release the bladder, I saw her intently studying my technique. In the weeks to come, when Bev and I did future C sections together, I let her take over as chief surgeon. I observed that she used that same technique that I had taught her. Imitation is the sincerest form of flattery, and Beverly's imitation of my surgical style was very satisfying. I was beginning to more fully appreciate what Dr. Griesy must have felt when he first handed me the suture and asked me to put a stitch in that man with the chain saw laceration many years earlier.

We finished the C section and Bev retreated to the nursing desk to write the post-op orders. I headed toward my call room to sneak in a nap before the night got crazy. On the way there I was called by the ER resident – he had a patient in shock. He apologized for calling me directly – this was Bev's call to field – but he explained that it was definitely not an intern's case– this was life or death urgent. He elaborated: he was puzzled. He was only in his second year of the ER residency, and hadn't seen this situation before. He explained that he had a 21-year-old girl who was in shock, with a blood pressure of 80/50, and a pulse of 130. She had abdominal pain and a hemoglobin of 3, and the curious thing was that she had a positive urine pregnancy test. He had done an ultrasound in the room and there was nothing in the uterus. He asked me to come down to ER to do a consult.

I realized instantly that this was a girl with a ruptured ectopic pregnancy. An ectopic pregnancy is one in which the fertilized embryo doesn't arrive in the uterus to implant and start the pregnancy, but rather it gets stuck in the fallopian tube or somewhere other than the uterus. Sometime later in the first trimester, it grows so large that it bursts the fallopian tube. Then the ruptured tube and pregnancy bleeds massively, and it can frequently be fatal. With such a low hemoglobin, and shocky vital signs, it was obvious that she was bleeding out. I told the ER resident that I would NOT be coming down to the ER. I ordered him to send her immediately to the OR, where I would meet her with my crew. We were going to operate STAT. At this point, since I was the senior resident, my word carried more weight, and the ER resident agreed to send the patient directly to the operating room before I had even evaluated her. It was a gutsy move on my part, but I felt so sure of my diagnosis, and so aware of the need for quick surgery, that I acted decisively.

The patient couldn't sign informed consent because she was in shock.

Beverly and I scrubbed quickly and had the anesthesiology resident put her to sleep. His staff physician was working right alongside him. Once the endotracheal tube was secured in place, I instructed the scrub nurse to splash her with betadine, because there was no time for a proper surgical prep. She did as I ordered, and I asked her also to call my staff physician on call, Dr. Weed.

Dr. Jack Weed, the gynecologic oncologist, was definitely the surgeon's surgeon. Anytime one of the regular staff surgeons from the OB/GYN department had any crisis in the OR, they called Dr. Weed. He was always cool and calm under fire. He was a Rear Admiral in the U.S. Naval Reserve. The license plate on his Chevy Suburban read RADM USN.

284

One of the biggest contrasts to the residency I had done at St. Luke's, when there was rarely a staff physician available for emergencies on call, was that here at KU med center we routinely had a staff member at our disposal if the situation warranted their backup. This situation certainly called for Dr. Weed.

Once the scrub nurse had splashed the betadine across the girl's abdomen, and the drape was in place, I made a long midline incision from just above her belly button all the way down to her pubic hair. I then dissected the underlying tissues with my intern assisting me. I expected Dr. Weed any minute, and I knew he would want me to begin the operation as soon as feasible in light of the exigent circumstances.

I finally got beyond the muscle and fascia layers and opened the inside of the abdomen, the peritoneal cavity. I expected to see blood, but the amount of blood I saw was overwhelming. There were large clots, and Beverly and I scooped them out in handfuls, and employed many packs of lap sponges to mop out the blood. Just then, Dr. Weed arrived in the room. He had scrubbed at the sink, and the nurse then assisted him in getting his sterile gown and gloves on.

I had just finished scooping out most of the blood clots, but I had not yet found the source of the bleeding. I knew that it would be on one side or the other. I would find a fallopian tube that was fat, with a pregnancy inside it that was bleeding and ruptured. I wasn't able to see it yet because of all the blood I was scooping out. I was relieved that Dr. Weed was here, so he could take over and sort out the root of the disaster.

Just then, I glanced sideways to look for Dr. Weed, and I noticed that he had moved over to the corner of the room. His was sitting on a chair in the corner, staring at the operating room floor with his hands held together to keep his sterile gloves clean. Then it dawned on me. He wanted me to fly solo. I had never done that before, except for C sections, but Dr. Weed had operated with me enough that he knew I was capable at this point in my training.

I felt a shudder go through me, but realized that he was right there in the corner if I needed him. I finally had enough blood out of the abdomen that I could see the swollen right fallopian tube, and I quickly clamped off the bleeding and removed the tube, with the ectopic pregnancy in it. I allowed my intern Beverly to do most of the closing of the abdomen, as my senior resident had done for me the year before.

Afterward, I thanked Dr. Weed for letting me operate without him.

"You were ready for this," he told me. To this day, I have never forgotten the moment he handed me the keys to drive the car for the first time.

(*Editor's note:* back in the 1990s when I did this residency, the common way of performing this surgery was to make a long incision in the patient's abdomen to complete this surgery. In the modern time, I perform this surgery laparoscopically, with three tiny ½ inch skin incisions. The surgery is the same on the inside, but all accomplished with a laparoscope, and tiny instruments. As a result of having only tiny skin incisions, the patients leave the hospital the same day that they come in for surgery. Minimally invasive laparoscopic surgery has been one of the most significant medical advances on the 21st century.)

One of the problems I confronted during my second year in Kansas was that my Family Practice Recertification Board Exam had to be taken. It was required every 7 years, but we were advised to take the exam on the 6th year, so that if we failed, we could take it again in year 7. If we didn't pass the exam by year 7, we were no longer Board Certified. Most hospitals require a doctor to be Board Certified in their specialty in order to admit patients to that hospital. The only exception is for doctors fresh out of residency training who are waiting to take their Board Exam. They are referred to as "Board Eligible" and they receive a hospital waiver to admit patients while they are waiting to complete their exams.

My Family Practice exam was coming up in three months, and I was very apprehensive, because of the breadth of material it covered. Currently I was immersed in an OB/GYN specialty which consumed my focus. I decided that I would have to do something to broaden my medical exposure so that I could re-immerse myself in family practice. I applied to work in a local Urgent Care, and spent four hours in the evening once a week seeing a variety of patients with concerns that had nothing to do with OB/GYN. It was refreshing, and forced me to remember how to manage hypertension, diabetes, etc.

One morning, close to lunch time, I was headed to the KUMC cafeteria when I received a page on my beeper. The number was unfamiliar. I answered the page and it was the private office of Dr. Kermit Krantz. He informed me that he had an earache and he wondered if I would swing by to take a look at it. If there is one area I feel totally comfortable with, it is the ear exam. After all, I examine two ears on every single person I ever see as a patient. As opposed to the other OB residents, who have no interest in the ears, or the lungs or heart exam, I always start at the top of the patient and examine the ears, listen to the heart, and eventually get around to the gynecological exam.

I was overjoyed that Dr. Krantz would trust me to render an opinion on his ears. But why not? I had examined tens of thousands of ears already in my career. I took a look, told him that the ear looked fine, there was nothing wrong with the canal or the eardrum. He nodded with approval and thanked me for my time. I walked out of his office feeling some modicum of worth as a human being.

That was often not the case as a resident. I recall a day when we were sitting in a conference with our staff physician, discussing how to manage a patient. The staff person was speaking, and a senior resident had interrupted with a comment about another way of managing the problem. Right then, the staff physician raised her voice. "Do you realize who I am?? I'm STAFF, dammit!! I don't give a flying fuck what you think!!"

At that moment the room had gone silent and everyone remembered where they stood in the pecking order. After all, this was a university teaching hospital, with a very well-defined pecking order.

The pecking order began with the staff physicians, and below them were the fellows, who had completed a residency and were taking additional training, and underneath them were the senior residents, then junior residents, then medical students. The train of people following a staff physician could include all different levels of hierarchy. It was commonplace to see seven or more people enter a patient's room during rounds.

I remember one such train of doctors, residents and students when I was in medical school. I was on my orthopedic rotation at a hospital in St. Paul. We did rounds with the entire entourage, including 3 staff physicians, all the senior and junior orthopedic residents, and finally 4 medical students. We entered one room where a patient had had a long leg cast placed for a leg fracture. The staff all marveled at the cast, and the pulley device that held it securely in place. We spent 10 minutes in the room discussing the specifics of the fracture and the cast, not ever once addressing or talking with the patient. Finally after the train of students and staff docs had left the room, a nurse in the hallway approached my resident and informed him that the patient had died an hour ago. And nobody had even noticed!!

I spent three months of getting extra family practice experience by working the Urgent Care which was located two miles up the road from the house we were renting. Now it was time to take my Recertification Boards for Family Practice. I had studied diligently, despite my exhaustion from the

OB residency. I felt extreme pressure to pass this exam, because if I didn't, I would have to study it all over again the following year, and re-take the exam, at the same time I would be taking my written board exam for the OB residency. A month after I did the exam, I was notified that I had passed.

Whew! That was a great relief.

Once I had escaped the two main challenges to my second year of residency, by first winning my lawsuit and then passing my Family Practice Boards recertification exam, the year concluded uneventfully. I was now entering my third and final year of this OB/GYN residency, and it appeared that I was going to make it, despite all the bets against me by my former partners in Minneapolis. I was succeeding because of the strategy I had laid out for my survival:

1. I was sleeping whenever possible, even choosing to sleep over eating.

2. I was treating this challenge like a marathon, taking it one day at a time and pacing myself, not looking for the finish, just getting through the day.

3. I was running whenever possible, to defuse my mental stress as well as maintain my stamina for being on call.

4. I was reminding myself that mistakes were likely, and that instead of beating myself up over them, even if they hurt patients, I would learn from them. In order to minimize mistakes, I wasn't afraid to ask for help whenever I felt uncomfortable with what I was doing.

And most of all, I was learning how to adapt, or die. This residency was so unlike the other one at St. Luke's because surgeons are different from family doctors and internists or pediatricians. Those other specialties are more cognitive, oriented toward problem solving through mental deliberation. I had to adapt to the mindset of the surgical residency training. These OB/GYN surgeons were more interested in becoming proficient in surgical technique than in knowing how to choose a medication for a serious bowel infection.

Early in my last year of residency, I was taking call one night with my junior resident Beverly Tong again. Bev told me that she had plans to return to her home town of North Dakota when she graduated from residency training. I told her she was nuts to endure those cold winters. As I was heading over to the OB wing to check on Bev's management of the laboring patients, I swung by the NICU (neonatal intensive care unit) to see a preemie we had delivered several weeks before. A "preemie" is an infant born before the typical 40 weeks of a full-term pregnancy gestation. The nurse told me about another baby who was struggling in the next isolette over from my preemie baby. She told me that this little guy was born at 24 weeks, just on the cusp of what is considered viable. He had been here outside the womb for several weeks already. He would have a long road ahead of him, and there was a moderate chance that he wouldn't make it out of the hospital before succumbing to a seizure or infection or some other serious problem.

At the moment, his problem appeared to be a respiratory issue. His oxygen saturation was dropping, and she couldn't keep his oxygen level stable. She was confused. She had called the pediatric resident, but he had informed her that he was too busy to come up to evaluate the infant. She knew that I had been in family practice, so she asked if I had any ideas. I suggested bringing the ultrasound machine from the OB unit to scan his heart.

I scanned his heart with our small OB unit ultrasound, and noted a large clear ring around the borders of the heart. His nurse was giving him hyperalimentation, basically giving him nutrition though a central IV line; I suspected that it was causing a pericardial effusion, which is a collection of fluid inside the sac that surrounds the heart. It can restrict the ability of the heart to function properly. I asked the nurse to relay this information to the senior pediatric resident. She did.

I left the NICU to continue my OB ward duties, and an hour later I received a frantic call from the NICU nurse. This baby was crumping, dying before her eyes, and none of the peds residents were able to get up there to evaluate. They were tied up in ER. She told me she suspected that they were blowing her off, and didn't seem to grasp the severity of this baby's struggles to oxygenate. She wondered if they had written this baby off because of its severe prematurity and overall medical struggles.

I walked back to the NICU with the ultrasound machine, and my scan determined that the fluid-filled circle around the baby's heart was more pronounced. I noted that his oxygen saturation was dropping severely. It called for drastic action. I called the peds senior resident and asked if I could take action for this apparent pericardial effusion. He agreed to let me use my best judgement. I was going to draw that fluid out from that fluid-filled sac immediately outside of the baby's heart. I had done that on several occasions at St. Luke's, with older adults who had pericardial tamponade. I asked the nurse for a 22-gauge needle, and I stuck it through the ribcage near this tiny premature infant's sternum, and I used the ultrasound machine for guidance. On the ultrasound I could see my needle approaching the sac around the baby's heart. I was nervous but strangely calm, as is typical for me when I am doing something that is a matter of life and death. Just then I saw the IV needle squirt some milky fluid out, and the clear ring around the heart disappeared. Almost immediately the oxygen saturation rebounded to its previous level, and the nurse was able to dial down his oxygen flow. It was a dramatic response to my very scary needle aspiration of his pericardial sac.

A week later I received an official letter of gratitude from the KUMC Pediatrics department and the NICU. That baby eventually made it out of the hospital.

*

It was now only two months before I graduated from KU medical center. To my dismay I was never called "Captain C section", the title I had aspired to, but I had earned the respect all the same. Instead, my fellow residents called me "Zorro" because my appetite for surgeries was insatiable. I was on call one evening and Mary brought the kids over to meet me in the cafeteria of the hospital so that we could spend a few minutes together. Our son Isaiah was three, and daughter Mary Claire 18 months old.

I ordered my usual French fries, because Isaiah loved them. I enjoyed this small respite spending twenty minutes eating with my family. What a difference from the days at St. Luke's in Milwaukee, when I had no family!! At least my home life was settled, and that provided huge emotional and psychological support when I needed it most. After our quick visit, I waved goodbye to them at the entrance to the hospital. I was walking the stairs back to the OB floor to check on my junior resident Randy Barnes, who was managing several people in early labor. Ever since my elevator disaster the prior year, I was taking the stairs everywhere, even if it meant eight flights of stairs. I was getting in great shape. While I was still in the stairwell, I was paged STAT to the main OR, which was located on second floor. Our OB ward had its own OR, which was quite convenient for when our laboring patients required a stat Cesarean section. It eliminated the risk of the patient being stuck in an elevator while transporting to the main OR rooms on second floor. In fact, our OB floor was a locked unit, because a year earlier a baby had been stolen from our unit. The baby had been whisked away by a mentally retarded couple who had driven out of state before they were finally apprehended by law enforcement. A multimillion-dollar lawsuit ensued, and within a few weeks all of the OB units across all of Kansas City had locked units. Our OR suite on the OB floor was sufficient for many of the cases we did, but our main gynecological surgery such as hysterectomies was done on the second floor, and that's where I was paged to, STAT.

I arrived in the OR to see a female, 24 weeks pregnant, who was undergoing emergency pelvic surgery for a fractured pelvis. She was bleeding severely and she was in shock. The orthopedics residents had already put her asleep and were attempting to fix her pelvis and stop her from bleeding to death, but they realized that the baby needed to be removed before they could do anything more to save her life, hence, they called me.

She had been brought in by ambulance after she had been involved in a serious car accident. She had driven over a hill on a busy highway, where she was hit head-on by another car who had crossed into her lane intentionally just at the top of the hill. It was a game the local teens played, called "hill-topping", where they would drive blindly over a hill at high speed in the lane for oncoming traffic, and just hope no one was there – like Russian roulette.

In this case, it was four young white guys who had crashed into this young black female who was barely into her sixth month of pregnancy. I glanced in at the patient lying on the table as I passed by the scrub sink. There was no time for scrubbing my hands. In my mind I played the Foreigner song "Cold as Ice"– it was a time for being cool under pressure and I was making a habit of humming that song at times like this. I observed that this poor girl had a compound fracture in her upper leg and a distorted pelvis from the fracture. I noticed that the lower half of the operating table was soaked in blood. I got in my gown and gloves rapidly and made a long midline incision from her belly button down to the pubis and dissected the layers with my hands as fast as I could – we trained for emergency extractions like this-and I had the baby out in less than 90 seconds. I then closed her abdomen very quickly and let the orthopedists attend to her serious bleeding. They were able to save her life.

After the baby was delivered, I handed it off to my junior resident Randy and directed him to get the baby to the NICU stat. However, I didn't clarify with the NICU team if they would be back up on our locked OB unit, or standing by downstairs outside the main OR. Randy ran the baby upstairs to our locked unit on 7th floor, and then discovered that the NICU team was downstairs just outside the 2nd floor OR where I was working. By the time he brought the 24-week infant back down to the NICU team, it was obvious that the baby was in bad shape. The baby only lived for a few minutes, and then they stopped resuscitation. As I considered that in retrospect, I realized that I should have clarified this with the NICU ahead of time, to avoid the confusion about where they were located. I don't believe that it would have made any difference for this severely premature baby's chances of living, but I will never know. It was one more potential skeleton to add to my closet. I vowed to learn from that mistake, and never commit it again. I would always clarify with the NICU where they intended to receive the baby. Mistakes in medicine, whether large or small, frequently lead to root cause analysis by a team of doctors and nurses, so that they can be avoided in the future. However, the people who commit those errors can never escape the pain of the guilt that accompanies them.

I feel so terrible for that poor mother who was the victim of the hilltopping. As soon as her relatives found out about the four white guys, all of whom were in the hospital with injuries of their own, a rumor went out that they would be coming to exact revenge on these murderers. Security was called in to lock down that entire floor of the hospital until all of the boys were released a few days later. After that, their security was their own problem.

*

As a resident I was "volunteered" to provide free care to a number of indigent clinics throughout the area, mostly to see OB patients on Medicaid or medical assistance programs for prenatal care. Most of them were unmarried and had no intention of marrying because they would then forfeit their medical benefits. The waiting room would be filled with 15-20 patients, all waiting to be seen without an appointment, just in order of arrival. One such a clinic was located in Leavenworth, Kansas. As I would drive into the town each week, I noted a prominent sign on the outskirts which stated that it was the home of Amelia Earhardt, famous aviatrix.

One day as I was fulfilling my voluntary shift in that public health clinic I was working alongside an internal medicine resident from KUMC. We hadn't met before. We struck up a conversation about running, and he informed me that he had been a Division 1 athlete in college, and had participated in the Drake Relays, in Des Moines, Iowa. His favorite event had been the mile race. Out of politeness more than anything I inquired about his race time for the event. He blithely replied: "3:59:40 "

I blurted out my surprise: "ARE YOU KIDDING ME?? YOU RAN A SUB 4 MINUTE MILE??"

His reply: "Yeah, and I took 7th in the race." (yes, that's not a typo, he took seventh place!)

I couldn't comprehend what he was telling me. It was beyond belief. To think back to the days when Roger Bannister had been the first person to run a mile under 4 minutes, and now there were seven in one race. I asked him to sign my OB/GYN compact reference guide – it was the only thing I had with me.

Then he told me something I didn't expect to hear. He said that his running wasn't his greatest life's accomplishment. He said that running was easy, but getting accepted into medical school was hard. He considered that a much greater achievement, as well as being a good husband and father.

That put it in crisp perspective for me. I was the guy who always wanted more out of my marathon career than my body was ever able to deliver. I had a better appreciation for myself that evening. I was a doctor, and that should matter more to me than my deflated marathon aspirations.

Sometimes I tended to downplay my academic achievements, because they seemed to come easily. Here was a guy who really appreciated his medical education and what it meant.

On the last Saturday of my residency training, we had our senior graduation banquet for the University of Kansas Medical Center. It was held at a fancy hotel banquet room at the Crowne Plaza in Kansas City, Missouri. On the way to the event, I reflected on the differences between this OB/GYN residency at KUMC and the family practice one I had done previously at St. Luke's in Milwaukee. One of the biggest differences was that this was a residency of surgical experiences. I learned Cesarean sections, and hysterectomies, and many other surgical procedures. St. Luke's had been focused upon medical management of patients, such as caring for stroke and heart attack victims. I had learned to intubate, and place chest tubes and central lines, all of which had served me well out in the tiny town of Madison. But now I was so darned happy to have attained the additional surgical skills – it was an awesome feeling that overcame me as I drove to this awards banquet. My former partner Tom Blankenship reminded me that I now possessed a special skill set, a hybrid blend of family practice cognitive breadth and of OB/GYN surgical prowess, which would open doors for me that very few people had access to.

I was given the Outstanding Senior Resident Award by the KUMC faculty, and my favorite intern Beverly Tong was awarded the outstanding junior resident. I decided to celebrate by drinking wine. In the space of an hour

I drank three glasses of wine and ate only some au gratin potatoes for supper. Throughout the entire three years of residency, I never drank alcohol, so these three glasses of wine represented the release I felt after having disciplined myself for such a long journey. However, it was way over my limit. I was so dizzy that Mary drove us home. When we arrived, everything was spinning as if I had been on a roller coaster too many times. I was too sick to even enter the house. It was a warm night in June, and I was wearing a suit and tie. I decided to lie down on the front lawn and promptly threw up all my au gratin potatoes. I then passed out on the lawn, in my suit and tie, and slept there overnight, right next to the regurgitated au gratin potatoes. I woke on Sunday morning and dragged myself into the house and had a miserable headache-filled day. Since that day I have not had more than a token half a glass of any alcoholic beverage. That experience taught me for the final time that I am a lightweight, and I don't ever want to be that sick again.

LAST DAY

June 30, 1999 We're not in Kansas anymore, Dorothy…

Ask any boat owner, and they will tell you that the best two days of owning a boat are the day you buy it and the day you sell it. In most instances, the same can be said about residency training. Usually the first day goes easy on you, unless, as in my case, you get stuck with being on call. The last day is almost always a breeze. Such was the case at KUMC, definitely the best day of residency – EVER.

I was back on the obstetrical service as the senior resident, but my junior was informed that she would be leading rounds in the morning. I slept in for the first time in three years, and arrived at 9 a.m. – three hours later than usual. I spent two hours on the OB ward with the team, and then the other graduating seniors and I headed over to the Jazz bar and grill across the street from the hospital, where we had lunch, and then talked for three hours. Our residency director had informed us that since we are Kansas state employees, we had to remain on hospital grounds until 3 p.m. if we wanted our last paycheck. It was a paltry $800 for my last two weeks of slave labor, but I needed it badly. The Jazz bar and grill was close enough to the KUMC campus to qualify as being on the hospital grounds. We had seen the previous ranks of seniors do this, so it was a tradition that we eagerly awaited. In fact, I had been counting down the past 100 days waiting for this moment to arrive. It was a glorious and lazy afternoon luncheon, and I was imbued with a feeling of freedom and relief as if I had just escaped from incarceration.

By 3 p.m. I drove home from the hospital to Mary and our three young kids. Isaiah was still 3. Mary Claire 2. Thomas Gerard only 7 months. We packed up our stuff and we left our house in Fairway Kansas (4827 Mohawk Drive) at 5 p.m. We drove to Princeton, Minnesota. Along the way, we pulled off at the exit for Lamoni, Iowa, where three years earlier on a day in April 1996 I had discovered that Mary was crying her eyes out because I had been accepted to the residency. I had promised her then that after residency, we could begin the next chapter of our life anywhere that she wanted to. It was a special moment to stop again at the Lamoni exit, and I was almost tearful to realize that I had made it through an exhausting and very taxing residency, despite the insecurities about my age. I was finished!! I was now an OB/GYN surgeon!! I could have my own office!!

And nobody would be able to tell me that I couldn't deliver babies again. And better yet, now I could do a Cesarean section if the situation demanded it, and if that went awry, I could also do a hysterectomy to remedy the complication. The training had secured for me tremendous latitude to define my own practice parameters, immune to the scrutiny and sanctions I had endured with my former partners.

Mary and I had deliberated about where to start our new life together now that residency was over. There was an opening in the small town of Princeton, Minnesota. The opportunity seemed perfect. The clinic and hospital had about 20 docs, but no OB/GYNs. I would finally get to combine my family practice skills with my newfound OB/GYN surgical skills. And best of all, I would be practicing in a small town again, as a small-town country doctor. Things were definitely looking up. The three year bone-crushing residency now seemed to be reaping benefits beyond my wildest dreams.

CHAPTER 7
The Eagle Has Landed

1999 Princeton, MN, Fairview Clinic

I arrived in Princeton, Minnesota to work for Fairview Medical Center, a large group comprised of 10 twin cities hospitals and which was affiliated with the University of Minnesota hospital and medical school. It was such a relief to have finished that long grueling OB/GYN residency. I likened it to finally reaching shore after swimming overnight through a turbulent, dark ocean. I had been on call every third night for three whole years. There were times that I fell asleep sitting upright in a chair in the middle of the day during a lecture. During those twenty minutes asleep I would usually have three or four rapid, bizarre dreams, a sure sign that I was sleep deprived. If ever I would lie on a bed, I could sleep instantly. There were times when I came critically close to quitting due to sleep exhaustion, as had been the case of the resident whose position I assumed after she quit. I am not sure why sleep is so critical to our well-being, but it is quite apparent that sleep is the wonder vitamin that keeps us whole.

Since I was the only OB/GYN in this new practice in the small town of Princeton, I was anticipating that I would be called upon frequently for emergencies. Little did I know that it would start in my first week in town.

I was still unpacking boxes in the garage of our rented home in downtown Princeton, three minutes from the hospital. I was called on our land line, the only phone we owned. We did not yet have cell phones. The nurse from the OB floor merely said, "Dr. Mayerchak, they need you in here STAT."

The urgency in her voice said all I needed to hear. I didn't ask for any more information – I just dropped what I was doing and bolted to the hospital.

I arrived on the OB floor to find Tracy Lester lying in her hospital bed which was entirely soaked with blood from the bottom of the sheet all the way up to her chest. She had just delivered a baby and the uterus was sitting

297

outside of her vagina, inverted. In other words, it was inside out. And it was lying between her legs, bleeding profusely. After the baby was born, the placenta had delivered, and when it came out, it was still attached to the uterus and it had turned the uterus inside out, which caused it to rapidly lose blood. Dr Chris Pensinger had delivered the baby, and he thanked me for getting my butt in as quickly as I had. He had tried to re-vert the uterus and put it back inside the patient's vagina, but he had failed. I could tell that there was extreme panic in the room. That type of scenario happens only once in a thousand deliveries. I hadn't seen one in residency. But I knew what to do. Nobody knew me, nor I them. It was my first week in town. I could see they were sizing me up, trying to assess whether I was up to the toughness that this situation demanded. After what I had been through at KU, I felt strangely calm and collected. This was no worse than what I had seen with the "hilltoppers" who had killed that baby in Kansas City when they fractured the mother's pelvis – I had seen a lot more blood in that situation. I noted that the nurse anesthetist was in the room, and I asked him to give her some sedation in her IV, and then I explained to her that I was going to try to invert the uterus again to its normal position, but that it might be painful for her. After she was sedated, I tried to push the uterus back to the normal anatomical orientation, but it was in a spasm and it wouldn't budge. In the meantime, she had 2000 cc of blood on her sheets. She had already lost about a third of her blood volume. I informed her husband that we would have to take her quickly to the OR and that I might need to perform a hysterectomy. He agreed and gave me verbal consent to do whatever was necessary, and then we wheeled her bed urgently to the OR on the main floor of the hospital. Back at that time there was no OR in the labor department, as there is now. It was cases such as this that finally won our argument that a labor ward needs to have an OR immediately accessible in the same area of the hospital.

However, on this particular day, we had to wheel her bed into an elevator, and ride down a floor, then wheel her into the OR, and all the while her uterus lay in between her legs, outside of her vagina, and bleeding profusely. As she arrived in the OR, we placed her on the operating table and Dr. Robin Fischer, another family practice doc, arrived to help us with the surgery. Ironically, Dr. Fischer had been a resident at Broadlawns Hospital in Des Moines, the place that had fired me just before the start of my family practice residency so many years earlier after I had injured my

298

back. Now, fate had brought us together.

I scrubbed my hands hastily at the sink just outside the operating room, humming Foreigner's "Cold as Ice" in my mind. When I stand at the scrub sink, it is my moment to prepare mentally for the surgery at hand. When I was an intern at KUMC, my senior resident bore the responsibility for how the surgery turned out. And in fact, the faculty member was ultimately responsible for the outcome, and we could always call for assistance if we needed it. I would often daydream at the scrub sink back then, or make meaningless conversation with my senior resident. In contrast, by the time I became a senior resident, that scrub sink time had evolved to a concerted pause in which I would concentrate my focus on the task at hand. That was a natural consequence of being handed more responsibility for the outcome of the surgery. And now at this scrub sink I was fully aware of the gravity of my situation: I was in a small town now, with no university professor surgeons at my beck and call. The outcome of this surgery – and the life of this patient – was entirely on my shoulders. This patient had already bled down to half her blood volume. I steeled myself for the challenge in front of me, and reminded myself that I was her best chance of survival. It was time to sink or swim. My mind flashed back to when I had operated on the girl in shock from the ruptured ectopic pregnancy, with Dr. Weed sitting in the corner, tacitly vouching for my competency. I told myself that I was ready for this. I strode through the OR door with a look of confidence on my face which betrayed any nerves I felt. I had the nurse anesthetist put her all the way to sleep, and I tried one more time to punch the uterus back to its normal, non-inverted anatomy, but I couldn't get it done. I then decided that a hysterectomy was the only way to save her life. I made a long midline incision from above her belly button down to her pubic hair, and began dissecting tissues as fast as I could, until I could see the uterus and bladder and all of the pelvic anatomy. Over the next hour and a half, I performed the hysterectomy, my first surgery of this magnitude in Princeton, while transfusing her with 8 units of blood and praying that she would stay alive through the surgery. The blood vessels around the uterus were huge, and when I cut them they bled profusely. Although I respected them greatly, I no longer feared them as I once had. All the while, I maintained my calm demeanor, spoke in a soft voice, and earned the respect of the operating crew and the OB nurses who were present. She did survive, and left the hospital four days later with her newborn baby. It was the first time I was called upon to prove myself in front of my family practice colleagues, and it was the most dramatic of circumstances under which to perform. Just after I finished dictating my operative note, it struck me that this had been my Whitney Houston moment come to life – "I want one moment in time, when I'm more than I thought I could be... when all of my dreams are a heartbeat away, and the answers are all up to me..."

This was only the first of many traumatic occasions I would inevitably be asked to rise above. I was grateful that I had succeeded.

Two years passed. On a warm day in October I was pacing in a parking garage in Dallas, Texas. I was very focused and pensive. I barely noticed my surroundings. Suddenly, the hair on the back of my neck began to bristle, and I sensed that I was not alone. I glanced up from the card I was reading and suddenly I realized that there were six grown men slowly circling me.

At first they were a hundred feet away, and then fifty, and now twenty. The circle around me was closing ever tighter. I noticed that one of them had a gun in his hand, partially concealed behind his back. I surveyed my situation. I was on the third floor ramp, and there was nowhere to run. I began to sweat...

Two years after my arrival in Princeton, it was time for my oral OB/GYN Board Exam. In order to prepare for the exam, I was required to keep a list of all the patients I managed in the clinic, and a separate list of all of the patients I operated upon in my first 2 years of practice. I submitted the lists to the OB/GYN Board, and after reviewing my lists, they agreed to admit me for the oral exam.

In previous years, the exam had been held at the Drake Hotel in Chicago.

It was an annual ritual that applicants dreaded. I had heard horror stories. The setup was such that there were three sets of two examiners. Each set of two examiners would meet with the OB/GYN Board candidate for one hour, then the next two examiners would meet with him or her, then the last two examiners would have their turn. The examiners actually met the candidates IN THE CANDIDATE'S HOTEL ROOM, as strange as that sounds. In each pair of examiners there would be a "good cop" and a "bad cop". One would grill the candidate with merciless intensity, and the other examiner would have a softer tone.

One such candidate, I was told, was met by the first two examiners in her Drake Hotel room, and she immediately broke down under the pressure from the "bad cop", who was grilling her about a surgery she had done. It was 15 minutes into the hour the examiners had with her. She asked if she could be excused to use her hotel bathroom, then retreated into the bathroom and took a shower. She emerged 45 minutes later when their time had expired. Needless to say, she failed the exam.

Knowing what I knew about the intensity of this exam process, I hired Dr. Wendell Wall, a recognized expert in oral boards preparation, to augment my preparation. He charged me $8,000 for his exam prep study materials, and he met with me on three occasions to personally grill me as the examiners would.

The exam preparation by Dr. Wall was very thorough and complete. In retrospect, it was well-worth the $8,000. His first question to me was: "Rich, I want you to take a drop of blood as it exits the left ventricle of a pregnant woman's heart. Trace it through her arteries down to her uterus, through the placenta, down through the fetus; how does it travel through the fetus, in which direction, and then back all the way to the woman's heart. "

I stumbled my way through it, and he corrected me several times as I described the path the blood would take. It was questions such as those that identified exactly what I knew and what I didn't. Gradually I developed more confidence in my responses to his questions, and a sense of confidence in my degree of preparation for the exam.

It is understandable why the method of examining candidates in their Drake Hotel rooms was doomed to be criticized. Eventually, the OB/GYN Board changed the venue to Dallas, Texas, where I was to have my exam. I was in the first class of the new arrangement. Our exam was held in a testing center, a much more neutral and less intimidating environment.

However, the balance of the exam was unchanged. It would require two examiners each hour, for 3 hours. And there would be a "good cop" and a "bad cop", although the Board didn't acknowledge that fact.

I drove to Dallas, Texas a week before my exam was to be held. As soon as I arrived in my hotel, I realized that I'd forgotten to bring my good suit. I couldn't be caught taking the exam without a good suit of clothes, so my first stop was to the local mall where I purchased a brand new suit for $500 and paid extra to make sure I had rapid tailoring in time for the exam.

I then spent the entire week cramming for the exam. I had a list of all of my surgeries done in the first 2 years in Princeton. I knew that they would focus on the most intense disasters, and also the youngest hysterectomy. It was considered taboo to perform a hysterectomy on any woman under the age of 30, but I had one who was 29. She had been a true emergency, someone in labor who had bled after a Cesarean section performed by one of my family practice partners. Nevertheless, I knew I would be crucified for taking away her childbearing at age 29. I prepared my defense.

Also I would be asked random questions about any and every OB/GYN topic. I would have to have the answer ready on the tip of my tongue.

People regularly failed this exam. I would have to impress these examiners that I was ready not only to perform surgery competently, but also that I could act as a consultant to any of my FP colleagues who needed my help. I was forewarned that if they asked me: I had just cut a ureter in surgery, now what would I do? I was not allowed to tell them I would call in the urologist to fix the injury. They would tell me "the urologist is in Hawaii on vacation."

Every specialist I might ask to help with any situation they would throw at me would all be on vacation in Hawaii that week.

And so I spent that entire prep week in my Dallas hotel room, cramming for the oral exam with a stack of 5 x 8 notecards riddled with facts. I had over 2,000 notecards loaded with trivia. I took some breaks from the confines of my hotel room to wander the grounds of the hotel.

On one such break, I was pacing in a parking garage of my Dallas hotel. I was very focused and pensive. I barely noticed my surroundings. Suddenly, the hair on the back of my neck began to bristle, and I sensed that I was not alone. I glanced up from the card I was reading and suddenly I realized that there were six grown men slowly circling me. At first they were a hundred feet away, and then fifty, and now twenty. The circle around me was closing ever tighter. I noticed that one of them had a gun in his hand, partially concealed behind his back. I surveyed my situation. I was on the third-floor ramp, and there was nowhere to run. I began to sweat...

Finally one of the men walked right up to me and asked me for identification. I told him I had nothing on me, because it was all in my hotel safe. He informed me that he was a police officer, and the other 5 men were from hotel security, and that there had been a series of parking lot robberies, and I appeared very suspicious, with my aimless wandering. I showed them my OB/GYN index cards, with all the trivia. I explained that I was preparing for the biggest oral exam of my life. After looking at the cards, and verifying that I was a guest at the hotel, they realized that I was not the bandit.

On the morning of the exam, all of the candidates met in the large conference room of the new Board Exam Center. To a person, we were all extremely anxious. The head examiner recognized that fact, and welcomed us to the new exam facility. He began by spending 20 minutes telling jokes. He started by telling us some famous Yogi Berra sayings, like:

Yogi Berra was giving directions – "and when you get to the fork in the road, take it."

Yogi Berra was asked if he wanted his pizza cut into 4 pieces, or 8. "You'd better make it 4", he said – "I don't think I can eat 8."

Yogi Berra said: "50 percent of baseball is 90% mental."

We were all laughing as he loosened the candidates by telling these jokes.

Then we were ushered into separate small rooms in which sat two examiners, dressed in suit and tie, much as I was in my brand-new tailored suit. They wasted no time getting into the specifics of my surgical case list.

Sure enough, as predicted, I had several hypothetical questions about having cut a ureter on a patient during a hysterectomy, and now what was I going to do about it? As I was reminded by my staff docs many times during residency, "there are two types of OB/GYNs: those who have cut a ureter, and those that are going to." So now I had to tell the examiners what I would do to fix it. Of course I began by telling them I would call the urologist. And of course they answered by saying that he or she was in Hawaii at a conference. I then described the many techniques for repairing a ureter, depending upon where in the woman's anatomy it was severed.

After three long hours, it was over. Yes, there had been a good cop and a bad cop. I discovered midway through the process that I was actually enjoying it! I had studied so long and thoroughly for this exam that I actually relished regurgitating this information to someone other than myself. It was surprisingly cathartic!!

As I drove home to Princeton that afternoon, I was supremely relieved. I had good feeling in my gut that I had satisfied these examiners that #1, I was competent to perform safe surgery, and #2, that I was competent to serve as a consultant to my family practice partners.

A month after the exam I received a letter in the mail informing me that I had passed my oral exam. I was now Board Certified in OB/GYN as well as Family Practice. Two specialties!! Double Boarded!! My vindication was complete. My former Minneapolis clinic partners who had told me that I could no longer deliver babies be damned! I was immunized against any such future pronouncements. They had predicted that I would fail in my attempt to finish the residency. But I "wanted it more", and I prevailed.

CHAPTER 8
EPILOGUE

Proverbs: 29:18: "Where there is no vision, the people perish."

When I was four years old I announced to my father that I wanted to become a doctor. When I was a teenager, I watched an old movie on television one night called *"The Tin Star"*. It was a 1957 film which featured Henry Fonda as the seasoned sheriff in a small town, alongside his sheriff-in-training, played by Anthony Perkins. Their drama was not the focus of my attention, but rather, the town's doctor. He was a small town country doc who did house calls. I remember seeing him drive his horse and buggy to deliver a baby one night. The following day, as the town was staging a celebration of his medical career, they discovered that he had been shot by an outlaw on his way back from the delivery. My imagination had been ignited by that story, and I could see myself becoming the town doctor that everybody revered and loved.

Now, 50 years after watching *"The Tin Star"*, I am finally in that small town, delivering babies and caring for them as they grow up, just like that country doctor did. I traveled quite an unlikely road to arrive at this wonderful juncture. After being fired from my first residency in Des Moines, I had to adapt. I found a second chance to begin my residency training at St. Luke's hospital in Milwaukee – and almost walked away on the first night. After finishing that residency, I passed up a $200,000 signing bonus from my dream job in the small town of Clarkfield to stay in Milwaukee for Michelle, and then she dumped me. Next I spent 18 months in the small town of Madison, Minnesota, as one of only two doctors in town. The townspeople embraced me, and I them. It had been in many ways the realization of that *Tin Star* movie I had watched. I was the small-town doc. But I had no wife, and no family to round out my fulfillment. So I failed in my first attempt to be a country doc. Yet again I had to adapt or die. I abandoned Madison, and all of its career satisfaction, for the trappings of city life.

Returning to the city introduced me to my wife Mary, the best thing that ever happened in my life. But it also burdened me with the ugly pitfalls of city practice, including the hoarding of patients by specialists guarding their medical turf. I could no longer deliver babies, or see kids, or do cardiac stress tests. I failed at being a city doc. That confinement of practice forced me to think outside of the box and take a big chance, and I bravely dove back into an OB/GYN surgical residency. I knew it would be difficult, considering my age. But I had the wisdom that comes with having completed a previous residency. I treated it as a marathon and took it one day at a time. Above all else, I slept whenever possible. I ran as often as I could. I learned from my mistakes. When I emerged from that nightmare of additional training, I brought with me with much more diversity to my skills and qualifications. Now I would no longer be told that I couldn't do the procedures I enjoyed.

Since moving to Princeton, I have delivered thousands of babies. A few years later I have given these same kids their shots before entering kindergarten. I have then coached them on the tennis team in high school. They have come back to see me to get their medical exams before entering college. I have performed thousands of hysterectomies on their mothers when their reproductive organs have rebelled. When I walk into our local grocery store, I smile with deep satisfaction as I see the cashier and the boy bagging my groceries, and I realize that I was the one who welcomed them both into this world.

So, do you think you have what it takes to become a medical doctor? Medical training is a marathon. It is mentally, emotionally and physically challenging. It cannot be conquered quickly, or without a strategy for success. I have shared mine. If you treat your medical education as a marathon, pacing yourself by taking it one mile at a time, and keep yourself in good physical condition, you already stand a good chance at succeeding. Add some leniency on yourself when you make costly errors, and get enough sleep, and you are well on your way. But most of all, learn how to adapt to your circumstances, or you will perish from any of a thousand pitfalls along the road. Good luck! I wish you great success.